MW01132075

MAINE
HOME COOKING

MAINE
HOME COOKING

175 Recipes from Down East Kitchens

SANDRA L. OLIVER

Photography by
JENNIFER SMITH-MAYO

MAINE

Interior Design by Jennifer Anderson
Cover Design by Miroslaw Jurek
Photographs by Jennifer Smith-Mayo

Library of Congress Cataloging-in-Publication Data
Oliver, Sandra L. (Sandra Louise), 1947-
Maine home cooking : 175 recipes from
Down East kitchens / by Sandra Oliver.
p. cm.
Includes bibliographical references and index.
ISBN 978-1-60893-180-4 (alk. paper)
1. Cooking, American--New England style. 2. Cooking--Maine. I.
Title.
TX715.2.N48O438 2012
641.59741--dc23
2012011461

Printed in China

5   4   3   2

Down East
Books • Magazine • Online
www.downeast.com
Distributoed to the trade
by the National Book Network

To my editors Letitia Baldwin, Aimee Thibodeau, Kathleen Fleury, and Toby Martin, and all those generous home cooks who shared their recipes and wisdom: my affectionate gratitude.

Contents

Introduction

In April 2006, Letitia Baldwin, then the style editor at *Bangor Daily News*, called me and asked if I would write a weekly column based on recipes garnered from newspaper readers in response to queries for how to make a certain dish. I said I would give it a try.

Letitia mostly knew me as a food historian. Some years ago she wrote an article for the *Boston Globe* about how I put together a traditional Thanksgiving dinner. Her time in the kitchen with me showed her my somewhat easygoing, slapdash style of home cooking coupled with a fascination for kitchen traditions. She thought it was a suitable style for something written for other home cooks.

Letitia named the column "Taste Buds," which I began by asking friends and neighbors if there was any recipe they wished they had. Sure enough, they did. Sometimes the query was for a recipe remembered from childhood, or one for something they ate somewhere and thought tasted good.

Wonderful letters came from all over eastern Maine, many from older women who had been cooking for their families for decades. Often they provided a bit of family history with the recipe, or told of a particular memory associated with the dish. Plus, they passed along advice on how to make the dish, and shared their experiences and kitchen wisdom. Many names have become familiar over the years, and I feel like those who write to me are old friends. My life has been enormously enriched by this connection to Maine's home cooks. They are part of a terrific conversation about cooking that I still do my best to share in the column.

Even though I solicited further queries with each column, inevitably there were gaps in recipe requests. One week I called Letitia and said, in a bit of a panic, "I don't have any recipe requests for this week. What do I do?" Letitia's answer was, "Just tell them what is happening in your kitchen." That began a second type of conversation, a bit one-sided as I told of what was growing in my garden and how I cooked it, or how I found a great dish at a potluck or enjoyed one at a friend's house. I became a recipe scavenger, prowling constantly, tasting as I went, and asking for recipes.

One reader captured my column's intent exactly when she wrote, "I like your recipes because you use what you can get in season and local, and you call for ingredients that normal people have in their kitchen."

Over the years, many readers have told me that they clip the column and save the recipes stuffed in a box or drawer, that they have added recipes from the column to their family's repertoire. If you are a column clipper, with this book in hand, you can empty your drawers and ditch the box of yellowed newspapers, because nearly all of "Taste Buds" is right here, indexed even. Whether you have been a longtime column reader or not, I hope you will spatter this book with batter and spills, dust the pages with flour and sugar, and mark it up with penciled annotations. Let it be an old, hard-working friend to keep you company in your kitchen.

Home Cooking in Maine

HOME COOKING IN MAINE

Home cooking is alive and well in Maine. Like most of my Islesboro island neighbors, and many others in Down East and inland Maine, I am a home cook with no professional culinary training. Being a food writer has required me to pay attention to some aspects of professional food practices, but in my heart of hearts, cooking is how I take care of family and friends, use what I grow in my island garden, and live responsibly on the earth. Like you, I have the daily chore of figuring out what to make for dinner. I never think of myself as a chef: to be a chef means you are the boss in the kitchen, with someone to do what you say, and I don't know about you, but there are only cats in my kitchen, and they don't take orders.

I hear a lot about how no one cooks any more. Some of my friends even tell me they don't cook, but I notice they are feeding their families and they look reasonably healthy to me. When I ask how they do it, they say, "Well, I just roast a chicken and boil some potatoes and make a salad." Why they think they aren't cooking baffled me until I realized that they thought cooking was assembling twenty-seven ingredients and spending half a day in the kitchen, plus probably getting a fry pan to flare up suddenly like TV chefs do.

Lots more people cook in a modest, daily, simple fashion than the professionals give us credit for. If you picked up this book, I'll bet you are a home cook, too.

Why Use Recipes?

Ironically, in daily home cooking, I don't often use recipes. I open the fridge, pantry, or look in the garden to see what is ripe and ready, and throw it all together. For many people, cooking is slavishly following a recipe, but I can hardly discipline myself to stick to one. Still, here are lots of recipes. You will see I spend as much time explaining how to work around the recipes as how to follow them. Some in this book are barely recipes at all. Feel free to tinker with them, substitute, add, and subtract.

Don't worry too much about details. For example, a recipe might call for one-half cup of a vegetable, but if I end up with a dab of something leftover or conversely come in a little shy, I round quantities up or down to the nearest whole vegetable. Veggies and most meat products don't come with little marks showing the half-cup line, so I decided long ago not to sweat the details, and nothing terrible has ever happened because of it.

Cook to taste. If you don't like a certain seasoning or minor ingredient, leave it out. If you really enjoy one, add more. Don't eat onions? Unless onions are the whole point, leave them out. Really like garlic? Add more. If you have a sweet tooth, use the sugar quantity recommended; if you prefer it less sweet, cut it back.

If you don't cook much, or even feel a little shy about it, but want to do more, get back in the kitchen, open this book, and let all the home cooks quoted here coach you along.

Please just let these recipes inspire you and help you make that daily what-to-have-for-dinner decision just a little more easily.

What to Expect of This Book, Philosophically Speaking

I believe in frugality, using leftovers, and not eating junk. Sure, you can make an exquisite dish if you use pricey ingredients imported from far away or wildly out of season. I'd rather use fruits and vegetables in season. I prefer to grate my own cheese over buying pre-grated bagfuls. I add my own water to orange juice concentrate rather than buy bottled orange juice that is made from concentrate. I seldom if ever recommend a particular brand, so you are free to buy just about any brand you prefer or can afford and you should get a satisfactory result.

I like having leftovers because they can save prep time and can serve as a starting place for menu planning. I throw away precious little, and even then my chickens get to eat it. Lots of recipes in this cookbook suggest ways to use leftovers.

If I can't pronounce the ingredient named on the package, I don't eat it. I prefer to use ingredients that have an identifiable source in nature—animal, vegetable, or mineral. I prefer using the least processed food possible and so always prefer butter over margarine and real whipped cream over that frozen whipped topping.

Otherwise, I try not to be too snooty about my grub.

WHY IS THERE FOOD HISTORY IN THIS BOOK?

As you read along, you'll find boxes marked "History and Memories" of some dishes. Why do I include these? I've stopped more conversations dead by answering the "what-do-you-do" question by saying that I am a food historian and freelance writer. Obviously, this is a modern cookbook, and not a work of history. Part of my work is writing about modern food and living sustainably. And I have been researching and writing about American food history for over forty years, specializing in food of New England, where I grew up.

Most of the time in this book I keep the history down to a dull roar, but whenever I think you might be interested in the back story on a particular recipe or foodstuff, I've shared what I've learned. I hope you enjoy it. If you find what I say is interesting, check my biography for the other books I've written. I give talks in Maine and New England on food history topics and teach anyone who is interested how to cook in a fireplace or how to conduct food history research.

NUTRITION INFORMATION

If you are watching your diet for calories, cholesterol, carbohydrates, sodium, and all that, you probably are one of the people who reads the nutrition label on the back of most food products in the grocery store, everything except things like heads of lettuce or apples.

Some cookbooks and magazine recipes will sum up nutrition information, made possible by a special software program, at the end of the articles. I had a note from Florence Turek, in Garland, who suggested that I provide nutrition information for the recipes I offer you here. I understand many people like to have that information, and I also understand that many of you, like me, hardly ever follow recipes as written, so with a mere tablespoon of butter we are likely to blow a recipe's fat grams right out of the water or tip over the fiber percentage by a substitution of brown rice for white. The good news is that if you want to calculate nutrition facts you can do it by going on-line to one of the many recipe analysis sites, like recipecalc.com. If you cook professionally, there are many software programs you can buy, some quite inexpensive, through which you can run your recipes to obtain the nutrition facts.

MY ISLAND GARDEN AND KITCHEN

Of course, you don't have to live on an island to have a garden and kitchen like mine, and I'll bet a fair number of Mainers live as I do, heating with wood, gardening all summer to produce food for the year, raising chickens and occasional livestock, even butchering their own meat. One of the great things about moving here twenty-two years ago from Connecticut, where I grew up, was discovering that lots of my peers made pickles, put up preserves, canned, and froze produce. I had been a bit of an oddity in Connecticut, where the only people I knew who did that were all forty years my senior.

My house dates to the very early 1870s and the kitchen has barely been changed since the 1940s, in some parts unchanged since the early 1900s. Most days I like that. My eighty-year-old Dual Atlantic combination wood and propane stove keeps my kitchen and adjacent spaces warm in winter while I make soup at the same time. In summer, I use gas. An electric oven in an adjacent space compensates for the inefficiencies of the gas stove whose oven I gave up on.

There is a generously sized pantry with my gram's old canister set and glass jars full of flour, sugar, rice, beans, oatmeal, corn meal, nuts, and seeds. I have oils, vinegars, and various sauces on hand as well. There are two stores on our island, and I can usually purchase whatever I need in either place as long as I think of it before closing time, although I am a member of the Belfast Co-op, where I do my shopping for bulk items like rice and nuts.

The house is blessed with a stone-walled and dirt-floored cellar perfect for storing winter vegetables. In addition, I have a pair of freezers. I do my food shopping in my garden in summer and in my cellar in winter.

The two-thousand-square foot kitchen garden is literally a stone's throw from the kitchen door. It is fenced to exclude the too-numerous deer that, frankly, I'd prefer to eat than watch grazing. I grow all the usual suspects as far as beans, peas, onions, corn, potatoes, salad stuff, broccoli, cabbage, beets, carrots, summer and winter squashes, cucumbers, and spinach are concerned. I also have a hoop house where I can grow greens in winter and heat-loving tomatoes, eggplants, peppers, and cantaloupes in summer. Peach trees, high-bush blueberries, strawberries, and asparagus occupy a second garden space. I pick apples in my yard and in abandoned orchards on the island.

Like many rural places, the island has a small population of folks who work together to make the community a good place to live. We know each other by sight, if not by name. Most of my friends and neighbors have contributed recipes. They know if they see me barreling down on them at a potluck supper or refreshment table, I am very likely to solicit the recipe for something I just ate. I've learned a lot about cooking from them.

SHELF ONE:
Couscous, Jacob's
cattle beans, white
and brown rice, and
popcorn for watching
movies, all are part
of my staples.

SHELF TWO:
Cornmeal, rye meal,
and homemade granola
are in easy reach.

SHELF THREE:
Bread and cake pans,
two kinds of salt, one
a coarse sort, the
other, fine sea salt.
The instant coffee
is for flavoring icing
or puddings.

SHELF FOUR:
You never know what
size baking dish or
pie plate you will need.
Don't forget Bakewell
Cream from Maine.

A Guide to This Cookbook

Instead of trotting out recipes in the old usual soups, main dishes, and salads fashion, I think you will enjoy reading this cookbook organized according to themes. If you are looking for a particular recipe, or have a specific ingredient you want to use, you will want to turn to the index right away instead of thumbing through the whole cookbook.

The first chapter is about Maine's classic recipes, like chowder, baked beans, lobster stew, and whoopie pies, as they are still being made in Maine. I often add bits of information about the history of some of these dishes, because over the years people have asked me questions about them, and I think you may be curious, too.

The next chapter is called "Homey Favorites" and is mostly about comfort foods, plain, tasty, home-cooked fare for families. My goal with this chapter is to provide simple recipes for basic dishes that even a new cook can follow painlessly. There's lots of advice in here from cooks who have years of practice with economical, uncomplicated, and popular dishes.

"Contemporary Maine Cooking" follows, and here are some dishes that have cropped up in the past thirty or so years, lots of ethnic contributions and new wrinkles of the sort that I encountered in my middle age but never knew about in my youth. Some of you will have grown up with pesto, salsa, and sushi, but most of these recipes will not have appeared in, say, a charity cookbook in Maine before the 1970s.

After some homey favorites like scalloped potatoes and some modern fare like enchiladas, we will want dessert! The "Desserts of Maine" chapter includes all sorts of cakes, cookies, pies, crisps, and puddings. Even though I no longer eat dessert as often as I prefer, I turn to this collection all the time for recipes like the kick-butt Key Lime Pie or the Golden Glow Cake, both so good they'll knock your knee caps off!

Because I cook all the time from my garden and my winter-stored supply of vegetables, I offer you a chapter called "Fresh and Seasonal" that walks you through the year with recipes for all sorts of vegetables straight from the garden. That chapter is followed by "Well Preserved and in a Pickle." I hope I am well preserved, and often find myself in a pickle, especially when there are too many vegetables at once and I have to get them into jars or the freezer tout suite or feed the fruit flies. This chapter tells how I do it and how you can, too.

The very last chapter is "Do It Yourself," with collected advice and wisdom for making home versions of some commercial products. You will also find some other good cooking ideas that readers have shared over the years.

MAINE'S HOME COOKS

Why does Maine still have a strong home cooking tradition? Much of Down East, Maine, like swaths of Middle America, is still rural, and fast-food alternatives are fewer and farther between. Some of us think we'd rather spend our hard-earned cash on stuff besides food we think we can make ourselves. You'd expect older people like me to be home cooks, but I find even younger Mainers will cook a meal for their families after a day's work. They prefer, as much as they are able, to be in charge of what goes into a meal and their children's mouths.

I know this because readers of my weekly *Bangor Daily News* column, "Taste Buds," responded enthusiastically whenever I put out a call for a recipe for the kinds of dishes we all make for our families. Not only did they send recipes, but they also sent stories about how they learned to make the dish, or recalled a memory of eating it or the person who taught them how to put it together. Recipes became mini-memoirs, and Down East, Maine, is rich in personal cooking stories, as you will soon see.

MY CO-AUTHORS

I have numerous co-authors, the wonderful folks who have shared recipes and ideas, memories and advice. Since April 2006, these cook-contributors to the "Taste Buds" column have taught me a lot and inspired me every week. Some of these folks are my neighbors and friends on Islesboro Island. Others are old friends, many from Stonington and North Stonington, where I lived for twenty years. Many more are "Taste Buds" readers in the *Bangor Daily News*.

Some of these folks wrote me letters sent through the mail. Some sent emails. In some cases, especially emailed letters, I did not discover what town they lived in and so that information is omitted.

I have tinkered with their recipes, averaged them out, and offered up their collective wisdom. To all of them, thank you. Without you, there would be no book for us all to share. I am delighted and proud to be associated with all of you. For a full list of my co-authors see page 276.

Classic Down East Dishes

CLASSIC DOWN EAST DISHES

Old-fashioned, traditional homemade dishes and the cooks who learned how to make them from mothers, grandmothers, neighbors and friends thrive Down East, where locals and visitors alike expect flavorful, chock-full-of-seafood chowder, toothsome dark brown baked beans, and creamy finnan haddie. They look for whoopie pies, needhams, and perfect lobster stew. These are our famous dishes.

Then there are almost-forgotten favorites that crop up in collections of family recipes, sometimes reflecting ethnic heritage like brambles, date nut bread, tourtiere, and molasses cookies, or recipes handed down by word-of-mouth like salmon and peas, venison pot roast, and red-flannel hash.

Fish & Shellfish

HISTORICALLY SPEAKING, COASTAL MAINERS ate a lot of fish, partly because in earlier times many fished for subsistence, and because there was a time, long gone, when fish was fairly cheap and Mainers scratching out a living could afford it.

A fillet of a fairly bland white fish (cod, tilapia, haddock, cusk, hake, striper, and even pollack) is fine for chowder, for baking, as a fish casserole. Salmon and Maine shellfish are wonderful on their own and in some of the classic dishes that follow.

Fish and Potatoes

{ SERVES 3 }

This dish is not handsome, but it tastes just fine, and the leftovers are handy for making fish cakes. I usually allow about a third of a pound of plain white fish and one medium potato per person. Feel free to season the dish with fresh or dried chives or parsley, or even a bit of garlic. I save and freeze the cooking water to use for chowder making.

3 MEDIUM POTATOES

1 POUND FILLET OF WHITE-FLESHED FISH

SALT AND PEPPER, TO TASTE

CHIVES, PARSLEY, OR GARLIC, TO TASTE (OPTIONAL)

¼ CUP (HALF A STICK) BUTTER, MELTED, OR ¼ CUP OLIVE OIL

Peel and cut the potatoes into quarters. Boil them in barely enough water to cover them until they are tender. Lay the fish on top and simmer until the fish flakes apart. Drain the potatoes and fish, then add the salt, pepper, and herbs. Mash it all together with a potato masher. Serve with melted butter or olive oil dribbled over the mixture.

Salmon Loaf

{ SERVES 2 TO 3 }

Salmon Loaf and Salmon and Peas (page 26) are two classic dishes, and while both are made these days with canned salmon, certainly leftover baked or poached salmon works as well. Time was when canned salmon was cheap; at least it is still nutritious.

Several cooks contributed their recipes. Evelyn Stinson, from West Enfield, got hers from a dear friend, Carolyn Burton, of Detroit. Emily Anderson, of Holden, uses her mother Cathy's recipe. Nancy Tracy, of Brewer, has one from her husband's aunt, Elizabeth Tracy Copperthwaite, of Winter Harbor. Patricia Reynolds, in Hermon, has her mom Madaline Roberts Leathers' recipe, in the Roberts family for years. Minnie McCormick, in Dover-Foxcroft, has her family's old recipe. Susan White, in Bangor, picked up her recipe from her Columbia

Gas Company bill back in the 1970s. Gina Doyle, from Corinna, sent her recipe, and Phyllis Whittier, from Dover-Foxcroft, sent hers along with an egg sauce to go over it.

ONE (14-OUNCE) CAN OR TWO CUPS COOKED SALMON

¼ CUP (MORE IF YOU USE DRIED BREAD CRUMBS) JUICE FROM
   SALMON CAN AND/OR MILK

2 EGGS, BEATEN

1 CUP FRESH BREAD CRUMBS

1 SMALL ONION, FINELY CHOPPED

1 TABLESPOON LEMON JUICE OR JUICE OF HALF A LEMON

SALT AND PEPPER, TO TASTE

DILL, PARSLEY, OR CHIVES, TO TASTE (OPTIONAL)

PAPRIKA

Preheat the oven to 350 degrees. Grease a 7x3½x2-inch loaf pan or a square baking pan. Drain the salmon, reserving the liquid. Remove the bones and skin, and pull the fish apart into flakes. Combine the fish, liquid, eggs, bread crumbs, onion, lemon juice, salt and pepper, herbs and paprika, mixing until they are evenly distributed. Put the mixture into the pan and shape it into a loaf. Bake 50 to 60 minutes, until it is solid to the touch and slightly golden on top.

Phyllis Whittier's Egg Sauce:

2 TABLESPOONS BUTTER

2 TABLESPOONS FLOUR

½ TEASPOON SALT

¼ TEASPOON PEPPER

1½ CUPS MILK

2 HARD-BOILED EGGS, DICED

{ MAKES 2 CUPS }

Melt the butter in a heavy pan, stir in the flour, salt, and pepper, and cook until it is smooth and bubbly. Gradually add the milk, stirring constantly, and let boil a minute. Stir in the eggs and heat through. Pour sauce over the loaf and serve.

Salmon and Peas

An old-fashioned dish like salmon and peas, traditionally made with canned salmon and canned peas for two or three generations of Mainers, still is comfort food when made with freshly cooked or leftover salmon and new peas or frozen ones. Serve it on baked potatoes or on toast with a salad alongside.

2 TABLESPOONS BUTTER (OR ONE OF BUTTER AND ONE OF OLIVE OIL)

2 TABLESPOONS FLOUR

1 CUP MILK

2 CUPS, MORE OR LESS, COOKED SALMON

·1 OR MORE CUPS COOKED OR FROZEN PEAS

SALT AND PEPPER, TO TASTE

1 TABLESPOON PREPARED MUSTARD (OPTIONAL)

MINCED PARSLEY (OPTIONAL)

Heat the butter or butter and oil in a heavy saucepan, and whisk in the flour, cooking it over a medium heat until the mixture bubbles. Gradually add the milk and continue cooking until the sauce is slightly thickened and heated through. Break up the salmon and add it to the sauce, then add the peas. Reduce the heat and cook until the peas are cooked through and the salmon is warm. If the mixture thickens too much, add milk. Taste and add the salt, pepper, and mustard. Spoon over baked potatoes or toast and sprinkle parsley on top.

Miriam Hart's Port Clyde Sardine Sandwiches

{ MAKES 4 SANDWICHES }

Mainers consume most of their sardines straight from the can with crackers. Nothing is a simpler, more portable snack or noon meal, whether for a worker's lunch box or for hunters', fishermans, or sailors'. However, there are several ways to use them in recipes.

One Maine sardine industry cookbook recommended sardines in tossed salad, potato salad, spaghetti sauce, rarebit, and sardine pizza, in case you can't convince anyone to go for anchovies. Sharon Frost, in Calais, said she has used recipes for Fish a La Reine and Creamed Sardines that she collected when she was "a teenager and sardines were plentiful and cheap." And Miriam Hart, in Hampden, shared Port Clyde Sardine Sandwiches. Miriam's recipe, which she labeled as "original," I think might appeal to many of you, though, alas, we no longer have Port Clyde sardines to work with.

1 CAN SARDINES, DRAINED

2 HARD-BOILED EGGS

1 RIPE AVOCADO

1 OR 2 TABLESPOONS LEMON JUICE

2 OR 3 TABLESPOONS PLAIN YOGURT

SALT, TO TASTE

4 SLICES THINLY SLICED CHEDDAR CHEESE

8 SLICES WHOLE-WHEAT BREAD

ROMAINE LETTUCE

Combine the sardines, eggs, avocado, lemon juice, yogurt, and salt. Lay the cheddar slices on four slices of bread; spread the sardine mix, then add the lettuce, and finally four more slices of bread.

SARDINE MEMORIES

When the Prospect Harbor packing plant closed in the spring of 2010, Maine lost the last sardine cannery in America, but Mainers lost neither their taste for nor memories of them. Jane Basely loaned me a charming little sardine cookbook, *Fifty-Eight Ways to Serve Sardines Hot and Cold*, produced in Lubec by the Seaboard Packing Company in 1947. Jane wrote, "I grew up in Lubec and all our parents and grandparents worked in the factories. It was a different era then, and one I will always cherish. Small towns had all that anyone needed, from movie theatres to clothing stores and local newspapers, etc." She recalled "the whistle blowing certain numbers when the fish had arrived or when it was time for the packers to return to work." From creamed sardines in a spinach ring to hot sardine mousse, the booklet is full of recipes that I'll bet hardly anyone ever tried, although it is beautifully laid out with photographs of the sardine dishes.

JoAnn Fuerst, in Mount Desert, proprietor of Wikhegan Antiquarian Books, sent a Maine Sardine Industry cookbook called *Uses and Preparation of Maine Sardines, America's All-round Seafood*, published in 1952. Sardines were touted as nutritious and delicious in "rugged he-man specials" as well as "dainty feminine canapés."

Shortly after the Prospect Harbor plant closed, the Maine State Museum collected cans, labels, equipment, business records, and memorabilia from the old factory in order to preserve this aspect of Maine's history.

Baked Fish with Mustard Mayonnaise

{ SERVES 3 }

I learned to make a tasty mustard-mayonnaise sauce from my long-time friend Mary Hughes. I was so surprised when she told me how simply she did it — it tasted like it ought to be more complicated. Allow about a third of a pound of fish per serving. Though I like grainy Dijon mustard, any sort will do. Choose one to suit your own taste, and if you wish, increase the proportion of mustard to mayonnaise to taste.

1 POUND FILLET OF WHITE-FLESHED FISH

SALT AND PEPPER, TO TASTE

¼ CUP MAYONNAISE

1 TO 2 TABLESPOONS GRAINY MUSTARD

Preheat the oven to 350 degrees. Grease or lightly oil a baking pan. Lay the fillet in the pan. Salt and pepper it lightly. Mix together the mayonnaise and mustard and spread it evenly on the fish. Bake the fish for 15 minutes, then test for doneness. If the fish flakes apart when you test it with a fork, it is done.

Haddock Casserole

This haddock casserole helps jolt me out of my baked-or-broiled-fish rut.
Pat Southard, of Howland, and Ruth Thurston, in Machias, both sent
recipes, and the one that follows is a hybrid of Pat's that called for noodles,
and Ruth's Fish Scallop with cream sauce, a bit of cheddar, and crumbs
on top. Pat's recipe called for uncooked fish and Ruth's called for cooked,
and I chose uncooked, though if I had leftover fish I would use it instead. I
bought about a pound of fish and discovered that this recipe actually could
take a little less or a little more, depending on how many servings you want.

{ SERVES 4 }

I chose to keep the noodles down to a dull roar, but you might like
more. Perhaps more cheddar is to your taste. Consider adding peas or
any other vegetable you like. You can make your cream sauce with fresh
or sour cream. Pat's recipe called for mayonnaise, which you might enjoy
in the sauce.

¼ CUP (HALF A STICK) BUTTER

1 SMALL ONION, MINCED

2 TABLESPOONS FLOUR

1 CUP MILK OR CREAM

4 OUNCES EGG NOODLES, COOKED ACCORDING TO
   PACKAGE DIRECTIONS

1 POUND HADDOCK, CUT INTO BITE-SIZE PIECES

¼ CUP GRATED CHEDDAR CHEESE

½ CUP SOFT BREAD CRUMBS

Preheat the oven to 350 degrees. Melt the butter in a heavy pan; add
the onion and cook until just tender. Stir in the flour and cook until the
mixture is bubbly. Add the milk and whisk together until the sauce is
smooth and thick. Remove from the heat. Grease a casserole dish, and
make a layer of noodles, then fish, and then sauce, and repeat. Top with
cheddar cheese and bread crumbs. Bake about 30 minutes, until the
casserole bubbles and the fish is cooked.

Oyster Pie

{ SERVES 4 TO 6 }

Native Americans gathered in Damariscotta millennia ago to eat oysters now raised there commercially. They ate enough to build small hills of the shells. They didn't make pie, though.

Kathleen Schneider, of Lincoln, started our search for a "delicious oyster pie" recipe like the one her husband's grandmother made with two crusts, oysters, potatoes, and hard-boiled eggs. Vivian Stuart, in Brooklyn, and Mary Landis, up in Millinocket, shared their recipes on which the following is based.

This recipe makes a generously sized pie, filling a two-quart casserole practically to overflowing. Consider halving the filling to bake in a deep pie plate. You can also use this recipe with clams instead of oysters.

2 POTATOES

4 CARROTS

2 HARD-BOILED EGGS

1 PINT OYSTERS, DRAINED, LIQUOR RESERVED

4 TABLESPOONS BUTTER

8 TABLESPOONS FLOUR

3 CUPS MILK

1 MEDIUM ONION, CHOPPED

2 TABLESPOONS FINELY CHOPPED GREEN PEPPER (OPTIONAL)

⅛ TEASPOON NUTMEG

1 TABLESPOON CHOPPED FRESH PARSLEY

SALT AND PEPPER, TO TASTE

ONE (9-INCH) PIE CRUST

Cook the potatoes and carrots ahead of time. Peel and chop the eggs. Drain the oysters, reserving the liquor to add to the milk later. Preheat the oven to 375 degrees. Grease a 2-quart casserole.

Melt the butter in a saucepan, and when it bubbles, whisk in the flour. Mix together the milk and the oyster liquor and add to the butter and flour and whisk it until smooth, cooking it over a medium heat until the sauce has thickened somewhat. Add the oysters and cook until the oysters' edges curl, about 2 to 3 minutes. Add the vegetables and mix together, add the nutmeg, parsley, and salt and pepper to taste.

Pour the mixture into the casserole and put the pie crust on top, crimping it to the edge of the casserole. Bake for 25 to 35 minutes, until the crust is brown and the filling is bubbly.

Lobster

Maine's most famous seafood is lobster, and anyone who drives through the York toll booths is practically required to buy one. For a while, Mainers drove around with a red lobster on their license plates, the only state in the union to sport cooked food on its tags.

So obviously Mainers are expected to know how to cook lobster. The advice varies on time and method. Some firm believers in steaming instruct us to bring two inches of salt water to a boil and stand the lobster on its head in that. Others recommend quite a lot more well-salted cold water with the lobsters in it brought gradually to a boil. There is advice about how to relax lobsters by rubbing their foreheads before plunging them into a cookpot. Everyone agrees that you must watch out for the snapping claws.

Most cooks today say that it is far too easy to overcook lobster. For a pound-and-a-quarter lobster, 8 to 10 minutes is right; for a pound-and-a-half crustacean, 10 to 12 minutes. A two-pound lobster will be done in 12 to 15 minutes.

Boiled Lobster

Bring cold, well-salted water to a boil in a covered pot large enough to hold both your lobsters and sufficient water to cover them. When the water boils, add the lobsters head first and allow to come again to a boil. Reduce the heat to medium, maintaining a steady bubbling, and begin timing.

Remove the lobsters when the time is up, and, if needed, rinse off the cooking scum with cold water. Serve with melted butter.

{ ADVICE }

If you wish to freeze cooked lobster for use another time, follow advice from Eleanor Campbell, of Gouldsboro. She suggested breaking off the claws, legs, and tails, and freezing them in the shell inside a plastic bag! "When you take them out," she says, "it is just like having freshly cooked lobster."

Lobster Stew

{ SERVES 4 }

A good lobster stew has a divine color, and it is good to make it ahead. A young Canadian friend visiting in the States a few years ago ordered a lobster stew at a diner and reported to me later her astonishment that there were no vegetables. She was accustomed to carrots, potatoes, peas, and onions in stews, mostly meat ones. This reveals a historical shift from stew as a verb instead of a noun. Lobster "stewed" is what we have here really, or oyster, scallop, and others, as past tense of stew. Where people in past times "stewed" we are likely to say "simmer" or "reduce the heat and cook slowly."

Whether you use the tomalley or not is up to you. If there are eggs in the lobster, called coral, add it to improve the color. Cook your lobster just as you normally would and take the meat out of the shell. Leave most of it in generous bite-sized pieces.

2 ONE OR ONE AND A HALF POUND LOBSTERS

½ STICK OF BUTTER

1 QUART OF HALF-N-HALF OR LIGHT CREAM

NUTMEG TO TASTE

Cook the lobsters and take the meat out of the shells. Cut into generously sized pieces. Reserve the tomalley if you wish, and the coral (eggs) if there is any. In a heavy bottomed pan, melt the butter, and add to it the tomalley and coral if you use them stirring to blend. Then add the lobster and cook gently over a low heat for ten minutes. Gradually add the half-n-half or light cream, stirring the whole time. Heat the mixture thoroughly, and add a grating or two of nutmeg. Set aside for several hours in the refrigerator to age. Reheat gently until hot. Serve.

Finnan Haddie

The term finnan haddie conjures up the dish made with it. But the fish can also be used to make chowder or fish cakes, or used any other way that savory smoked fish is used. Warmed in white sauce with hard-boiled eggs crumbled into it, it is delicious. Prepared simply in cream, it is nearly a fast food.

The traditional way to serve finnan haddie is in a soup plate, just as you might serve lobster or oyster stew. It is fine served over a baked potato, toast, or crackers.

¼ POUND FINNAN HADDIE (SMOKED HADDOCK) PER PERSON
½ CUP MILK OR CREAM PER PERSON
BUTTER (OPTIONAL)

Soak the fish in cold water for an hour, or lay it in boiling hot water off the heat for 5 minutes.

Baked method: Preheat the oven to 350 degrees. Place the fish in a baking dish, cover with cream or milk, and bake until the fish flakes apart, 20 to 30 minutes, depending on the thickness of the fish.

Top of stove method: Simmer the fish in a large sauté pan over a medium-low heat until it flakes apart. Serve with a dot of butter on top, pepper to taste, over potatoes, crackers, or toast.

FINNAN HADDIE HISTORY

The fish in question is haddock; the time and place is late eighteenth-century Findon, Scotland. The fishwives of Findon salted haddock lightly then hung it in the chimney to be smoked by peat fire. Haddocks, "haddie," from Findon became quite popular and desirable, and the product spread from Findon to Edinburgh and beyond, and the name Findon haddie eventually corrupted into finnan haddie.

Between 1860 and 1880, New Englanders caught and smoked haddock, but most of it was sold to the Canadian maritime provinces. Nearby Nova Scotia and New Brunswick, settled by a fair number of Scots in the nineteenth century, sent a number of fishermen and even industrial workers to New England, from Boston to Maine, who came with a taste for finnan haddie. Some married Yankee women who learned how to cook the smoked fish, and by the early 1900s, most New England cookbooks had directions for fixing it.

Chowder & Its Variations

RICH, FLAVORFUL, BROTHY but thick-with-ingredients chowder is a Mainer's birthright, or at least ought to be.

Chowder, like many dishes, has variations on its basic structure. Chowder traditionally begins with salt pork, fried out to make fat on which cooks layers of onions, potatoes, and fish (usually a white fish like haddock or cod, or shellfish); then one adds water and, lastly, milk. The ingredients' kind and quality makes the difference in chowder flavor, and personal taste is a guiding principle. Generally, I do not buy chowder mixes at the supermarkets, being suspicious about the origins and quality of the flabby-looking little pieces I too often see there, but I would trust a mix from a fish market.

Basic Fish Chowder

My basic chowder is built with one medium potato per person, plus a third of a pound or so of fish or shellfish per person, and one medium onion for every two people. A small piece of salt pork, about an inch square, finely chopped, per person is sufficient, or a tablespoon of oil or sometimes bacon fat. The fat from salt pork or bacon gives a rich flavor, which is why I prefer it.

{ SERVES 3 }

Some like to cube potatoes, but I belong to the slicing school of thought, and I usually slice the potato so that I have a thin edge and a thick one. The thin edge cooks off and helps thicken the chowder.

1 TO 2-INCH SQUARE SALT PORK, FINELY CHOPPED, OR A COUPLE
    TABLESPOONS BUTTER, VEGETABLE OIL, OR BACON FAT
1 MEDIUM ONION, CHOPPED
2 OR 3 MEDIUM POTATOES, SLICED
1 POUND FISH OR SHELLFISH, OR A COMBINATION
FISH STOCK OR WATER
ONE (14-OUNCE) CAN EVAPORATED MILK, OR UP TO 2 CUPS OF
    LIGHT CREAM, HALF-AND-HALF, OR WHOLE MILK
SALT AND PEPPER, TO TASTE

Fry the salt pork in a heavy-bottom pot until you have crispy bits, which you can remove and set aside or leave in. Add the onion, potatoes, and fish in layers. Add just enough water or stock until you can just see the liquid at the surface of the ingredients. Cook until the potatoes are fork tender, and then add the milk, cream, or half-and-half. Heat well, but do not allow it to boil. Taste and add the salt and pepper. Chowder is usually better if it stands overnight in the fridge and is eaten the next day.

Variations:

Corn Chowder

Substitute corn cut fresh from one cob per person for the fish or shellfish, or about ¾ cup of whole-kernel corn. Add it as you assemble the layers. If you intend the corn chowder to be a vegetarian alternative, use butter or oil in the bottom of the pot.

Corn and Lobster Chowder

Substitute corn cut fresh from two to three cobs of corn for the fish or shellfish. Pick the meat from two lobsters, more if you have it, large pieces cut into bite-size bits. Add the corn in the potato and onion layers, and when the potatoes are tender, add the lobster and milk, cream, or half-and-half.

Clam Chowder

Use a pint or more to taste of freshly shucked clams. Grind them coarsely or cut into pieces with a knife. Add them *after* the potatoes and onions have cooked together and the potatoes are tender. Cook only for five minutes in the chowder and do not allow the chowder to boil.

CHOWDER HISTORY

Before New England was settled, chowder was made at sea and relied upon the stored supplies on fishing vessels: salt pork and hardtack, to which the fishermen added some of the fish they caught. It was made with water, since obviously no milk was available.

Over time, common crackers, sometimes soaked in milk, replaced the hardtack, laid in with the fish, before potatoes were universally included, and for a while even after. While the crackers might cook apart a little, the result was densely packed with ingredients, but not gluey. Some recipes, even ones from the 1800s, call upon the cook to sprinkle a little flour into the pot over a layer of fish or potato.

Milk is more common in chowder recipes after the mid-1800s. In parts of New England, including a few locations in Maine, milkless chowder was still common even in the 1900s.

Bean Suppers

BAKED BEANS WITH BISCUITS OR BROWN BREAD, alongside ham or hot dogs and a dollop of coleslaw, is Maine's Saturday night menu at home or at bean suppers offered up by lodges, churches, and granges. In some households, sharp cucumber pickles, called muddy water pickles, accompanied the baked beans.

Baked Beans

In Maine the standard baking bean is the lovely large yellow eye, though the purple-speckled Jacobs cattle, soldier, and others have their adherents. Down East Marifax, a flavorful all-brown bean, is a favorite. As far as I am concerned, molasses, sugar, mustard, and pepper are merely flavorings and you can add them to taste. In the recipe that follows, there is not much sweetening, so taste it after it has baked a couple of hours, and if you prefer something sweeter, add more molasses or brown sugar.

3 CUPS DRIED BEANS

¼ TO ½ POUND STREAKY SALT PORK

½ SMALL ONION (OPTIONAL)

¼ CUP MOLASSES, OR TO TASTE

2 TABLESPOONS MUSTARD

SALT AND PEPPER, TO TASTE

Soak the beans overnight or use a speed-soak method. Drain the beans, cover with fresh water, and simmer until the skins burst. Put them into the bean pot with the salt pork, onion, molasses, and mustard, and fill the pot with hot water or the bean-cooking liquid, until you can just see liquid through the beans. Bake covered at 250 degrees for 4 to 6 hours. Taste after 3 or 4 hours and adjust the seasonings.

{ SERVES 8 TO 10 }

{ ADVICE }

Speed-Soaking Beans: If you don't plan ahead to soak your beans overnight, use this speedy soaking method. Put the beans in a pan and add water to about 2 inches over the beans and bring to a boil. Take them off the heat and let them sit for 1 hour. After that, bring them to a boil again and cook until they achieve the time-honored skins-bursting stage: pull up a spoonful and blow on them. If the skins peel back, then they are cooked enough to bake.

Open-Faced Baked Bean Sandwiches

Leftover baked beans are terribly useful and economical. While I usually have pint-size containers full of winter-baked beans in my freezer, when they are gone I am not embarrassed to buy a can of good old Maine baked beans to make a fast supper.

I've always liked cold baked bean sandwiches, merely mashed up and spread on hearty multigrain, whole-wheat, or rye bread with mayonnaise. Warm beans merely served on toast or an open-faced bean sandwich improved with onions and a bit of cheese and run under the broiler is an easy and comforting supper.

1 OR 2 SLICES OF BREAD PER PERSON

MUSTARD

HAM SLICED THINLY (OPTIONAL)

CANNED BAKED BEANS OR LEFTOVER HOMEMADE BEANS, DRAINED

ONION, THINLY SLICED

CHEDDAR OR SWISS CHEESE, THINLY SLICED

Turn on the broiler. Toast the bread lightly to prevent the sandwich from becoming soggy. Lay the toasted bread slices on a baking sheet. Spread with mustard if desired, and lay on the ham if you use it. Top with well-drained baked beans and lay a few rings of onion on top of that. Add the cheese last. Run under the broiler for five minutes, check to see if it needs more time, and remove it when the cheese is a little bubbly and the onions wilted.

BAKED BEAN HISTORY

Historically New England beans were not very sweet. Hardly any molasses was added in recipes from the early 1800s until the later 1890s or so. Heavily sweetened beans came to Maine with the introduction of commercially canned beans.

Traditional Mainers still make less-sweet baked beans, even in home-style restaurants. I once had baked beans for breakfast in a Machias restaurant and was delighted at the savory beans, with barely a hint of sweetness.

Baked Bean Soup

You can easily make baked bean soup by adding sautéed onion, stock or broth, and lively seasonings. Morsels of ham or bacon further improve the soup, as do a stray carrot or celery stalk. For the lively seasonings, it pays to keep an open mind because a squirt of ketchup, dollop of mustard, shake of chili powder, cumin, garlic powder, or pepper might do the trick. With a salad or coleslaw served on the side, the soup makes a very decent meal. Don't forget pickles.

{ SERVES 3 TO 6 }

1 LARGE ONION, CHOPPED

1 TO 2 TABLESPOONS VEGETABLE OIL

1 RIB CELERY, CHOPPED (OPTIONAL)

1 CARROT, SLICED (OPTIONAL)

1 ¾ TO 2 CUPS OR 1 LARGE CAN OF BAKED BEANS, DRAINED TO
    REDUCE THE SWEETNESS

TWICE AS MUCH BEEF OR VEGETABLE BROTH AS BEANS, OR TO TASTE

DICED HAM OR COOKED AND CRUMBLED BACON (OPTIONAL)

YOUR CHOICE OF POWDERED CELERY SEED, GARLIC, CHILI POWDER,
    CUMIN, RED PEPPER, MUSTARD, OR KETCHUP, TO TASTE

Sauté the onion in the oil, plus celery and carrots, if you choose them, for about 5 minutes until they are just softened. Add the beans, broth, meat, and your choice of seasonings. Bring to a boil and reduce the heat right away to a simmer. Cook all together for 30 minutes, taste, adjust seasonings, and serve.

Steamed Brown Bread

{ MAKES 2 SMALL LOAVES }

I found this recipe, a classic thirded brown bread with less sweetening, in the Knight Memorial Methodist Episcopal Church cookbook from Calais, dated 1922, donated by Mrs. W. E. Gibson.

1 CUP GRAHAM MEAL OR WHOLE-WHEAT FLOUR

1 CUP CORNMEAL

1 CUP FLOUR

1 TEASPOON SALT

2 TEASPOONS BAKING SODA

2 CUPS SOUR MILK

½ CUP MOLASSES

{ ADVICE }

I find brown bread recipes are pretty flexible, and can stand more molasses if you like the sweetness, or the substitution of sour milk for buttermilk or vice versa. Add raisins if you like them, and toss in a handful of chopped nuts if you want.

Put a pot of water on the stove to boil, and grease your molds or coffee cans. Put the graham meal or whole-wheat flour, cornmeal, flour, salt, and baking soda into a bowl and whisk them together well. Stir in the milk and molasses and stir only enough to moisten all the flours. Pour the batter into the molds or cans, dividing evenly if you use two, and position them on a rack inside the pot of hot water. Make sure water comes halfway up on the molds. Check the water level occasionally and add more hot water from a kettle as needed. Steam for 1¼ hours if you divide the batter into smaller containers, or for 3 hours if you do not. To test, insert a tester as you do for cake; if the skewer comes out clean it is done.

BROWN BREAD

Lots of Mainers steamed brown bread in coffee cans or lard pails. A double-boiler works very well for steaming. I have a lard pail I use for large breads, and a tube pudding mold for smaller ones. Since I have a wood-burning cookstove to heat my kichen and house, that's where I steam my pudding, and my island neighbor Linda Graf does, too, often making more than she needs right away and freezing a couple loaves for seasons when she isn't heating her house with wood.

Minnie McCormack, of Dover-Foxcroft, still makes brown bread, and if she is baking beans, she bakes the brown bread at the same time in greased cans in a water bath in the oven, an economical idea.

Old-Fashioned Brown Bread

Donald Marsh, in Holden, sent a brown bread recipe, writing, "This recipe is so easy that you won't believe it unless you try it." He found this hundred-year-old recipe in *The Maine Jubilee Cookbook*, submitted by Melvina W. Johnson, of Gorham.

Most of us do not equate bread crumbs with flour, but in past times bread crumbs were used to thicken sauces and substituted for flour in some baked goods. In this recipe stale bread and cornmeal with just a little bit of flour are the main ingredients.

If you are using day-old white bread crumbs you will need less milk than if you have stale whole wheat. If you have a food processor, consider pulsing the stale bread to get coarse crumbs. I steamed this one in a double boiler and included a generous handful of raisins. It's better than cake and is perfect for dessert.

¾ TO 1½ CUPS SOUR MILK

⅓ CUP SUGAR

¼ CUP MOLASSES

½ CUP CORN MEAL

4 SLICES STALE BREAD, TORN INTO SMALL PIECES

3 TABLESPOONS FLOUR

1 TEASPOON BAKING POWDER

1 TEASPOON BAKING SODA

½ TEASPOON SALT

RAISINS

Bring the water to a boil and preheat the oven to 325 degrees. Grease a pudding bowl, coffee can, tin mold, loaf pan, or, if you have one, lard pail. Combine the milk, sugar, molasses, and cornmeal and add the bread crumbs. Let soak. Meanwhile, sift together the flour, baking powder, soda, and salt. Stir the milk and crumb mixture, and if it is dry rather than dough-like stiff, add more milk. Add the flour mixture, stir to mix, and put the batter in the baking container. Put it in a hot water bath in the oven or in a steamer on top of the stove over low heat. Bake or steam for 2½ to 3 hours. It is done when it pulls away from the sides, and a tester inserted comes out clean.

Homemade Biscuits

{ MAKES 20 2-INCH BISCUITS }

Georgia Gray, nicknamed "the biscuit lady," of Verona, shared this recipe she uses to make biscuits for baked bean suppers, sometimes producing up to three hundred of them. Georgia recommended Maine-produced cream of tartar, Bakewell Cream, and commented that she always sifts the flour and uses Crisco shortening. I tried them with butter because I really like butter. She also said, "Cut through the dough with a spoon to get rid of air bubbles before you knead it." Don't over-handle the dough, and work quickly.

4 CUPS FLOUR

4 TEASPOONS CREAM OF TARTAR

2 TEASPOONS BAKING SODA

1 TEASPOON SALT

⅓ CUP COLD SHORTENING OR 5 TABLESPOONS BUTTER

1½ CUPS MILK

Preheat the oven to 430 degrees. Sift together the flour, cream of tartar, baking soda, and salt; cut in the shortening with a pastry cutter, two knives, or food processor until the mixture looks like coarse cornmeal. Add the milk, tossing the dough until all the flour is incorporated. Cut through the dough with a spoon in several places, then turn the dough out on a lightly floured board and knead quickly a couple of times. Pat the dough out to about an inch thick. Cut the dough in rounds and place them on a greased baking sheet or in a 9x13-inch baking pan. Bake 15 to 20 minutes, until golden brown.

Venison Pot Roast

{ SERVES 6 }

I am spoiled by having a wood-burning cookstove to do all my slow cooking on. In winter, I heat the house while I make soups, spaghetti sauce, chili, cook beans for baking, and do pot roasts. Blessed with avid hunter friends, I end up with generously sized pieces of venison perfect for the long, slow cooking that turns wild, lean meat into something that you can cut with your fork. I give it a minimum of 2 hours on top of the stove, and 3 at a slow simmer is better. The cooking time will vary depending on the cut of meat.

I have also used a pressure cooker for this, which works beautifully. The onions and garlic that I put in along with about a cup of water and the meat absolutely melt away during the cooking to become a rich, dark sauce with nuggets of mushrooms that I also add. My pressure cooker manual says 30 minutes for beef pot roast, but for venison an hour is better.

2 POUNDS VENISON

2 LARGE ONIONS, COARSELY CHOPPED

3 CLOVES GARLIC (OPTIONAL)

1 MEDIUM CAN MUSHROOMS OR 12 OUNCES FRESH MUSHROOMS,
   COARSELY CHOPPED

1 BAY LEAF

RED WINE (OPTIONAL)

SALT AND PEPPER, TO TASTE

Put the venison, onions, garlic, mushrooms, and bay leaf into a heavy pot with a tightly-fitting lid. Add water until there is at least an inch in the pot. Bring the pot to a boil and immediately turn down the temperature to a steady simmer. Check to make sure the water does not evaporate away. Cook for at least 2 hours, adding a splash of red wine for the last half hour. Test for tenderness and cook a little longer if necessary. Taste the gravy and add salt and pepper to taste.

Pressure cooker method: Put the venison, onions, garlic, muhrooms, bay leaf, and 1 cup of water into the pressure cooker. Add red wine, if desired. Bring the cooker up to a sufficient temperature that the pressure regulator knob rocks gently. Maintain that temperature for an hour. Let the pressure come down, and open to check the meat. If needed, replace the lid and cook longer, checking every 10 minutes until you have the desired tenderness.

Like many rural places in Maine, my island has a small population of folks who work together — and cook together — to make the community a good place to live.

Ham Loaf

If you serve your baked beans with boiled ham, you might have leftover ham for a ham loaf. Someone has joked that eternity is a ham and two people. When a ham meant the whole back leg of a pig, that would be true, but now a cook can acquire tiny hams, medium-size ones, and party-size spiral-cut numbers. Ham loaves are a way to help use up a big ham, and it is worth having enough ham to make one.

The following recipe is based on one from Ginny Hall, formerly of Islesboro, now a Maryland resident, passed along to me by island neighbor Ruth Hartley. The brown sugar, vinegar, and water poured over the top baked into a luscious glaze that went over very big in our household. We joked that I should bake the loaf in a big flat pan and double the glaze to make a kind of ham cake with brown-sugar-glaze frosting. The second glaze below provides the standard pineapple accompaniment to the ham.

1 POUND GROUND HAM

1 POUND GROUND PORK

1 CUP COARSE CRACKER CRUMBS

2 EGGS

1 SMALL ONION, FINELY CHOPPED

½ CUP MILK

½ CUP LIGHT BROWN SUGAR

¼ CUP VINEGAR

⅓ CUP WATER

1 TABLESPOON DRY MUSTARD

Preheat the oven to 400 degrees. Mix the ham, pork, cracker crumbs, eggs, onion, and milk together and pack into a greased loaf pan. For the glaze, in a separate bowl, mix together the sugar, vinegar, water, and mustard. Pour the glaze over the ham loaf and bake for 1½ hours.

Pineapple Glaze Variation:

2 TO 3 TABLESPOONS BROWN SUGAR

½ CUP CRUSHED CANNED PINEAPPLE, WELL DRAINED

Preheat the oven to 350 degrees. Mix the sugar and pineapple together and pat into the bottom of a loaf pan. Turn the ham mixture above into the pan and bake for an hour. Allow to cool for 15 minutes then turn out onto a platter.

Muddy Water Pickles

Some households served these very sharp pickles with baked beans and brown bread on Saturday night. The recipe harkens back to the 1700s and lives on today in some corners of the state. The pickles are made with dry mustard powder in a brine made mostly of vinegar, and they look like the very dickens, a mucky mess in a jar, hence the name "muddy." They are also called "riley water" pickles because we use the term "riled up" colloquially to describe something or someone disturbed or stirred up. Often when water is riled up it is also muddy.

My late neighbor Susie Wilbur gave me this recipe that she acquired from her Aunt Edna Durkee. She said, "These pickles have a real twang." They really do. They are not for the fainthearted. These pickles do not require processing in a canner.

SMALL CUCUMBERS

2 QUARTS CIDER VINEGAR

½ CUP SALT

2 CUPS SUGAR

¼ CUP DRY MUSTARD

Pack as many small, fresh cucumbers as will fit into sterile jars. Mix together the vinegar, salt, sugar, and mustard. Pour in the brine and close the jar. The pickles will be ready in a couple of weeks or so. Store in a cool place.

New England Boiled Dinner

A traditional New England boiled dinner is really about the vegetables. When corned beef is surrounded on a platter with white potatoes, yellow rutabaga, orange carrots, perhaps pale green cabbage, and brilliant deep red beets, the vegetables have the meat seriously outnumbered, and the smart cook makes sure that there are plenty of them for leftovers, because that's how we get to corned beef hash and particularly Red-Flannel Hash (see right).

I hold that the beets ought to be cooked separately from the other boiled dinner ingredients, because otherwise they will turn everything a ghastly pinkish red. I usually peel and cut the vegetables so that they will cook in a similar amount of time, but I am not scientific about this, and don't fuss if the carrots are more tender than the potatoes. I like my cabbage tender but you might like it firmer. I cook the beef alone until it is fork tender, then heave in the vegetables and let them sink to the bottom to cook, and let the beef sit on top to stay hot.

4 TO 5 POUNDS CORNED BEEF BRISKET

6 LARGE POTATOES

6 TO 8 LARGE CARROTS

1 SMALL RUTABAGA, OR HALF A LARGE ONE

1 SMALL CABBAGE, OR HALF A LARGE ONE

6 TO 8 MEDIUM BEETS

3 TO 4 SMALL ONIONS

Put the beef into a pot large enough to hold the meat and vegetables. Add water until it reaches half way up the chunk of meat. Simmer steadily for about 1 hour for each pound of meat, adding hot water if it boils away. Prepare the vegetables, quartering the potatoes and cutting the carrots into chunks 3 inches long, the rutabaga into chunks slightly smaller than the potatoes. Leave the onions whole. Add the vegetables 30 to 40 minutes before you wish to serve dinner, and add the cabbage 15 minutes before the end. Cook the beets separately, peel them, and reserve them, keeping them hot. Serve the dinner on one large platter, slice the beef against the grain, and pass mustard with it.

RED-FLANNEL HASH

Hash is a variable dish and depends largely on what you have for leftovers, though you can choose what to include or leave out. If you don't like beets, then make a simple hash of meat and potatoes. If you wish, cook with an egg on top to make a hearty breakfast or brunch dish.

Save the boiled dinner leftovers and chill them. When you are ready to make the hash, chop the beef and vegetables separately, but to your taste as far as texture is concerned. Toss them together in a bowl or mix on the griddle or frying pan. If you wish, add a small chopped onion to the mixture, which you fry on a heavy pan, turning it over when it crisps on one side. If the meat is lean, add oil as needed.

Serves as many as leftovers permit.

From Our Ethnic Heritage

OVER THE CENTURIES, MAINE has absorbed people from many non-English ethnic groups, beginning with the Germans who came to Waldoboro in the eighteenth century and who account for the famous Maine-made Morse's sauerkraut. Since then, French-Canadians, Scots from the Maritimes, Scandinavians, and Italians all contributed to Down East fare. Some dishes crop up only for holidays, like Christmas and Easter. Others are daily fare.

Ployes

Flat breads are found all around the world, made most simply with grain, water, salt, and baked flat on hot surfaces. Think about tortillas, lavash, pita, bannocks, and pancakes. Among French-Canadians, ployes are a traditional flatbread. Made of buckwheat flour, stacks of ployes were served on the tables of farm families, used as bread to sop up plates and fill out a meal. They are also served as pancakes with maple syrup for breakfast. A very handy ployes mix is made here in Maine from locally grown buckwheat, or you can mix your own using the recipe below.

> 1 CUP BUCKWHEAT FLOUR
>
> 1 CUP FLOUR
>
> 2 TEASPOONS BAKING POWDER
>
> 1 TEASPOON SALT
>
> 1½ CUPS COLD WATER
>
> ½ CUP HOT WATER

Sift together the flours, baking powder, and salt, then mix in the cold water. Let stand at least 5 minutes, then add the hot water and mix to make a batter. Drop by spoonfuls on a hot, lightly greased skillet. Bake until the tops are bubbly and dry. Flipping them over briefly is optional.

Lefse

Lefse was a daily bread for some Norwegians in the past, and like lots of ethnic dishes, it is now made for holidays as a remembrance of a family's heritage. An Islesboro neighbor of mine, Craig Olson, introduced me to this flatbread made from potatoes and flour with a bit of salt and cream or oil in it. Lefse is rolled out until it is quite thin and quickly baked on a flat griddle. Think of it as a Scandinavian tortilla.

Craig learned to make lefse from his grandmother, Thela Olson, who made a big batch before Thanksgiving when she served it for that holiday, and then froze half of it for Christmas. The Olsons have theirs with butter and cranberry sauce on it, but, like crepes, it can also be savory if you have a meat or seafood filling for it.

Learning to handle the dough takes a little practice. It helps if the potatoes are quite cool when you add the flour, and if the dough is kept chilled until you are ready to make the breads. A flat griddle is handy, too, and real Norwegians use a lefse stick, a long wooden blade with a flat and tapered end to slip under the breads to turn them over. I used the longest spatula I have, the one I use for icing a cake, and it works fine.

Craig described how his grandmother flattened each ball of the dough adeptly with the heel of her hand before rolling it out with a rolling pin. He advises using an uncovered rolling pin. Flour your work surface, and if the lefse is sticky, either while baking or drying, then you need to flour it a bit more.

3 PACKED CUPS COOKED POTATOES, RICED OR PUT THROUGH
A FOOD MILL

1 TABLESPOON SALT

1 TABLESPOON SUGAR

5 TABLESPOONS VEGETABLE OIL

1½ CUPS FLOUR

Mix together the potatoes, salt, sugar, and oil. Allow to cool. Knead in the flour until it is all incorporated and the dough feels smooth. Divide into 12 equal parts and roll each part into a ball.

Heat your griddle (if you have an electric one, set it for 450 degrees). Using a rolling pin, roll each ball into an 8 to 9-inch-diameter bread; it should be very thin. Place on the ungreased griddle. When it bubbles and browns, turn it. Then when it bubbles and browns a little on that side, lift it off the griddle, and, folding it in half, lay it on a tea towel and cover with another towel until you are ready to serve it.

Irish Soda Bread

{ MAKES 1 LOAF }

Soda bread recipes vary a great deal, but all are raised with baking soda and sometimes baking powder, too. Most of the time, but not always, they have oatmeal. All called for buttermilk and usually raisins or currants. Caraway seed did not occur in every recipe, but a descendant of Irish-Americans solemnly assured me that it wouldn't taste right without the caraway. It appears that you can use plain flour alone, or use part whole wheat.

Five folks sent recipes when asked: Jean Anderson, on Islesboro, and Ruth Thurston, in Machias, both sent recipes calling for flour and whole-wheat flour. My sister Sally Vaster, in Somerville, advised not to knead or handle the dough too much, to avoid toughness. A recipe from Patricia Estabrook, in Houlton, needed butter and an egg, currants but no caraway. Ethel Pochocki wrote about her favorite recipe, "I've tried others with eggs, shortening, whole wheat flour—but I always go back to this one." This turned out to be our favorite, too. Please note that there is one step that you need to do overnight, or at least for an hour, before you begin to make it. Like most quick breads and biscuits, it is best warm and eaten the first day.

1 ½ CUPS QUICK OATMEAL

1 ½ CUPS BUTTERMILK OR SOUR MILK

1 ¾ CUPS FLOUR

1 ½ TEASPOONS BAKING SODA

1 TEASPOON SALT

2 TABLESPOONS SUGAR

½ CUP RAISINS OR CURRANTS

1 TABLESPOON CARAWAY SEED

Mix the oatmeal and buttermilk together and let sit overnight, or for 1 hour if you are in a hurry.

Preheat the oven to 350 degrees. Mix the rest of the ingredients together in a bowl, and add the oatmeal and buttermilk mixture. Knead quickly into a soft ball of dough. On a floured surface, roll or pat out into a round loaf, 1½ inches thick and about 6 inches across. Using a floured knife, cut the dough into quarters, all the way through the loaf but without separating the sections.

Slide onto a lightly floured baking sheet. Bake for 55 to 60 minutes until it is well browned and has a hollow sound when tapped.

Tourtière

Tourtière, traditionally served in Quebeçois families after Christmas Eve midnight mass, *has* to have pork, potato, onion, garlic, cinnamon, salt, and pepper and be baked between two crusts. "There are probably as many recipes for tourtière as there are Quebeçois," wrote Peggy Gannon, of Palmyra. Most recipes call for cinnamon. Some call for cloves, and one for allspice. Sage, marjoram, parsley, thyme, and poultry seasoning all put in an appearance. One recipe I saw called for chopped celery cooked with the onion and garlic, which was omitted in a couple, while another called for celery seed. Clearly seasoning the pie is a matter of taste; just make sure you use cinnamon. Tourtière is good served warm or cold, and accompanied by cranberry sauce or applesauce. A couple of the recipes caution to cool the filling before putting it in the pie crust, a good idea because it will keep the pastry from softening too much while baking.

4 MEDIUM TO LARGE POTATOES

2 POUNDS GROUND PORK

1 LARGE ONION, CHOPPED

2 CLOVES GARLIC OR LESS, TO TASTE

½ TO 1 TEASPOON CINNAMON

½ TEASPOON CLOVES OR ALLSPICE

1 TEASPOON SAGE OR POULTRY SEASONING

THYME, MARJORAM, GROUND CELERY TO TASTE (OPTIONAL)

TWO (9-INCH) PIE CRUSTS

Put the potatoes on to cook, and while they are boiling, put the pork, onion, and garlic into a large skillet and cook them all together very well. Then add spices, cover, and reduce the temperature to low. When the potatoes are done, drain and mash them, adding milk and butter if you wish, just as if you were making mashed potatoes for dinner. Mix the pork and potatoes together very well, and put in a cool place to chill.

Preheat the oven to 425 degrees. Roll out the pastry, line your pie plate, and spoon the cooled pork mixture into the pie. Cover with the top crust. Bake for 15 minutes, then reduce the temperature to 375 degrees and bake an additional 35 to 40 minutes until the crust is golden brown.

TOURTIÈRE AND CHRISTMAS EVE MEMORIES

Tourtière recipes seem to come along with good memories. Jeanine Brown Gay, in Belfast, wrote to say that her parents "were the first of a large family to marry and have children, so the dozen or more relatives would gather at my parents' home after midnight mass for tourtière, wine, and coffee. My brother and I loved it, because the aunts and uncles would wake us up to open gifts that Santa had left for us under the tree."

Peggy learned to make tourtière by watching her French-Canadian stepmother make it, and Charlene Randall, in Bangor, found two recipes for it in her mother's recipe box. Charlene wrote that her mother, Jeanette "Odele" Lewis, was ninety-two when she passed away in 2002, and cooked for most of her life. Charlene reported, "Mother said these pork pies were a New Year's tradition in her home."

Sharon Goguen, in Belfast, sent along her family's interesting variation on tourtière, writing "My father's family was French-Canadian and we always had this on Christmas Eve. It is a little different from most recipes I have seen, as this one incorporates apples." Alice Rollins sent along three variations on the tourtière theme.

Latkes

{ SERVES 8 TO 10 }

Good old Maine potatoes are perfect for latkes, or potato pancakes, one of the dishes associated with Chanukah, the annual Jewish festival of lights. They are easily made, especially if you use a grater blade in the food processor to grate the potatoes, though hand-grating is fine, too. Usually they are fried in cakes 3 to 4 inches in diameter, and served with applesauce or sour cream. The Chanukah story celebrates the miracle of the oil in the temple lasting eight days when it was expected to last but one. So the latkes' significance lies in commemorating the oil required for frying them. A good, all-purpose, white-skinned potato is best for latkes.

> 4 CUPS PEELED, GRATED POTATOES
>
> 1 LARGE ONION, FINELY CHOPPED
>
> 2 TEASPOONS SALT
>
> 2 EGGS, BEATEN
>
> 2 TABLESPOONS FLOUR
>
> A FEW GRINDS PEPPER
>
> OIL FOR FRYING

Put the grated potato in a colander and press it against the sides to squeeze out the excess liquid. Put in a bowl, and add the onion, salt, eggs, flour, and pepper, and mix thoroughly. Heat a frying pan or skillet and add oil to cover the bottom, then drop large spoonfuls of the potato mixture onto it, flattening them with a spatula. Cook at a fairly high temperature until they are browned on one side, then flip them over and brown on the other. Drain on paper, and keep them warm in the oven until all of the mixture has been cooked.

Gamaldags Peparkakor

My Swedish-born grandmother, my mother, and now my sister Sally and I make these gingery, orange-scented cookies for Christmas. The family story was that the name meant Good Day Pepper Cakes, the "pepper" being spicy ginger. Ideally, we make them early in the holiday season, because their flavor improves as the month wears on. For years, we made them on Thanksgiving weekend when we gathered at Mom and Dad's house.

Be aware that the dough will be stiff to mix and that you need to chill it before rolling it out.

½ CUP BUTTER

¾ CUP SUGAR

1 EGG

¾ CUP MOLASSES

2 TEASPOONS FINELY GRATED ORANGE ZEST

3½ CUPS FLOUR

1 TEASPOON BAKING SODA

1½ TEASPOONS GROUND GINGER

1½ TEASPOONS GROUND CINNAMON

1 TEASPOON GROUND CLOVES

Cream together the butter and sugar. Mix in the egg, molasses, and orange peel. Sift together all the flour, baking soda, ginger, cinnamon, and cloves and add them to the butter and sugar mixture, until all the dry ingredients have been incorporated. The dough will be stiff and sticky. Cover and refrigerate overnight.

When you are ready to make the cookies, preheat the oven to 350 degrees and grease a couple of baking sheets. Generously sprinkle your cutting surface with flour. Roll out small, fist-size pieces of dough to about ⅛ of an inch thick, and cut your cookies. You may have to slide a thin-bladed spatula or knife underneath them to loosen them. Slip them onto the baking sheet and decorate as you wish. Bake for 8 to 10 minutes. Remove to a cooling rack and allow to cool completely before storing.

Creton

{ MAKES 1 LOAF }

French-Canadian creton shows up around the holidays, or at least when the weather turns cold. The flavorful combination of ground, spiced pork and pork fat cooked with onion and spread on bread is just the ticket for breakfast on a day that you intend to spend shoveling snow, cutting trees, or cross-country skiing. Deb Rollins and Ruth Thurston shared recipes, and Peggy Gannon sent her stepmother Merciale Fillion's recipe.

The recipes call for ground pork. You could grind your own, or buy it already ground. I cut my pork off a picnic shoulder, and add in a little extra fat. Peggy wrote, "I find this rather greasy so I sauté the pork lightly first and pour off the fat." You may wish to do that, too.

Virtually all the recipes suggested onion, allspice, salt, and pepper as necessary seasonings; some added bay leaf and garlic. I used allspice, salt, pepper, onion, and garlic. The flavor develops over a couple of days, but taste it anyway before it is done, because you may wish to get the salt and pepper up to speed and add a little more allspice. This recipe, which makes a small amount, is easily doubled.

1 POUND GROUND PORK

¼ POUND GROUND CLEAR PORK FAT

1 MEDIUM ONION

1 CLOVE GARLIC

2 TABLESPOONS BREAD CRUMBS

¼ TEASPOON ALLSPICE, OR MORE TO TASTE

SALT AND PEPPER, TO TASTE

Put the pork, pork fat, onion, garlic, bread crumbs, and ½ cup water in a heavy saucepan over a low heat and simmer together for 2 hours. Add the spices, salt, and pepper, and simmer an additional 15 minutes. Taste and adjust seasonings, bearing in mind that the flavor develops further in a couple of days. Pour into a bowl or a 5x8x2-inch loaf pan, cover, and chill. Serve with bread for sandwiches or for canapés or on crackers.

St. Lucia Buns

Louanne Littlefield, an Islesboro neighbor of mine, passed this recipe along to me. Whether or not you are descended from a Scandinavian, and Maine is full of them, and whether or not you observe St. Lucy's Day in December, as many do in this state, you might enjoy the *Lussekatter*, or St. Lucia Buns, that follow. You can also form the dough into loaves as Louanne did. The saffron is definitely a must. In fact, it is practically the whole point.

{ MAKES 2 DOZEN }

2 PACKAGES ACTIVE DRY YEAST

½ CUP WARM WATER (105 TO 115 DEGREES)

⅔ CUP LUKEWARM MILK (SCALDED THEN COOLED)

½ CUP SUGAR

½ CUP BUTTER, SOFTENED

3 EGGS

½ TEASPOON GROUND CARDAMOM

1 TEASPOON SALT

½ TEASPOON POWDERED SAFFRON

5 TO 5½ CUPS FLOUR

RAISINS FOR GARNISH

SUGAR FOR SPRINKLING

Dissolve the yeast in the warm water in a large bowl. Stir in the milk, sugar, butter, 2 eggs, cardamom, salt, saffron, and 3 cups of the flour. Beat until smooth. Stir in enough of the remaining flour to make dough easy to handle. Turn dough onto a lightly floured surface; knead until smooth. Place in a greased bowl, cover, set in a warm place, and let rise until double.

Preheat the oven to 350 degrees. Punch down dough; divide into 24 parts. Shape each piece into an S-shaped rope; curling both ends in. Put a raisin in the center of each curl. Place rolls on a greased cookie sheet. Brush tops lightly with butter; let rise until doubled. Mix the remaining egg with one tablespoon water, and brush buns lightly with the mixture. Sprinkle with sugar. Bake for 15 to 20 minutes.

Baked Goods & Confections

CAKES, BREADS, COOKIES, and other sweets fill some of our grandmothers' recipe collections and favorite cookbooks like the famous *Maine Rebekahs* cookbooks. After all, those recipes had to be written down to remind the cook just what the proportions were, where a soup or stew could more easily tolerate ingredient variability. Following are some of our most famous Maine baked goods.

Blueberry Molasses Cake

Molasses as a sweetening for all sorts of Maine-baked goods reflects a necessary frugality among Maine cooks. Little wonder that one variation on blueberry cake included a molasses version.

{ MAKES 1 CAKE }

Ethel Pochocki, of Brooks, sent me this recipe, which she collected about thirty years ago from a neighbor named Virginia Gray. Ethel reports that it has become one of her family favorites, and wrote, "Simple and doesn't need frosting, but whipped cream makes it even more delicious." Molasses does not overwhelm the blueberries as much as you might think.

2½ CUPS FLOUR, WITH 2 TABLESPOONS REMOVED

1½ TEASPOONS BAKING SODA

½ TEASPOON EACH OF YOUR CHOICE OF GROUND SPICES: CINNAMON, NUTMEG, OR GINGER

⅔ CUP MOLASSES

1 CUP SUGAR

½ CUP CANOLA OR VEGETABLE OIL

1 EGG, LIGHTLY BEATEN

1 CUP BOILING WATER

1 CUP LIGHTLY FLOURED BLUEBERRIES

Preheat the oven to 350 degrees. Grease a 9x13-inch pan. Sift the flour with the baking soda and spices. Mix together the molasses, sugar, oil, and egg. Add the flour and spices, then mix in the boiling water. Add the blueberries last. Bake for 30 minutes or until a tester inserted comes out clean. Serve with whipped cream.

Blueberry Cake

Blueberries are Maine's iconic fruit and Down East is generously spread with barrens studded with boulders and ledges where the little wild berry grows plentifully. I never heard of blueberry cake until I came to Maine three decades ago, and so I was particularly grateful for the education that lots of Maine cooks gave me in this classic Down East cake.

Quite a few of them dug around in their grandmother's or mother's recipe collections. Nancy Jordan, of Otis, found a sixty- to seventy-year-old recipe among her family's collection, from a now-forgotten baking powder company. Cheryl Spencer, from Old Town, shared her mother's forty-something-year-old recipe. Genevieve Delicata, of Prospect, got her recipe from her sister, who picked it up from their grandmother. Jan Dodge, who has family connections to my town of Islesboro, sent her mom's recipe, cut out of an old newspaper.

Sandra Tibbetts, in Brewer, shared a neighbor's recipe. Sonya Savage, in Enfield, found hers in a 1964 *Pilgrim Daughter's Cookbook* from the Lincoln, Maine, Congregational Church. Jan Dodge found another in the Ashville [Maine] Community Church cookbook. Even Maine Senator Margaret Chase Smith's recipe got into the act, one that Ruth Thurston of Machias had collected.

For June Jandraeu, in St. Francis, a blueberry cake recipe passed down four generations reminded her of "going to pick blueberries with Grammie so she could make this delicious cake. It seems to have taken forever to pick the two cups of berries because they were so small."

Among the solid advice coming from these cooks was the recommendation to separate the eggs and beat the whites to fold into the cake. Several recipes called for sprinkling cinnamon sugar on top for baking, but a struesel topping is better. Some cooks reported that frozen berries were fine to use if added in a fully frozen state. Others specified fresh only in order to avoid the dreaded blue batter.

Judy Boothby, of Bangor, wrote me, saying, "Fear not! Frozen blueberries are possible." To avoid a hideous color from mushy frozen berries, this is what Judy does. "Leave them in the freezer until the last minute. Measure all ingredients. Set aside ¼ cup of flour in a pie plate.

Blend the rest of the ingredients. Roll the berries briefly in the flour, fold in, and bake a little longer than for fresh."

Then blueberry grower Linda Long cautioned that if you use frozen berries, be sure to bake the cake a little longer and test for doneness. Good point.

For the topping:

¼ CUP BUTTER

⅓ CUP FLOUR

½ CUP SUGAR

1 TEASPOON CINNAMON

For the cake:

½ CUP (ONE STICK) BUTTER

¾ CUP SUGAR

2 EGGS, SEPARATED

1 TEASPOON VANILLA

2 CUPS FLOUR

2 TEASPOONS BAKING POWDER

¾ CUP MILK

1½ TO 2 CUPS FLOURED BLUEBERRIES

Prepare the topping first by cutting the ingredients together with a fork and set aside. Preheat the oven to 350 degrees. Grease and flour an 8- or 9-inch square pan. Cream together the butter and sugar and beat in the egg yolks. Add the vanilla. Beat the egg whites until stiff and set aside. Sift together the flour and baking powder and add to the butter and sugar mixture alternately with the milk. Fold in the whites and then gently add the berries. Distribute the topping or just sprinkle with cinnamon sugar. Bake for 40 minutes, slightly longer if the berries are frozen. The cake is done when the topping is golden brown and a tester inserted comes out clean.

Hot Water Gingerbread

{ MAKES 1 CAKE }

{ ADVICE }

I know someone who chops candied ginger finely and adds it to gingerbread. Sometimes I make an orange glaze, most easily done by melting marmalade. Otherwise add sugar to orange juice with extra peel grated in and heat until it is syrupy. With a jazzy glazing poured over it, you can get away with this for company dessert.

Lately, chocolate has unseated molasses as a comfort food flavoring. Before chewy chocolate chip cookies dominated the cookie jar, there were soft, luscious molasses cookies and before brownies took over, there was gingerbread. I get a real hankering for gingerbread sometimes, and this lovely cakey one with the crisp top came from my grandma. I used this recipe for a 4-H cooking project fifty years ago and got a blue ribbon out of it.

My family called it Hot Water Gingerbread because of the boiling water you add at the very end. It turns the whole thing into an alarming muddy mess, but forge on, bake, it and it comes out fine. It will have a crisp top at first, which turns soft overnight. I've served it with applesauce on top, or whipped cream.

2½ CUPS FLOUR

½ TEASPOON CLOVES

1 TEASPOON CINNAMON

2 TEASPOONS GROUND GINGER

1½ TEASPOONS BAKING SODA

½ CUP SUGAR

½ CUP BUTTER

1 EGG

1 CUP MOLASSES

1 CUP HOT WATER

Preheat the oven to 350 degrees. Grease a 9x9-inch pan. Turn on the teakettle to heat water. Sift together the flour, spices, and baking soda. Cream together the sugar and butter. Beat in the egg, add the molasses, and beat all together. Stir in the dry ingredients, and make a stiff batter, then add the boiling water, stirring out any lumps. Pour into the baking pan and bake for 30 to 35 minutes, until the center is raised and firm.

Graham Rolls

When Marilyn Hall, in Oakfield, asked about where to find graham to use in some muffin recipes, we learned that whole-wheat flour is seldom sold as graham flour anymore. Estelle Chipman, from Birch Harbor, discovered some in a dietary and special foods section of the grocery store sold as "All-Natural Stone-Ground Whole-Wheat Graham Flour."

Betty Mills, in Dexter, found the following Graham Rolls recipe in her Dexter-native grandmother Eula Towle's collection after Eula's death at age ninety. The recipe originally came from Eula's mother, Nellie Levenseller, and Betty believes the recipe is at least one hundred years old. Betty wrote, "When my grandmother made these, she used the original old-fashioned cast-iron muffin pans with the oblong curved logs." If you own a cast-iron muffin pan, by all means bake these muffins in it to create a toothsome crunchy exterior. When I use my cast-iron pans, I always preheat them for ten minutes or so in the oven as it preheats.

{ MAKES 12 }

1 CUP GRAHAM OR WHOLE-WHEAT FLOUR

½ CUP FLOUR

1 TEASPOON BAKING SODA

½ TEASPOON SALT

⅓ CUP SUGAR

1 CUP SOUR MILK

1 EGG, BEATEN

2 TABLESPOONS MOLASSES

2 TABLESPOONS MELTED BUTTER

Preheat the oven to 425 degrees. Grease your muffin tins. Sift together the dry ingredients and put into a medium bowl. Whisk together the wet ingredients and add to the dry, and mix them with a few swift strokes. Spoon the batter into the muffin tins and bake for 12 to 15 minutes until golden brown on top and a tester inserted comes out clean. Serve hot with butter.

Date Nut Bread

{ MAKES 1 LOAF }

{ ADVICE }

Marie Lorizio, of
Newport, shared her
date nut bread recipe.
Marie fortified her bread
with raisins and soaked
the dates and raisins
in flavor-boosting
strong coffee!

Close to forty years ago, the late, great Maine-born boat builder and maritime historian John Gardner told me about date nut bread as a memorable recipe from his youth in the early twentieth century. Over the years, several Maine recipe collections have come to me, some written by hand into notebooks, others on cards, and over and over in sections recorded in the first half of the 1900s, I find date nut bread. The recipe crops up in community cookbooks, too, the ones assembled by organizations like the Rebekahs and Granges. Then lo, in my personal copy of Marjorie Standish's *Cooking Down East*, published in 1969, the pages containing banana bread, lemon bread, *and* date nut bread are the book's most spattered pages.

Between the 1920s and the present, a couple of things have changed about date nut bread: the older recipes have less sugar and a little less shortening in them. Hmmm. By the 1960s, the proportions in the recipe below seem to have appeared and not changed very much since. Obviously, you can knock both the sugar and fat back a little and still get delicious bread.

1 CUP CHOPPED DATES

½ CUP RAISINS, OPTIONAL

3 TABLESPOONS BUTTER

1 CUP BOILING WATER OR BREWED COFFEE

1 ½ TEASPOONS BAKING SODA

½ TEASPOON SALT

2 EGGS

1 TEASPOON VANILLA

¾ CUP SUGAR

1 ½ CUPS FLOUR

½ TO ¾ CUP CHOPPED WALNUTS

Put the dates, optional raisins, and butter in a mixing bowl and cover with the boiling water or coffee. Let stand for about 20 minutes. Preheat the oven to 350 degrees and grease a 9x5x3-inch loaf pan. To the dates in the mixing bowl, add the baking soda, salt, eggs, vanilla, and sugar. Beat well, and then add the flour, mix thoroughly, then fold in the nuts. Pour the batter into the loaf pan. Bake for 60 to 65 minutes, or until a tester inserted comes out clean.

Whoopie Pies

Whoopie pies, the classic chocolate cake-like cookie sandwich stuffed with either a sweetened vanilla-flavored shortening or a marshmallow filling, have been on Maine's menu since at least the 1920s. Recipes contributed by readers included some a half-century old.

Along with recipes came baking advice. Jeanine Gay, of Belfast, uses Silpat (a non-stick fiberglass and silicone sheet pan liner); Helen Braley, of Plymouth, bakes them on ungreased pans, as does Gloria Bodman in Machias. Alice Rollins, of Guilford, cautions, "Remove them from the oven just before the cookies are completely baked so they aren't over-done."

Let's talk about shortening. Most recipes called for Crisco or Spry, white shortening in the can. Over the past few years I phased hydrogenated vegetable oils out of my kitchen, replaced with butter, oil, and lard from home-grown pigs, preferring shortenings that humans have known about, and that the human body has been digesting, for centuries, over relatively modern manufactured ones. Most recipes call for Crisco in the cookie part, but I substituted butter. Crisco surely is the classic filling ingredient for whoopie pies. Despite my reservations, I include it below, though personally I would greatly prefer one made with butter.

For the cookies:

2 CUPS FLOUR

½ CUP COCOA POWDER

1 TEASPOON BAKING SODA

½ TEASPOON SALT

⅓ CUP SHORTENING

1 CUP SUGAR

1 EGG

1 TEASPOON VANILLA

1 CUP MILK

For the filling:

2 EGG WHITES

2 CUPS CONFECTIONERS' SUGAR

½ CUP SHORTENING OR BUTTER

1 TEASPOON VANILLA

Preheat the oven to 375 degrees. Sift together the flour, cocoa, baking soda, and salt. Cream together the shortening and sugar, beat in the egg and vanilla, then add the dry ingredients and milk alternately. You will have a fairly stiff cake batter. Drop by large spoonfuls onto a greased cookie sheet, leaving room for them to spread somewhat. Bake for 10 to 15 minutes. Allow to cool slightly before removing them to a rack.

Beat the egg whites until they are fluffy, gradually adding one cup of confectioners' sugar. Then spoonful by spoonful add the shortening and the rest of the sugar to the egg white mixture until it is smooth and fluffy, and then beat in the vanilla. When the cookies are cool enough to handle, make pairs of similarly sized ones and spread the filling on one half and top with the other half. Wrap in plastic wrap or put into an airtight container.

WHOOPIE PIE MEMORIES

Whoopie pies delight year-rounders and summer visitors alike. In all likelihood, developed as the Berwick Baking Company's answer to Drake's Cake's Devil Dogs, whoopie pies may very well be descended from a Pennsylvania Amish confection called a "gob."

Jeanine Gay, in Belfast, sent Rollande's Whoopie Pies, a recipe, she said, "copied from my mother's sister about sixty years ago." In Owls Head, Brenda McLain's mom's recipe has served four generations. Alice Rollins, in Guilford, uses a fifty-year-old recipe, and Lois Farr's came from her mom's 1942 *Rebekahs Cook Book*. On Mount Desert Island, Ruth Watson made whoopie pies for her children growing up in the 1950s and '60s. Martha Alley, of South Thomaston, found her recipe in a 1978 Lincolnville Grange cookbook. Alice K night, in Rockland, reported that she taught from 1962 until her retirement in 1990, and her whoopie pie recipe was a great favorite with her Home Economics students. And in Veazie, Carol Thompson's recipe has served five generations!

Several recipes are well-traveled. Jennie Jones from Baileyville sent her recipe to her daughter in Mexico, where it worked perfectly. In 1964, Lucille White took hers to England, where she lived for two years. When Lois Farr lived in California, she "always made them when my son went on camping trips." Her son's friends had never eaten them before, but, she reported, "After the first time, his pals always said 'Be sure to have your mom make those chocolate things.'" Evelyn Greene, in Bangor, uses the same filling in whoopie pies and red velvet cake! Lucile White reports: "Guys really love them because I don't skimp on the filling."

Chess Cakes

{ MAKES 12 }

{ ADVICE }

I made these cakes in cupcake tins, but when I saw how large they were I thought they would be a better size if baked in mini-muffin tins. The original instructions said, "Mrs. Longley says the crust should extend half way up the sides of the pans. She uses her hamburger mold to cut dough for the proper size." You'll have to experiment to find the right diameter for your pans. I ended up inverting a small bowl and running a knife around the perimeter.

A little piece of Maine's political history floated up with this recipe. Marion Wright, in Bangor, asked about chess cakes, which she remembered her mother making. Marion recalled the basic process: line cupcake tins with pie pastry, put in a dollop of jam or jelly, and top it with cake batter. She needed the recipe for the cake batter and Ruth Thurston, in Machias, sent Governor James B. Longley's wife's recipe for me to try.

The batter that follows is sweet and acquires a nice golden top, and while some recipes say to frost them when they are done, you could get away with dusting them with confectioners' sugar. I was reminded of jelly-filled doughnuts when I bit into one. The following cake batter is half of Mrs. Longley's recipe, easily doubled.

DOUGH FOR A 2-CRUST PIE

1 ¼ CUPS FLOUR

½ TEASPOON SALT

1 SCANT CUP SUGAR

1 ¾ TEASPOON BAKING POWDER

⅓ CUP BUTTER, SOFTENED

1 LARGE EGG

½ TEASPOON VANILLA

⅔ CUP MILK

JAM OR JELLY

Preheat the oven to 350 degrees. Roll out the pie dough and cut it into rounds to line your cupcake tins. Sift together the flour, salt, sugar, and baking powder. Using an electric mixer, beat the butter into the dry ingredients until it is thoroughly incorporated, or use your fingers to rub the butter into the dry ingredients. Mix together the egg, vanilla, and milk, and add gradually to the flour and butter mixture, beating well between additions until you have a smooth batter. Drop heaping teaspoons of jam or jelly into the lined cupcake tins. Drop heaping tablespoons of batter on the jelly, covering it entirely, and filling the cups as you would for cupcakes.

Bake for 20 to 25 minutes or until a tester inserted comes out clean. Let cool for a while, then lift from the tins to finish cooling on a cake rack. Frost as you wish.

CHESS CAKE HISTORY AND MEMORIES

This is classic tea party fare. I didn't make the connection between chess cakes and maids of honor right away, but sharp-eyed Diane Clough, of Bridgewater, poked around in her mother's 1952 *Rebekahs Cook Book* and found a recipe entitled "Maids of Honor," submitted by Helen E. Brown of the Emerald No. 65 Lodge in North Anson. Sure enough, pastry, jam, and cake batter.

Maids of honor were a moderately popular little tart in the 1800s, but the filling in those days was lemon flavored and sugary and would remind a southerner of chess pies. (How they came to be called "chess" is a long story, but involves a shift in the pronunciation of "cheese," further confused by the fact that actually there was no cheese in it, but rather the filling curdled like cheese.)

Ruth Thurston, of Machias, sent along a copy of an old newspaper clipping that she reported had turned all yellow, entitled "Mrs. Longley's Chess Cakes." Ruth said she must have cut it out of the paper during Governor James B. Longley's administration. He was Maine's first Independent governor, in office from 1975 to 1979.

The Longleys' daughter, Susan, from Liberty, was Islesboro's representative to the legislature, and a good one, too. I called her up and asked her if she remembered chess cakes. She exclaimed, "I haven't thought about them for years. They were delicious." I asked her what jam or jelly her mother used, and she said she thought it must have been apple or peach, or "some light-colored one." As it happened, Susan said Mrs. Longley died only a few months before we spoke. So we remembered her with the recipe.

Needhams

{ MAKES 5 DOZEN }

Needhams, a chocolate-covered confection made with potato, sugar, and coconut are famous in Maine, and over the years Marjorie Standish's recipe from *Cooking Down East* has become the standard. I have never heard a convincing explanation for how needhams got their name. The most common is that they were named for a famous evangelist in Portland named Reverend George S. Needham. They seem to have been a commercially made confection that migrated into the home kitchen.

Millie Whiles, in Machias, advises that she does not use leftover mashed potatoes because they are likely to have seasonings in them. She also refrigerates the baking sheet full of candy overnight to harden. Louann Littlefield, my neighbor, sent her grandmother's version, and she said, "Grammie Leach used toothpicks to dip, but I love those Wilton dipping tools." (Wilton is a cake decorating and confectionary company.) Jo Andrews, in Brooksville, suggests sprinkling the tops of the candies with red and green sprinkles before the chocolate hardens up.

Paraffin is used to help harden the chocolate. Now, I know that paraffin is edible, but I couldn't help thinking, hmmm, is there a way to do without it? Sherry Ryan, whose recipe came from her great-grandmother, omitted the paraffin. Sherry doubles the chocolate and spreads a very thin layer in the bottom of the baking pan before adding the potato, coconut, and sugar mixture, then tops it with more melted chocolate before cutting them into squares.

I used Sherry's method myself, but remember you don't get chocolate on all sides of your needhams that way. The recipe that follows calls for the standard paraffin.

For the filling:

½ TEASPOON SALT

¾ CUP UNSEASONED MASHED POTATO

½ CUP (1 STICK) BUTTER

2 POUNDS CONFECTIONERS' SUGAR

½ POUND FLAKED COCONUT

2 TEASPOONS VANILLA

Add the salt to the mashed potatoes, and melt the butter in the top of a double boiler over boiling water. To the melted butter add the potatoes, sugar, coconut, and vanilla. Mix well and spread in a layer about half an inch thick in a buttered jelly-roll pan. Cool thoroughly until hard and then cut into 1 to 1½-inch squares. Prepare the chocolate coating.

For the coating:

12 OUNCES CHOCOLATE CHIPS

4 OUNCES UNSWEETENED CHOCOLATE

½ CAKE PARAFFIN (2 OUNCES)

In the top of a double boiler over boiling water, melt the paraffin, then add the two chocolates and stir to melt and blend. Dip the potato and coconut squares in the chocolate, allowing them to finish dripping before placing on waxed paper to harden.

NEEDHAM MEMORIES AND ADVICE

When Betty Jean Maybury, in Brewer, sent her recipe, she commented, "Bet you will get a lot of recipes." I sure did: fifteen needham makers, many of whom concoct the candy for the holidays, contributed their experiences. I had Christmas in mind when I asked for this recipe. Barbara Elward, of Mattawamkeag, said she "always makes needhams for Christmas," ("and Valentine's Day, etc.") Ruth Thurston, in Machias, said, "I used to make these every Christmas until the children grew up and I grew out." Dorothy Quimby used Marjorie Standish's recipe at Christmas "for years" and found it foolproof and delicious. Lois Farr, in Dover-Foxcroft, wrote, "This recipe belonged to my sister's father-in-law, he made them every Christmas. I make them myself at the holidays." Linda Senter, of Clifton, said, "Happy holiday feasting," so I bet needhams are a holiday treat at her house.

Geraldine Pelletier of Hampden wrote that she is eighty-three years old, "so you can see this is an old recipe." The recipe was old by the time Mrs. Standish incorporated it into her cookbook. I have a 1930 American Legion Auxiliary Cookbook from Thomaston, Maine, that has a recipe for "potato candy needhams" in it. In another, printed in 1926, from First Universalist Church of Machias, there's an identical recipe for something called "uncooked fudge," but they are needhams all right. When Mrs. Standish standardized the recipe, she introduced the paraffin for the coating.

Hermits

The Maine Rebekahs, the lodge affiliated with the Independent Order of Odd Fellows, publish one of the state's longest standing series of community cookbooks, updated all through the 1900s and now into the twenty-first century, too. Their fundraising supports a variety of charities in Maine and abroad, including the Odd Fellows' and Rebekahs' Home of Maine, a non-profit residential care and nursing facility in Auburn. The most recent edition featured a chapter of recipes from past presidents, and this hermits recipe from Alice G. Priest McNeil, whose presidential term was 1909 through 1910, caught my eye. I based the recipe below on hers.

Alice had a light hand with spices, and I doubled up on the quantities. The molasses reminds us of gingerbread, and the raisins are a welcome morsel to bite into. You can bake these in a sheet to cut into bars, or you can make drop cookies. If you make drop cookies, use a quarter cup less flour. I baked the hermits on a 10x15-inch jelly-roll pan, but you can use two smaller baking pans. Bake them a little longer if you make them thicker.

2¾ CUPS OF FLOUR (OR 2½ CUPS IF MAKING DROP COOKIES)

¾ TEASPOON SALT

1 TEASPOON CINNAMON

1 TEASPOON CLOVES

1 TEASPOON BAKING SODA

½ CUP BUTTER OR SHORTENING

1 CUP SUGAR

1 EGG

½ CUP MOLASSES

½ CUP COLD WATER

½ CUP FINELY CHOPPED WALNUTS OR PECANS

½ CUP RAISINS

Preheat the oven to 350 degrees. Grease and flour a baking pan. Sift together the flour, salt, spices, and baking soda and set aside. Cream together the butter and sugar, and then beat in the egg and molasses. Add the sifted dry ingredients alternately with the water, and beat to make a smooth batter. Fold in the nuts and raisins. Spread the batter in the pan or drop by teaspoonfuls on a baking sheet. Bake for 20 minutes if in a large sheet, or 15 if in cookie form. Cool and cut to a size you prefer.

Homey Favorites

HOMEY FAVORITES

Everyone I know says the hardest thing about daily cooking of the "what's-for-supper-tonight" variety is deciding what to have. The recipes that follow will give you some homey, easy, comfortable, and economical suppers suitable for beginning or experienced cooks. Most are even kid-friendly.

Potatoes

POTATOES ARE PRETTY INEXPENSIVE and lots of them are grown in Maine both for commercial production and in home gardens like mine. I could buy them, but I grow them, anyway, because I can't get over the thrill of sticking a spading fork in the ground and turning up dinner. The potato names Katahdin, Red Norland, and Kennebec conjure up Maine. My favorite all-purpose potato is Carola, which I grow every year in addition to Sangre or Red Norlands and occasionally All-Blues.

Garlic Mashed Potatoes

Sally Pappas was looking for a recipe for garlic mashed potatoes. "I have looked through a lot of my cookbooks but haven't found one we like yet." It is a new enough wrinkle in cooking that a lot of cookbooks don't include directions for it, and when I looked on the Web for some ideas I saw that there was no agreement about the proportion of garlic to potatoes. With garlic mashed potatoes it is really a matter of cooking to taste, and the question really is what to do with the garlic. Experiment until you find the way you like best.

Here are some of the methods I tried. Each produces a slightly different effect. Since I like garlic a lot, my rule of thumb is one clove of garlic to each potato, and sometimes I toss in even a little more.

{ADVICE}

Sometimes I substitute potato-cooking water for part of the milk in mashed potatoes. It is a little less rich, and tastes fine. As always, how much liquid you need depends on how mealy the potatoes are. If you use a dry potato, like a russet, you will want more milk.

■ For a milder-flavored garlic mashed potatoes, cook peeled whole cloves of garlic with potatoes, mashing them together when you add milk, butter, salt, and pepper. (I often save potato cooking water for soup, so I have a garlic-flavored broth when I do this.)

■ For a slightly more pungent garlic flavor, add pureed fresh garlic to the potatoes as you mash them.

■ For a garlicky-flavored mashed potato without the bite, mince the garlic finely and heat it with the milk and butter before adding to the potatoes.

■ My favorite way is to add roasted garlic to the mashed potatoes. To make roasted garlic, peel a bunch of garlic, dribble it with olive oil, put it into a small baking dish with a lid on it, and bake it at 300 degrees until it is soft enough to stir with a spoon. Roasting mellows garlic and preserves the flavor.

■ You can buy garlic paste in tubes and minced garlic in jars, remembering that you need so much garlic in mashed potatoes that this might be a costly way to go. I haven't tried using dried garlic powder, but if you were flat out of fresh garlic cloves and were really aching for garlic mashed potatoes, that might work.

Warm Potato Salad

In this salad the warm potatoes soften the goat cheese to make it smooth and creamy. Use a vinaigrette dressing and treat the goat cheese as an ingredient along with potatoes, onion, and parsley. As the cheese melts, it mellows out the dressing. If you want, you can add other blanched warm vegetables.

{ SERVES 4 TO 6 }

{ ADVICE }

Goat cheese is widely available. Just about any grocery store will carry the soft goat cheese needed in this recipe. If you shop at a farmer's market, you can often buy it directly from the maker.

1 ½ POUNDS RED POTATOES

1 SMALL RED ONION, FINELY CHOPPED

3 SPRIGS FLAT-LEAFED PARSLEY, MINCED

2 OUNCES SOFT GOAT CHEESE

VINAIGRETTE DRESSING, TO TASTE

SALT AND PEPPER, TO TASTE

Cut the potatoes into bite-size pieces and cook until tender. Drain quickly and, while they are still warm, add the onion, parsley, goat cheese, dressing, salt, and pepper, tossing all together gently until the cheese melts. Serve.

POTATO SALAD VARIATIONS

Sometimes a classic, plain, cold potato salad with celery, onions, boiled eggs, and a generous dollop of mayonnaise is just the ticket for a summery supper. Other times potato salad with a lower calorie count is really welcome. Fortunately, potatoes take kindly to all sorts of additions, and adapt themselves to warm or cold salads.

Most potato salads around my house are a free-for-all. One thing I do that gives a potato salad some character is sprinkle onto warm cooked potatoes some rice vinegar, white wine vinegar, or plain malt vinegar—the sort some Down Easters like to put on french fries. The vinegar soaks into the potatoes as they cool down.

I add blanched green beans, asparagus, broccoli, shredded spinach, pickles, chopped finely, cucumber, celery, red onion, pickled onions, shallots, scallions, parsley, the kitchen sink, though not all of these at one time.

For dressing, I use vinaigrette, mayonnaise, a garlicky homemade dressing that I am fond of, or blue cheese dressing. Sometimes I do a combination of dressings.

Scalloped Potatoes

{ SERVES 4 TO 6 }

{ ADVICE }

I always thought if scalloped potatoes had cheese in them, then they were really "au gratin" potatoes, but maybe this is being picky. Sprinkling cheese on the top certainly dresses up an otherwise fairly dowdy dish, and a sharp cheddar or nippy blue cheese adds needed flavor, too.

Here is our collected Down East wisdom on scalloped potatoes.

Use as many potatoes as you like. Janice Harrigan, from Houlton, favors russets. How about one medium one for each person? You can parboil them, and if time is an issue, that would probably be helpful; otherwise you are in it for at least an hour of baking time. Slice them thinly, a quarter of an inch or less. Sliced onions are required, and need to be laid between the layers of potato.

Vicki Landry, of Little Deer Isle, sent a recipe that she found in the Deer Isle *Island Nursing Home Volunteers Cookbook*. It called for mushroom soup thinned with a little milk. That guarantees a smooth sauce. Otherwise, use milk and flour and practice, practice, practice. If you want your potatoes to be low fat, do as Linda Jean Conn, from Bangor, does, and use skimmed milk. If you want to gussy it up, use sour cream, cheese, and whole milk. Season them with salt and pepper, garlic, and parsley. Warm the milk and add it until the milk comes up to the top layer of potatoes.

Jacqueline Thomas, in Bangor, however, favors starting the dish covered with foil in a 325 degree oven, and then taking the foil off and raising the temperature to 350 degrees. Jacqueline's recipe also recommends heating the milk and melting the butter in it before adding it to the potatoes.

Ruth Thurston, in Machias, suggested a potato casserole made with cold boiled potatoes, assembled scallop-style with cheese, butter, and sour cream.

4 MEDIUM POTATOES THINLY SLICED

1 MEDIUM ONION THINLY SLICED

3 TABLESPOONS FLOUR

SALT AND PEPPER, TO TASTE

1 CUP SHREDDED CHEDDAR CHEESE (OPTIONAL)

2½ CUPS MILK

¼ CUP BUTTER

1 CUP SOUR CREAM (OPTIONAL)

CHOPPED PARSLEY

Preheat the oven to 325 degrees. Grease a 9-by-13-inch glass baking dish. Lay in a thin layer of potatoes, sprinkle on about half of the onions, sprinkle in the flour, salt, and pepper, and, if you are using it, part of the cheese. Then repeat this until the potatoes, onions, and cheese are used up. Heat the milk and butter together in a saucepan until the butter is melted, and if you choose sour cream, stir it in until it is all smooth. Pour this over the potatoes in the casserole and watch for it to show through the topmost layer of the potatoes. Cover with foil and put the casserole into the oven. Check back in 30 minutes, and test the potatoes. If they are barely tender, remove the foil, and raise the temperature to 350 degrees and cook at least another 30 minutes or more until the potatoes are very tender and the top is slightly browned.

Baked Stuffed Potatoes

Baked stuffed potatoes are a great dodge for a quick supper as long as you have already baked potatoes on hand. I never bake them on purpose for this dish, but rather I bake more for dinner one night than I actually need, and have them a few days later. I scrape out the insides and do the stuffing, reheating as needed.

1 LARGE OR 2 SMALL BAKED POTATOES PER PERSON

A COUPLE SPOONFULS OF FILLING, MEAT, CHEESE, OR VEGETABLE

MILK, CREAM, BROTH, OR LEFTOVER GRAVY

SEASONINGS OF YOUR CHOICE (ONIONS, GARLIC, SALT, PEPPER, ETC.)

Slice the potato the long way and gently scrape out the insides, leaving a fairly firm outside about an eighth to a quarter of an inch thick. Mash together the filling and potato, dribbling in cream, milk, or broth. Season, tasting as you go along, until it is satisfactory. Pile the filling back into the potato halves, mounding them up. If you want a little color, sprinkle them with paprika, or top with a bit of Parmesan. Bake in a 350 degree oven until they are hot through, about a half hour.

{ ADVICE }

If it looks like you will have too much filling, don't worry. Just put it into a small dish to bake, or make it into patties to fry some other night. If your potatoes are mealy, that is, a bit crumbly and tender, as russets and other baking potatoes often are, you will need a little more of the moistening ingredient than if you use a waxier potato. You may wish to sauté your onions and garlic for the filling, or else mince them very finely. You are using Maine potatoes, too, right?

Chicken Galore

LOTS OF MY BEST CHICKEN RECIPES come from slender friends, and I am happy to share them with you. Even though I favor cooking chicken pieces with the skin on and bone in, many recipes following are made with boneless, skinless chicken breasts beloved of those watching calorie and cholesterol counts, but which run a constant risk of being tough and tasteless. Tweaking them so they have actual flavor is the trick.

Chicken Cacciatore

{ SERVES 4 }

Cacciatore is the chicken dish with tomato paste in it, an Italian recipe at its core, sometimes called Hunter's Chicken. Diane Ferris, of Harrington, helped me out with this one. A French woman taught her to make it and Diane said, "She told me two important things: one is to make sure chicken pieces are dry to the touch so they will brown in the oil. And the other is, if the sauce seems too thin, use tomato paste to thicken it up."

I tried it with chicken thighs, bone in, and skin on. It took about an hour in all to prepare. Serve it on pasta or polenta — fried mush to us Yankees.

2 POUNDS CHICKEN PIECES

2 TABLESPOONS FLOUR

2 TABLESPOONS OLIVE OIL

2 CLOVES GARLIC, MINCED

1 GREEN PEPPER, CHOPPED

1 MEDIUM ONION, CHOPPED

1 CUP SLICED MUSHROOMS

1 CUP CHICKEN STOCK

½ CUP RED WINE

¼ CUP TOMATO PASTE

1 BAY LEAF

1 TEASPOON BASIL

½ TEASPOON THYME

A FEW GRINDS OF BLACK PEPPER

SALT, TO TASTE

Pat the chicken dry and dredge it in flour. Heat the olive oil in a heavy bottom pot or deep-fry pan over a medium-high flame, and drop in the chicken pieces, skin side down, browning them about 5 minutes until the skin is golden. Remove them and keep them warm. Add the garlic, pepper, onion, and mushrooms to the oil and cook them for about 3 minutes, stirring occasionally. Then add the stock, wine, and tomato paste. Combine it all well, then return the chicken to the pan. Add the herbs, and simmer covered for about 30 minutes. Uncover and simmer for another 15 to 20 minutes to thicken the sauce somewhat.

Pan-Roasted Chicken Breasts with Balsamic Sauce

{ SERVES 4 }

The late Gail O'Donnell, of Belfast, food stylist by profession, collected chicken dishes. This one is quick and tasty. Serve it with a green vegetable, like broccoli or some green beans, and rice to soak up all the sauce.

The tarragon is a key ingredient. You might find it in the produce section among fresh herbs. Otherwise, plan on using 1 teaspoon of dried crumbled tarragon for the 1 tablespoon of the fresh.

4 BONELESS, SKINLESS CHICKEN BREASTS

2 MEDIUM TOMATOES, DICED

1 LARGE ONION, DICED

1 CLOVE GARLIC, DICED

3 TABLESPOONS OLIVE OIL

3 TABLESPOONS BALSAMIC VINEGAR

2 TABLESPOONS TERIYAKI OR SOY SAUCE

1 TABLESPOON CHOPPED TARRAGON

SALT AND PEPPER, TO TASTE

Preheat oven to 400 degrees. Place the chicken, tomatoes, onion, garlic, oil, vinegar, teriyaki sauce, salt, and pepper in roasting pan. Bake, uncovered, for 20 minutes or until the chicken is done. Remove chicken from the pan and cover it to keep it warm. Add chopped fresh tarragon to juices in the pan and bring them to a boil on a surface burner. Remove from heat. To serve, put the chicken on a platter and spoon the sauce over it.

Parmesan Chicken

My Islesboro neighbor Donna Seymour gave me this recipe. She suggested, "Before serving, add olive slices or crossed slivers of sundried tomato on top of melted cheese for presentation!" I'd save that gambit for company.

This recipe says you can use just about any kind of crumbs you like. I used those famous Panko crumbs, but you can grab any dry bread stuff you have. Donna's idea of crushed croutons is helpful, if you have some around, and sometimes they have seasonings added. Generally I make my own croutons, but you do whatever you like about this. Also, I decided to use buttermilk as the dipping medium because it is thicker than plain milk, and is tangy, too.

4 SKINLESS, BONELESS CHICKEN BREASTS (CAN BE CUT IN HALF FOR MORE APPEALING PORTION SIZE)

OLIVE OIL OR MILK SUFFICIENT TO COAT THE CHICKEN

¾ CUP, MORE OR LESS, BREAD CRUMBS

¾ CUP, MORE OR LESS, GRATED PARMESAN CHEESE

4 TO 8 teaspoons coarsely shredded PARMESAN CHEESE FOR TOPPING

PAPRIKA

Preheat the oven to 350 degrees. Grease a baking pan lightly with olive oil. Coat the chicken with the olive oil or milk. Roll in the breadcrumbs, seasonings, and grated Parmesan cheese. Place them in the baking dish and sprinkle with paprika. Cover with aluminum foil, bake for 40 minutes, remove foil, add 1 to 2 teaspoons of coarsely shredded Parmesan cheese to each piece of chicken to melt on top, and continue baking until the cheese is melted and the chicken is golden, 5 to 10 minutes.

Chicken and Bean Stew

{ SERVES 8 }

{ ADVICE }

The recipe calls for half peppers, but it works fine with whole ones. I substituted red for the yellow. Feel free to increase the cumin and chili powder amounts, and to use a zippier picante sauce, too. You can substitute almost any kind of bean you like in this recipe: kidney, cannellini, fava, even black beans. The helpful thing about the pintos is that they break up a little and help thicken the stew. If your bean of choice doesn't readily do that (like black or kidney beans) you might mash a few before adding them.

When Libby King's numerous children and grandchildren descend on her Islesboro summer home, she cooks up a batch of this flavorful, plentiful, and low-fat stew.

Round the can sizes to the nearest amount you can find so that you can come as close to 4 cups of tomatoes and 2 cups of cooked pintos as possible. If you serve this on rice, you can feed more people, but it makes enough for eight as is. I think it would be perfect with corn chips on the side or broken and sprinkled on top. Or serve it with cornbread.

2 TABLESPOONS OLIVE OIL

4 BONELESS, SKINLESS CHICKEN BREAST HALVES CUT
    INTO SMALL PIECES

1 LARGE ONION, CHOPPED

2 TO 3 CLOVES GARLIC, MINCED

½ GREEN PEPPER, CHOPPED

½ YELLOW OR RED PEPPER, CHOPPED

TWO (14.5-OUNCE) CANS STEWED TOMATOES OR
    ONE (28-OUNCE) CAN

ONE (15-OUNCE) CAN COOKED PINTO BEANS, DRAINED AND RINSED

¾ CUP MEDIUM HEAT SALSA

1 TABLESPOON GROUND CUMIN

1 TABLESPOON CHILI POWDER

SALT AND PEPPER, TO TASTE

Heat the oil and add the chicken, onion, garlic, and peppers, and cook until the chicken is done. Add tomatoes, beans, salsa, and seasonings, and cook at a simmer all together for at least an hour. Serve with sour cream and grated jack cheese.

WHITE CHILI

Libby's stew turns easily into white chili by leaving out the tomatoes, salsa, red pepper, and substituting white beans for the pintos. Add a small can of green chilies and chicken broth. Flavor with cumin.

Chicken Fricassee

Apparently there are two kinds of fricassee, a white one and a brown one. Hannah Allen, from Bangor, pointed out that a quick version of this can be made with good old cream of mushroom soup fortified with canned mushrooms. Hannah turns the fricassee into a tetrazzini by serving it over spaghetti and topping it with Parmesan cheese.

Fricassee is another way to warm up leftover roasted chicken. The recipe works well with turkey, too. But if you have chicken quarters or a split breast or three lying around and you don't know what to do with them, fricassee from scratch isn't hard at all. In fact, you can keep your Crockpot (er, slow cooker) employed for a while with this one.

{ SERVES 4 TO 5 }

{ ADVICE }

Feel free to jazz this up with garlic, thyme, and parsley. Add a splash of sherry toward the end. If you want to veggie it up a bit, add peas, shredded spinach, even cut green beans or broccoli. Serve it on top of toast, baked potato, noodles, rice, or biscuits.

- 5 POUNDS CHICKEN BREASTS AND THIGHS, OR A WHOLE CHICKEN CUT UP
- 3 CUPS CHICKEN BROTH, OR WATER
- 1 CARROT, COARSELY CHOPPED
- 1 STALK CELERY, COARSELY CHOPPED
- 1 SMALL ONION, COARSELY CHOPPED
- 3 TABLESPOONS BUTTER
- 3 TABLESPOONS FLOUR
- SALT AND PEPPER, TO TASTE
- MILK OR CREAM (OPTIONAL)

Put the chicken pieces into a deep, heavy bottom pot with the broth and the carrot, celery, and onion. Bring just to boiling, then reduce the temperature and allow the pieces to simmer without boiling for about 2 hours, until the meat is tender. Take the meat out of the cooking liquid, and, if you wish, remove the skin and bones and discard them.

In another heavy pan, melt the butter and add the flour, stirring with a whisk until it bubbles. Gradually stir some of the cooking broth into the flour and butter mixture, whisking until you have smooth, thick gravy. Cook it, thinning it with milk or cream, until it is the consistency of sauce. Taste, and adjust seasoning with salt and pepper, and any herbs you favor. Add the meat and warm it through in this mixture before serving it over your choice of starch.

Libby's Lemon Chicken

Libby King makes this for company and family suppers alike, and even though it has a few dressy refinements, it really is quite simple to put together and is a great do-ahead dish.

Present this generously sprinkled with parsley on a big platter with the lemon slices all strewn around. Serve with rice, a pilaf, couscous, small pasta, or, in summer, potato salad. Bright green vegetables, like asparagus in spring, broccoli or green beans in summer, are lovely accompaniments, and a great addition is bright yellow ones like sweet potatoes, squash, or carrots.

2 POUNDS BONELESS CHICKEN

¼ CUP FLOUR

SALT AND PEPPER, TO TASTE

OLIVE OIL

3 TABLESPOONS CAPERS WITH JUICE

1 CUP WHITE WINE

1 LEMON, THINLY SLICED

SEVERAL STALKS OF PARSLEY, FINELY MINCED

Slice each piece of boneless chicken horizontally. Put the slices between two pieces of waxed paper and pound them gently with a mallet or rolling pin. Toss together the flour, salt, and pepper, and dip each piece in the mixture, shaking off the excess. Put a little olive oil in a heavy skillet, and make it quite hot. Cook the chicken slices for 3 to 4 minutes each side. Remove them to a baking dish. Add the capers and wine to the pan and cook until you can scrape up the little stuck-on bits. Pour it over the chicken in the baking dish. Lay the lemon slices all over the chicken.

Preheat the oven to about 350 degrees and put the chicken into the oven for 25 to 30 minutes or until it is heated through. Lay the chicken on the platter, pour the juices over it, and distribute the lemon slices. Sprinkle with minced parsley.

Baily's Chicken Wings

{ SERVES 3 TO 4 }

These chicken wings led me off a vegetarian path one day years and years ago. I was visiting with Baily Ruckert, of York, who served them for lunch. I was hungry and I ate. Later when I gave up vegetarianism, a gradual process, I recalled the wings, which I always called "Chicken Wings the Way Baily Does Them," and I wrote and asked her for the recipe.

This is an exceedingly simple process, but you have to plan ahead to allow for marinating. They are best hot from the oven, but are fine cold. The long baking time makes for great-tasting skin, which I suppose is what chicken-wing-eating is all about. Sometimes I disjoint the wings.

¾ CUPS OF SOY SAUCE

½ CUP OF BROWN SUGAR

DASH OF GARLIC POWDER

DASH OF WORCESTERSHIRE SAUCE

10 TO 15 CHICKEN WINGS

Mix the soy sauce, sugar, garlic powder, and Worcestershire sauce together in a large shallow bowl until the sugar dissolves. Add the wings and turn them until each is covered with marinade. Cover and place them in the refrigerator to marinate for at least 3 hours, and flip them around every once in a while.

Preheat the oven to 375 degrees. Lay the wings on a rack in a large pan in a single layer. Bake them for 1½ hours , turning them, and brushing with marinade every 15 minutes.

Soy Sauce and Wine Simmered Chicken

{ SERVES 4 TO 6 }

I learned this way of fixing chicken in an adult education class we had here taught by a contractor who learned to make it from his sister. I always call it Pete's Sister Shirley's Chicken, which doesn't give details, hence its name above. It is best made with chicken legs or thighs, but this recipe can make a chicken breast tasty and stay moist, too.

- 4 TO 6 CHICKEN LEGS OR THIGHS (OR FRYER PARTS)
- 1 TABLESPOON WHITE WINE
- 6 TABLESPOONS SOY SAUCE
- 4 TO 6 SLICES GINGER ROOT
- 2 SCALLIONS CHOPPED
- 1 TABLESPOON SUGAR

Put the chicken, wine, soy sauce, ginger root, and scallions, plus a ¼ cup of water into a cook pan with a tight-fitting lid. Bring to a boil, and then reduce the temperature to low and simmer for 1 hour, turning the chicken pieces over half way through. Sprinkle the sugar in for the last 15 minutes. If you wish, garnish with a little more chopped scallion.

Honey Mustard Chicken

Because mustards vary, taste the sauce mixture to see if it is snappy or sweet enough for you. Add more mustard or honey accordingly.

{ SERVES 4 }

- 4 BONELESS CHICKEN BREASTS
- 1 TABLESPOON OLIVE OIL
- 1 CUP CHICKEN GRAVY
- 4 TABLESPOONS DIJON-STYLE OR OTHER NON-YELLOW MUSTARD
- 3 TEASPOONS HONEY
- SALT AND PEPPER, TO TASTE

Sear the chicken on both sides in olive oil over a medium high heat for about 5 minutes. Mix together the gravy, mustard, and honey, and cover the chicken with the sauce, and simmer an additional 8 to 12 minutes until it is done. (If you choose to cook bone in chicken, plan on simmering or baking it for closer to 40 minutes.)

Beef & Venison

BEEF IS EVER POPULAR almost anywhere and in Maine it is joined by venison, either deer or moose meat. You can find locally produced, largely grass-fed beef in lots of locations. One butcher shop I buy from doesn't even market their meat as local; they just do it, and it's tasty, cut the way you want it, and reasonably priced.

On Islesboro Island where I live, the only predators that deer have are earnest and patient bow hunters and cars. Most deer meat in my freezer was given to me by generous hunter friends. Mainers have a vigorous hunting tradition that puts wild venison like deer steaks and mooseburger on lots of our tables. Venison is low in fat and cholesterol compared to domesticated meat like beef and pork, and if you handle it properly, can be cooked to be very tender and toothsome. Ground venison is great for chili and meat sauce for pasta, where its low fat content doesn't pose a toughness problem. I like venison steaks marinated, grilled rare, and thinly sliced.

Leslie's Chili

Dottie Gagne, of Greenville, asked for "any chili recipe as long as it is GOOD." Nobody sent in a recipe, so I decided to go hunting for one. I asked all around — at my bank, at a graduation party — and after a while I noticed the general drift of conversation went something like this: "Well, I don't really have a *recipe* for chili," and "Oh, I just use one of those chili kits," the kind with alarming names on them. So it wasn't an excess of modesty that prevented a deluge of favorite family chili recipes; it's just that good old seat-of-the-pants cooking most of us do quickly before hungry people show up looking for supper.

Then I remembered a delicious chili I ate once at my friend Leslie Fuller's Cushing home. I arrived shortly after she got home from work, and she assembled it while her husband, Ben, several cats, and I milled around the kitchen. It was richly flavored and satisfying and I remember thinking, "Gosh, this is good. How come I don't make chili more often?"

1 ONION, CHOPPED

2 CLOVES GARLIC, MINCED

1 TABLESPOON COOKING OIL

1 POUND LEAN GROUND MEAT

TWO (14-OUNCE) CANS KIDNEY OR BLACK BEANS

ONE (28-OUNCE) CAN TOMATO SAUCE

¼ CUP SUGAR

1 TABLESPOON CHILI POWDER

1 TABLESPOON CUMIN

¼ TEASPOON CAYENNE

SQUIRT OF KETCHUP

Brown the onion and garlic in oil in a large heavy pan. Add the meat and brown it, then add the rest of the ingredients and cook for ½ an hour or so. Taste occasionally and adjust seasoning. It's always better the next day.

{ SERVES 4 TO 6 }

{ ADVICE }

Leslie suggests using beans of two colors (black beans and kidney beans or light kidneys and dark red kidneys), and always draining them, then adding sugar, and a squirt of ketchup. She says it is better when you soak the beans yourself and then you can use a Crockpot, because canned beans fall apart too easily if you cook them long. She likes using cut-up beef chuck best, but will use ground meat. Leslie also said to add "heat to taste, sometimes I use hot sauce." Start with the amount the recipe specifies, then add more gradually until it is as hot as you like it.

Meatballs

From Mount Desert, an old friend offered the oven-baking idea. She wrote, "The biggest 'tip' I can give is quit frying (I used to do it, too). Too hard on my back and the meatballs." She said to put them on a broiler pan and bake them "til brown and crusty, then dump the done meatballs right into the simmering sauce." She reports that she has turned as much as twenty pounds of meat — a combination of pork, chuck roast, sirloin, and turkey and "copious" amount of Parmesan — into meatballs. She varies the seasoning — curry for an Indian accent, and five-spice powder for Chinese. "A couple times a year," she wrote, "I make a million tiny meatballs — freeze them loose on trays and then bag — which throughout the year I throw into soups or use as appetizers." Good idea!

A-ha! The secret is Parmesan cheese! How did I miss that all those years? I treated meatballs as if they were just a small, round kind of meatloaf, and I don't put Parmesan in meatloaf. But there it was in the recipes you sent me when I moaned and groaned about not making very good meatballs. That, plus baking the little buggers in the oven instead of standing around and frying them. Heavy lifting on this came from Sharon Ray, in Brewer, and Machias' own Ruth Thurston.

2 POUNDS GROUND CHUCK

1 CUP DRY UNSEASONED BREADCRUMBS

2/3 CUP GRATED PARMESAN CHEESE

1/2 CUP MILK

1/2 CUP BEEF BROTH OR WATER

3 EGGS, BEATEN

1/4 CUP FINELY CHOPPED PARSLEY

2 TABLESPOONS DRIED OREGANO

3 GARLIC CLOVES, MINCED

2 TEASPOONS SALT

1 TABLESPOON BLACK PEPPER

2 TEASPOONS DRIED BASIL

1 TEASPOON CRUSHED RED PEPPER FLAKES (OPTIONAL)

Mix all ingredients together very well. Preheat the oven to 425 degrees and lightly oil or spray a baking pan. Form the meatballs into 2-inch balls and place them, not touching, in the pan. Bake them for 15 minutes, turn them, and bake another 15 minutes. Add directly to your sauce, or cool them and freeze on a baking sheet and bag for later use.

Venison Bourguignon

Here recommended by Mitch Hutchison, the wife of Philo, one of Islesboro Sporting Club's founders, is yet another venison variation on a beef recipe. Mitch borrows from elegant beef bourguignon recipes, then substitutes venison and sometimes moose meat for the beef.

{ SERVES 6 TO 8 }

Serve bourguignon on rice or noodles, or even polenta (fried cornmeal mush to us Yankees). This is actually an ideal dish for preparing ahead and leaving in a slow-cooker on low all day, to be finished a half hour before dinner. Use fresh mushrooms because they add more flavor than canned.

4 SLICES BACON (OR TWO TABLESPOONS OLIVE OIL)

3½ TO 4 POUNDS OF CUBED VENISON

4 CLOVES OF GARLIC, CRUSHED

1 CARROT, CHOPPED

1 MEDIUM ONION, CHOPPED

2 CUPS RED WINE

3 CUPS BEEF STOCK OR BROTH

2 BAY LEAVES

2 TABLESPOONS OLIVE OIL

3 CUPS SLICED FRESH MUSHROOMS

1 POUND PEARL ONIONS, SKINNED AND PARBOILED

Put the bacon slices in the bottom of Dutch oven and fry until crisp. Remove them. Brown the meat in the bacon fat (or use olive oil if you prefer). Add the garlic, carrot, onion, wine, stock, and the bay leaves. Cover and let simmer for about 6 hours. If you plan to use a slow cooker the next day, cook the mixture for 30 minutes and put aside in the fridge. In the morning, put the ingredients in the slow cooker and set it on low for the day.

An hour before dinner, put 2 tablespoons of olive oil in a large sauté pan and cook the mushrooms until they all are soft. They will shrink. Add the mushrooms and pearl onions to the meat. Cook uncovered until dinnertime, about 45 minutes or so, to allow the sauce to thicken. Taste and adjust for salt and pepper. Remove the bay leaves and serve.

Venison or Beef Stroganoff

One of my favorite things to do with venison is to make a stroganoff. I use a basic beef stroganoff recipe and substitute venison. I have used a pot roast and stewing meat, even steaks. Like many dishes of this sort, it is better the second day.

2 TABLESPOONS OLIVE OIL

1 ½ TO 1 ¾ POUNDS VENISON CUT INTO STRIPS

1 LARGE ONION, CHOPPED

2 TABLESPOONS BUTTER

3 CUPS MUSHROOMS, SLICED

1 CUP BEEF BROTH OR WATER

½ CUP WHITE WINE

1 CUP SOUR CREAM

SALT AND PEPPER, TO TASTE

Heat the 2 tablespoons of olive oil in a heavy pot (a Dutch oven is ideal) over a high heat, and quickly brown the venison. Remove it, then put the onions in the pot, reduce the heat to medium high and cook them until they are soft. Remove the onion and reserve it. Melt the butter in the pot and add the mushrooms. As soon as they are soft, put the meat and onions back into the pot, and add the broth and wine. Simmer over a low heat for 1 hour, add the sour cream, taste, and add salt and pepper to taste.

Pork

WHEN I GREW UP IN THE 'FIFTIES, there were pork roasts and chops. Maybe there were tenderloins and ground pork, but I don't remember as many as there are now. And no one I knew thought that pork was "the other white meat." Never mind. It's all good.

New Year's Pork and Sauerkraut

{ SERVES 6 TO 8 }

{ ADVICE }

The applesauce is not supposed to be a sweetened version; merely stew it with the skins on to give it color before you run it through a sieve or food mill.

My Islesboro neighbor Alice Girvin grew up in Harrisburg, Pennsylvania, near the Pennsylvania Dutch area of Lancaster County where her German neighbors ate pork and sauerkraut on New Year's for good luck and prosperity in the coming year.

The sauerkraut and pork are cooked together, the potatoes are boiled and mashed and served with the applesauce in side dishes. Alice said, "As a kid I used to put down a layer of sauerkraut, then potatoes, on top then I frosted it with applesauce. That's how I ate the three layers." She says she outgrew it, but you might enjoy eating it that way.

5 POUNDS SAUERKRAUT

5 POUNDS PORK, TENDERLOIN OR RIB ROAST

11 POTATOES

8 POUNDS APPLES

Preheat the oven to 325 degrees. Spread the kraut on the bottom of a 9-by-13 baking pan, then place the pork in it, add a little water, and cover the pan. Bake for 25 minutes a pound. Keep it covered and moist; it is not supposed to brown. Boil and mash the potatoes just as you usually do. Prepare the apples by coring and stewing them. Run them through a food mill.

Barbecue Sauce and Spare Ribs

Steve Merchant's barbecue recipe calls for the sort of thing most of us have in the house except maybe for liquid hickory smoke. He uses Heinz ketchup, and asserts rather vigorously that it has to be Heinz or else. He likes light brown sugar and prefers the honey to be orange blossom.

{ MAKES 1 PINT }

One principle of barbecuing is "slow and low," that is, you cook your ribs or pork shoulder or whatever for a long time at a low temperature. They are supposed to be smoke-cooked, that is, enough smoke for flavor, cooked through, tender on the inside with a flavorful crisp exterior. The purpose of the sauce is to keep the meat from drying out. If you are not cooking on a grill, then the only way to have the smokey flavor will be to use liquid smoke.

You can use Steve's sauce on chicken, pork loin, even pork chops, if you don't want to do spareribs. The sauce is not as sweet as you might think it would be.

1 CUP HEINZ KETCHUP

½ CUP LIGHT BROWN SUGAR

⅓ HONEY (PREFERABLY ORANGE BLOSSOM)

¼ CUP DISTILLED WHITE VINEGAR

1 TEASPOON GARLIC POWDER OR ½ TEASPOON PUREED GARLIC

1 TEASPOON DRIED BASIL

2 TEASPOONS LIQUID SMOKE (OPTIONAL)

Blend all ingredients and let sit at least 1 hour before using it or heat it in the microwave and whisk thoroughly. If making ribs heat the oven to 260 degrees, spread the ribs generously with the sauce, and set them concave side up on a rack over a panful of hot water. After 45 minutes, turn the ribs over, and spread the sauce on the other side. Continue baking for another hour and a quarter. Check and brush on additional sauce if the surface looks a little dry.

Pulled Pork

Pulled pork cooks for a long time, but you can ignore it for hours. My island neighbor Melissa Olson puts a fresh pork shoulder in her large capacity Crockpot, slaps the lid on it, sets it at high, and leaves it for five or six hours until it is very tender. At that point she takes it out and removes the bones, picks the meat out, separates it from the fat, and shreds it with her fingers, pulling apart the tender strands. Then she adds the barbecue sauce and reheats it a bit.

You can make your own barbecue sauce or help yourself to one of the dozens concocted by various makers large and small. Melissa and her husband, Craig, were introduced to their favorite commercial sort when a summer resident left them with a part bottle of it. (I imagine quite a few of us have been the beneficiaries of summer refrigerators, with samples of all sorts of interesting stuff.)

Melissa serves pulled pork on burger rolls with baked beans and coleslaw on the side and apple crisp for dessert. The pork would work well on soft corn or flour tortillas, too, and as a filling for burritos or tacos.

FRESH PORK SHOULDER, PICNIC ROAST, OR FRESH HAM

2 TO 4 OR MORE CUPS BARBECUE SAUCE

Put the fresh pork roast in a large capacity Crockpot or into a covered roasting pan. Set the Crockpot temperature at high to cook it for 5 to 6 hours, or at low to cook it for 7 to 8 hours. Or put the roaster into a 250 degree oven for 5 to 6 hours. When the meat is so tender that it comes away from the bone, take it out of the pot and cool it to enough to handle. Remove the bones, pull off every particle of fat, and discard. Add barbecue sauce to taste, and return to a low heat until you are ready to serve it.

Cheese

GOOEY, RICH, and—when you choose aged cheddar or blue or smoked—robustly flavorful, cheese adds a comforting element to many dishes and is a perfectly useful main ingredient, too. It is indispensable for appetizers.

Cheese Balls

{ MAKES 3½ CUPS }

When my friend Susan Hess, in Georgetown, invited me to supper after a holiday concert she sang in, she offered this marvelous mixture as an appetizer before dinner, demonstrating that we all can use delicious little items to whip up in advance and pull out whenever people show up. Serve it rolled in chopped parsley or in chopped walnuts or pecans, with crackers or toasts to spread it on. It is rich, so a little dab'll do you. This recipe makes enough for a large gathering, or you can divide it up into smaller balls, wrap each in plastic wrap to roll later in the coating of choice, or to press into a ramekin.

The recipe calls for beer. You don't need very much, so my advice is to open a beer, and drink it while mixing the cheeses so you can just add a couple splashes from the bottle. You could probably even leave out the beer, but then you'll need something like cream to thin the cheese mixture a little.

> 1 POUND CREAM CHEESE
>
> ¼ TO ⅓ POUND BLUE CHEESE
>
> 1 JAR PREPARED CHEESE SPREAD OR 4 OUNCES FINELY GRATED CHEDDAR
>
> 2 TO 3 TABLESPOONS BEER

Let the ingredients come to room temperature and beat them all together very well. Refrigerate. Serve as needed, rolled in chopped nuts or parsley, or served plain with crackers.

Rinktumdiddy

Burke and Midge Welldon, of Islesboro, don't know why their family called this dish rinktumdiddy, and neither do I, but I have seen a similar variation of Welsh rarebit that was called Pink Bunny. I even Googled rinktumdiddy, and the search engine scratched its head for a couple of nano-seconds before flashing the "returned no results" message. In fact, the Welldons went so far as to make up a little pan full that they dropped off at my house letting me off the old what-to-have-for-supper hook for one night. They even supplied the crackers. Delicious. Add a salad, and there you go.

{ SERVES 3 }

2 HEAPING CUPS GRATED CHEESE

BUTTER THE SIZE OF AN EGG (ABOUT 4 TABLESPOONS)

2 TABLESPOONS WORCESTERSHIRE SAUCE

1 ½ CUPS CANNED TOMATOES, DRAINED

¼ TEASPOON BAKING SODA

1 WELL BEATEN EGG

SALT, TO TASTE

PAPRIKA, TO TASTE

CRACKERS OR TOAST

Put the cheese and butter into the top of a double boiler. Melt them together. Add the Worcestershire sauce, tomatoes, and soda, and whisk together. Add the beaten egg last and whisk until it is fairly smooth, then add the salt and paprika, adjusting the seasonings to your taste.

BUTTER THE SIZE OF AN EGG

Now there is in this recipe one of those famous early measurements, "butter the size of an egg." Modern people get their tails in a twist over instructions like this. Just take an egg and hold it next to a stick of butter and it will dawn on you gradually that it is roughly equal to a quarter cup, or half a stick of butter. Piece of cake.

Cheddar Crisps

{ ADVICE }

When I mix up a batch
of cheese crisps, I form
variously shaped logs
of dough, wrap them in
waxed paper or plastic,
and store them in a
plastic bag in the fridge
or even freezer, until I
need them. Shape the
dough into a round log, or
flatten all four sides for a
square, make rectangles
with a flatter lengthwise
shape, or even triangles
by turning the log into
a three sided one. To
bake them, you just slice
them off and put them
on a baking sheet for only
fifteen minutes! (The
edges do soften as they
bake, so the shapes will
have slightly rounded
corners.) You can of
course, just roll small balls
between your palms, and
flatten them with a fork
on the baking sheet,
but then people think
they are cookies.

I could not have been more surprised at the ingredients of these little homemade crackers. The secret is the crispy rice cereal that turns into a lovely little nugget of crunch. My island neighbor Marcy Congdon made these for an open house she had and I asked for the recipe, thank goodness. You can make them now and bake them later.

Since you choose the cheddar you use, you can make this recipe with a very sharp one, or if you prefer, a mellow one. Consider using flavored cheeses: jalapeno, garlic, dill, etc. You can adjust the amount of mustard, add other spices like garlic, mustard, coarse black pepper, poppy, sesame, or toasted cumin seeds. You could even sprinkle the tops with a coarse salt and press it gently into the surface.

You can bake them only an hour ahead of serving them. If you bake them days before you need them, store them in a tin or plastic container with a tight-fitting lid. They do not require refrigeration after baking.

1 POUND BUTTER, SOFTENED

1 POUND GRATED SHARP CHEDDAR CHEESE

4 CUPS FLOUR

3 TEASPOONS SALT

1 TEASPOON CAYENNE OR OTHER SPICE, OPTIONAL

4 CUPS CRISPY RICE CEREAL

In a mixer bowl, with a dough hook, beat together the softened butter and the grated cheddar. Toss the flour, salt, and cayenne together in a bowl or put into a sifter, and add it to the butter and cheese mixture, continuing to beat. Fold in the crispy rice cereal last and mix until it is blended all through the very stiff dough. Divide the dough and form logs no more than two inches in diameter. Wrap and chill.

To bake, preheat the oven to 350 degrees and grease a baking sheet very lightly. Cut off slices no more than a ¼ inch thick and arrange on the pan. Bake for 15 minutes. Remove and let cool. Store in a tightly sealed container or serve immediately.

Side Dishes

SIDES IS A FUNNY NAME for these lovely combinations. Just because they don't have meat, I suppose they are relegated to a lesser status. Sometimes side dishes with their combinations of vegetables and grains are much more interesting than the entrees.

Green Rice

{ SERVES 4 }

Diane Ferris, of Harrington, who winters on Islesboro, made this for dinner one night and I fell in love with it, green with parsley, rich with cheese and eggs, and a crusty top. Perfection.

Whenever I cook rice, I always make more than I need because leftover rice is so handy. I put it into pancakes, scramble eggs into it, do a vegetable stir fry, and dump rice in that. Here is another way to use leftover rice.

2 CUPS COOKED RICE, WHITE OR BROWN

1 SMALL ONION, DICED

¼ CUP (1 HALF STICK) BUTTER

2 EGGS, BEATEN

1 CUP MILK

1 CUP PARSLEY, MINCED

2 CUPS CHEDDAR CHEESE, SHREDDED

Preheat the oven to 350 degrees. Grease a baking dish or casserole very well. Combine all the ingredients and pour into the baking dish. Bake for 45 to 50 minutes or until the center is set and the top is a golden brown.

Creamed, Hard-Boiled Eggs

Hard-boiled eggs in the fridge are like money in the bank, good for making deviled eggs, egg salad sandwiches, slicing into a spinach salad, and for creamed eggs, a favorite of mine, and an oddly neglected recipe for a lunch, brunch, or light supper dish. It is wonderful on toast or a baked potato, and on rice.

{ SERVES 3 }

Once you make the creamed eggs, you can do all sorts of things like add asparagus, peas, spinach, or slivers of smoked salmon. The following three recipes walk you through the white or cream sauce to creamed eggs to kedgeree. You'll see that they follow each other right along.

White or Cream Sauce:

{ MAKES 1½ CUPS }

2 TABLESPOONS BUTTER

2 TABLESPOONS FLOUR

1 CUP MILK OR CREAM

SALT AND PEPPER, TO TASTE

Melt the butter and whisk the flour into it and cook until it is bubbly then whisk in the milk or cream, and cook until thick and smooth. Add salt and pepper to taste.

Creamed Eggs:

1 BATCH OF WHITE OR CREAM SAUCE

4 BOILED EGGS

SALT AND PEPPER

ADD-INS LIKE ASPARAGUS, PEAS, HAM, SMOKED SALMON, OPTIONAL

TOAST, BAKED POTATO, OR RICE

Cut the eggs in slices or chop them and stir into the white or cream sauce. Season with salt, and pepper, paprika, or curry to taste. Heat through and serve on the toast, potato, or rice.

Curried Creamed Eggs with Spinach

Creamed, curried eggs on toast, with lots of shredded spinach added to it, is a quick and comforting brunch, lunch, or supper dish. You can make this dish even more quickly if you keep a supply of already hard-boiled eggs on hand. Already boiled eggs are handy for sandwiches, for crumbling onto salad, or grabbing to eat on the way to work in the morning. Boil up a few when you are fixing supper some night, and you are all set for a while.

- **2 TABLESPOONS BUTTER**
- **2 TABLESPOONS OLIVE OIL**
- **½ ONION, CHOPPED**
- **1 TABLESPOON CURRY POWDER, OR TO TASTE**
- **2 TABLESPOONS FLOUR**
- **4 OUNCES SPINACH, STEMMED AND SHREDDED**
- **1 CUP MILK AND MORE AS NEEDED**
- **3 HARD BOILED EGGS, CHOPPED COARSELY**
- **SALT AND PEPPER, TO TASTE**

Melt the butter in a heavy sauté pan and add the olive oil. Cook the onions over a medium heat until they are just soft, about 5 minutes, then stir in the curry powder and flour and cook until the flour bubbles slightly. Add the shredded spinach and stir into the mixture in the pan until the spinach is wilted. Add the milk, stirring to prevent lumps, and cook until it is thickened slightly. Add the eggs. If you like a looser mixture, add more milk. Taste and adjust seasonings with salt and pepper and more curry powder. Serve on toast or baked potatoes.

{ SERVES 2 TO 3 }

{ ADVICE }

I swear, if my kitchen scissors disappeared, I'd be in a bad way. The older I get, the less easy it is for me to claw into various kinds of packaging—the tough plastic that meat is sometimes packed in, or bags and even boxes are such a challenge. Out come the scissors and I snip, cut, and stab my way into them. What scissors are really good for is shredding and snipping green stuff. In this recipe I cut the spinach into fine shreds with them. I also use scissors on herbs like parsley and basil.

Bloody Mary Aspic

Aspic is old fashioned, I know, but when it shows up at a potluck I and, I notice, a lot of others, greet it with joy.

Island neighbor Bonnie Hughes brought tomato aspic to a sewing circle potluck luncheon, but said that she was a little unhappy with her recipe that she made with packaged gelatin dessert. She said, "I think aspic ought to taste like a good Bloody Mary." I agreed, and Bonnie and I each tried to come up with a version that matched our ideas of a Bloody Mary. I suppose I could've bought a bottle of Bloody Mary mix, but why pay someone else to add Worcestershire sauce to tomato juice?

A few email consultations with Bonnie and poking through a few recipes online showed me that there was a huge variety of Bloody Mary mix ingredients: clam juice, lime juice, lemon, horseradish, liquid smoke, brown sugar, celery, beef broth can all be added to tomato juice. The following made very fine aspic. I suppose if you were feeling a little rascally, you could, in the spirit of Jello-shots, add vodka to your aspic to make a real Bloody Mary on a plate.

2 TABLESPOONS OR 2 PACKETS GELATIN

½ CUP COLD WATER

1 ½ CUPS TOMATO JUICE

½ CUP CONSOMMÉ

1 TABLESPOON WORCESTERSHIRE SAUCE

1 TABLESPOON VINEGAR

2 TABLESPOON SUGAR

1 TEASPOON HOT SAUCE, TO TASTE (OPTIONAL)

JUICE OF HALF A LEMON OR LIME

2 RIBS CELERY, FINELY CHOPPED

HALF A GREEN OR RED PEPPER, FINELY CHOPPED (OPTIONAL)

Soak the gelatin in cold water, then mix it into all the other ingredients except the celery and peper. Taste and adjust seasonings. Allow to begin to set up, then fold in chopped vegetables and pour into a mold or serving bowl to finish setting up. Serve with a bit of mayonnaise if desired.

Skillet Suppers & Hearty Casseroles

ASSEMBLE THESE DISHES IN ONE POT OR PAN, toss a salad, and call everyone in for supper. Practically every one of these recipes can be made in half an hour from scratch or assembled ahead of time for reheating just before it's time to eat.

Kedgeree

Another leftover rice dish, kedgeree was in past times considered a suitable breakfast dish, and I think it works for supper, too. Apparently the name is a corruption of the word "kichiri" adopted in India by the British during the Empire when so many English lived there. Curry and chutney found their way into British cookery, and American, too, during that time.

{ SERVES 4 TO 6 }

- 2 BATCHES WHITE OR CREAM SAUCE
- 4 HARD BOILED EGGS, CHOPPED
- 2 CUPS COOKED FISH (HADDOCK, SALMON, FINNAN HADDIE)
- 2 CUPS COOKED RICE
- CREAM OR MILK
- SALT, PEPPER, AND CURRY POWDER, TO TASTE

Mix all together in a heavy sauce pan or double boiler, adding more milk or cream as needed to keep it from becoming stiff. Heat through. Taste and adjust seasonings.

Cold Tuna Noodle Salad

{ SERVES 4 }

Tuna noodle casserole transmogrified. It comes out like a salad if you make a cold dish instead of a hot one. Use all the same main ingredients — tuna, noodles, celery, onion, peas but substitute salad dressing for the white sauce and put potato chips on top. I left the celery raw, minced the onion finely, and blanched the fresh peas. I used mayonnaise with a little of a favorite homemade creamy garlic dressing, page 223, to thin it somewhat, though if you are a fan of ranch dressing that would work well in this dish. Feel free to add other flavor enhancers like herbs, pickles, or olives. I used dill and parsley.

6 TO 8 OUNCES FLAT NOODLES

1 LARGE CAN TUNA FISH, DRAINED

2 TO 3 STALKS CELERY, FINELY CHOPPED

1 SMALL ONION OR 2 TO 3 SCALLIONS, FINELY CHOPPED

1 CUP FRESH PEAS, BLANCHED IN HOT WATER (OPTIONAL)

FINELY MINCED PARSLEY AND DILL (OPTIONAL)

MAYONNAISE OR SALAD DRESSING

SALT AND PEPPER, TO TASTE

CRUSHED POTATO CHIPS

Bring a pot of water to a boil and cook the noodles for the time recommended on package. Drain and cover with cold water to cool down. Drain well, and put into a large bowl and add the chopped vegetables and herbs. Add enough mayonnaise and salad dressing to bind to your taste. Add salt and pepper to taste. Put into a serving dish and sprinkle crushed potato chips on top.

POTATO CHIP MAGIC

When I was little – five or six years old – potato chips were a very special treat, rarely purchased in our household, reserved as a picnic treat or offered up on Fourth of July. One time my family went to visit Uncle Carl and Aunt Hazel. Hazel made tuna noodle casserole for our dinner and I watched entranced as Aunt Hazel crushed up a whole bag of potato chips and sprinkled them on top of the casserole. I had never seen that before and it was magical.

Fried Rice

I really like to have cooked rice on hand. I often cook twice as much
as I need, so there are leftovers for a fast stir fry and rice supper, or for
fried rice. Fried rice is terrific at absorbing all kind of leftovers and stray
bits as long as you don't get all obsessive about authenticity. Obviously,
chicken, pork, tofu, little bits of beef, and most kinds of shellfish, but
also lots of vegetables, especially greens. So the recipe below will give
you the basic fried rice into which you can stir shredded bok choy,
spinach, beet greens, chard, or even kale. Fry up some onion or scallions,
celery, red or green pepper to add, garlic if you like it. If there are
leftover green beans, or peas, or carrots, in they go. A handful of cashews
boosts the protein level. Add soy sauce or tamari at the table, sometimes
with a little red pepper and garlic paste stirred into it.

> 3 OR 4 SCALLIONS
>
> 2 LARGE EGGS
>
> 4 TABLESPOONS OIL
>
> 4 CUPS COLD COOKED RICE
>
> HALF A HEAD BOK CHOY OR CHINESE CABBAGE SHREDDED
>
> OTHER VEGETABLES OR MEAT OF YOUR CHOICE (OPTIONAL)
>
> SOY SAUCE

Chop the scallions. Beat the eggs as for scrambled eggs. Heat a wok
or large fry pan and put in half the oil. When it is hot, add the eggs,
tipping the wok or pan to spread the egg into a large thin layer. Cook
until it is firm, then turn out onto a cutting board. Put the rest of the
oil into the pan and add the rice, stir frying it until it is hot through.
Meanwhile, shred the cooked eggs. When the rice is completely heated,
add the shredded bok choy and other ingredients. Sprinkle and stir
in soy sauce or tamari until the rice is a light brown, and stir fry until
everything is hot, then add the eggs and scallions.

Green Tomato Fajita Casserole

{ SERVES 6 TO 8 }

{ ADVICE }

Being the frugal cook that I am, I try to do an end run around prepared taco cheese. I have a really high resistance to letting someone else grate cheese for me, and, besides, I've never liked the mouth-feel of those cheeses straight from the bag: they taste like they have sawdust on them. The ingredients for taco cheese are cheddar and jack cheese mostly, with a little asadero and queso blanco mixed in. A simple combination of cheddar and jack cheese would work just fine. Our own State of Maine Cheese company (cheese-me.com/) produces a pretty zippy pepper jack that would work fine here, too, and blended with cheddar, it would turn up the heat on the whole dish.

Sandra Burke, in Dedham, Maine, sent this recipe along. It appealed to me because zucchini and green tomatoes happen together in my garden, a can of black beans is usually in the cupboard, and I usually have corn on hand, either fresh or frozen.

If you like heat, Sandra pointed out, you can add chopped jalapeños. You can use a prepared fajita sauce if you like or as Sandra said, taco or enchilada sauce are workable substitutes. Or you can use the fajita sauce recipe following; make it hotter using jalapeños.

Then, too, Sandra said, this dish can be extended to become a Mexican lasagna. "Just line the bottom of a greased baking pan with corn tortillas, spread half of the vegetable mixture, sprinkle with cheese, top with another layer of corn tortillas, then the rest of the vegetables, then top with cheese again." Bake that at 350 degrees for 30 minutes or so.

1 MEDIUM ONION, DICED

⅛ TO ¼ GREEN PEPPER, DICED

1 MEDIUM OR 2 SMALL ZUCCHINI, DICED

VEGETABLE OIL

2 CUPS DICED GREEN TOMATOES (2 TO 3 LARGE ONES)

½ TEASPOON DRIED OR 1 TABLESPOON FRESH MINCED CILANTRO

½ TEASPOON DRIED OREGANO

½ TEASPOON DRIED THYME

1¾ CUPS COOKED, OR ONE (14-OUNCE) CAN BLACK BEANS, DRAINED

1 CUP CORN KERNELS

1 CUP TOMATO SAUCE

¼ CUP FAJITA OR ENCHILADA SAUCE (RECIPE FOLLOWS)

2 CUPS TACO CHEESE OR 1 CUP GRATED CHEDDAR PLUS 1 CUP

  GRATED MONTEREY JACK

Preheat the oven to 325 degrees. Sauté the onion, green pepper, and diced zucchini in a little oil until the onions are translucent, about 5 minutes. Then add the tomatoes and herbs, and cook together for 5 minutes. In a large bowl, combine the beans, corn, tomato, and fajita sauce. Add the cooked mixture and mix well. Spread in a 9-by-13-inch baking dish, top with the cheese. Bake for 45 to 50 minutes.

Homemade Fajita Sauce:

½ CUP LIME JUICE

¼ CUP VEGETABLE OIL

1 ONION, CHOPPED

2 CLOVES OF GARLIC MINCED

¼ CUP CILANTRO, FINELY CHOPPED

1 SLICED HOT PEPPER (JALAPEÑO, GREEN CHILI, ETC.)

1 TEASPOON CUMIN

SALT AND PEPPER, TO TASTE

{ MAKES 1 SCANT CUP }

Mix. Refrigerate whatever you don't use right away.

Turkey Casserole

{ SERVES 4 }

{ ADVICE }

Turkey has got to be a working girl's best friend. Even if all you have is a breast, you can roast it for dinner on the weekend, and then shave off thin slices for sandwiches or to add to a lunch salad. If you make gravy, hot turkey sandwiches are a possibility. If you do the whole bird, there will be enough for more hot meals and glorious soup, too.

This turkey casserole, my absolutely favorite turkey leftovers dish, is the main reason to have Thanksgiving dinner. I learned to make this forty-plus years ago when I lived with a young family with three moderately fussy eaters under twelve. Those three youngsters loved this dish made of cooked turkey, leftover gravy, and topped with leftover or freshly-made stuffing. The young people were still at a stage where most of their foods couldn't touch each other on the plate, so vegetables, if there were any, were segregated, squash in one spot, and the peas in another. Though I don't mind my food mixed up, I tend still to serve this with the veggies on the side.

4 CUPS COOKED TURKEY, LIGHT AND DARK MEAT, CUT IN
   BITE-SIZE PIECES
COOKED VEGETABLES, OPTIONAL
2 CUPS TURKEY GRAVY OR SAUCE
2 TO 3 CUPS PREPARED STUFFING

Preheat the oven to 350 degrees. Grease lightly a two quart casserole. Spread the turkey meat in the casserole, add vegetables if you wish, and pour the gravy or sauce over the top. Top with a layer of stuffing. If you wish, dot the top with bits of butter. Bake for 30 minutes or until the gravy is bubbling and the stuffing is toasted golden.

OLIVIA'S STELLAR S'MORES

Camp is also the only place I eat s'mores, and that is usually because I entertain young friends there. Olivia Olson showed me a way of putting together a s'more that was vastly better than the way I learned at 4-H camp fifty plus years ago.

Toast two marshmallows and when they are golden brown, lay one on one of the crackers, and top with a piece of chocolate. Then lay the other marshmallow on top of that, and finally the other half of the cracker. Press gently together so that the chocolate is buried in hot marshmallow.

Skillet Supper

Camp is one place where I use mixes and cook from cans because it is less handy to maintain a pantryful of ingredients there. If I am really organized before I go, I might mix up dry ingredients at home for favorite pancakes or muffins, and add the eggs, oil, and milk at camp. Even so, I am likely to bring potatoes, onions, and garlic from the home garden, and sometimes even frozen stuff.

The recipe calls for kielbasa, but I think that almost any kind of sausage you like would taste fine and work just as well, and I suppose even ground meat, though you might want to omit the oil, and cook the meat with the onions and garlic. The little can of chilies is what makes this different and delicious.

1 LARGE ONION, CHOPPED

2 CLOVES GARLIC, MINCED

2 TABLESPOONS VEGETABLE OIL

4 LARGE POTATOES, PEELED AND CUBED

1 POUND SMOKED SAUSAGE

ONE (4-OUNCE) CAN CHOPPED GREEN CHILIES

ONE (15¼-OUNCE) CAN WHOLE KERNEL CORN, DRAINED,
   OR SCANT TWO CUPS

Cook the onion and garlic in the vegetable oil in a large skillet over medium heat until they are just tender, about 5 minutes. Add the potatoes and cook them for about 20 minutes, stirring and turning them occasionally. Add the sausage and continue cooking until the potatoes are tender. Add chilies and corn and heat the mixture through.

Spaghetti Sauce

When Sharon, in Surry, wrote looking for "spaghetti sauce made from scratch and simmered all day," my Islesboro neighbor Adrienne Durkee sent along her recipe on which I embroidered. She starts with a quart of her own home canned tomatoes. You may prefer to start with fresh tomatoes peeled and seeded, on the premise that seeds make the sauce a bit bitter. Adrienne advised, "Don't add water, and do taste to see if more seasoning is needed."

1 MEDIUM ONION, CHOPPED

1 TABLESPOON OLIVE OIL

1 QUART OF HOME CANNED TOMATOES, OR 1½ POUNDS OF FRESH
  TOMATOES, CHOPPED, OR 1 LARGE CAN CRUSHED TOMATOES

1 LARGE CAN TOMATO PUREE OR 3 CUPS OF HOMEMADE PUREE

2 TO 4 CLOVES OF GARLIC, TO TASTE

1 GREEN PEPPER, MINCED (OPTIONAL)

2 TEASPOONS DRIED BASIL

1 TEASPOON DRIED OREGANO

1 BAY LEAF

TWO (7-OUNCE) CANS SLICED MUSHROOMS OR 3 CUPS SLICED
  FRESH MUSHROOMS

2 TABLESPOONS SUGAR OR 1 MEDIUM CARROT GRATED

SALT AND PEPPER, TO TASTE

SWEET ITALIAN SAUSAGE AND/OR MEATBALLS

Using a heavy 1-gallon stainless-steel pot, cook the onion for about 5 minutes in the olive oil. Add the tomatoes, puree, crush the garlic into the tomatoes, add the green pepper, herbs, mushrooms, sugar or carrot, and simmer it over a low heat for at least 3 hours. Alternatively, you can put the sauce in a slow-cooker on high for 6 to 8 hours.

About an hour or two before serving, brown the sausage and/or meat balls and add them to the sauce. As Adrienne says, "These will give flavor to sauce."

Let me tell a story on myself about spaghetti sauce and learning to cook. My mom was a straight-from-the-box-or-can kind of cook. Her spaghetti sauce consisted of a can of tomato sauce opened and a packet of Italian seasonings added. That was it.

When I left home at age twenty, I lived for a year with a single mom, Jane Keener, and her young family. I did childcare and fixed supper. One night Jane said, "Let's have spaghetti." I spent a frantic hour that day tearing through the cupboards looking for the little packet of seasonings, and finally in desperation, I went to the store and bought one because I didn't know how to make spaghetti sauce without it.

Jane was very good-natured when I told my tale that evening, and merely opened the *Betty Crocker Picture Cook Book* to pages 384-385, where to my astonished eyes, I saw that tomato sauce for spaghetti had onion, green peppers, garlic, salt, and pepper added to three and a half cups of cooked tomatoes or a #2½ can. What a revelation! Another cookbook she had suggested grated carrots, basil, oregano. Who knew?

Soup Suppers

GIVE YOURSELF A MEAL PLANNING break by declaring soup night once a week. Add some bread, a salad, and a couple cookies for dessert. Several of the soups that follow are hearty enough to be a meal all by themselves. Make a double batch and freeze some for a fast supper another time.

Cabbage Beef Soup

Frugal, delicious, healthful: this Cabbage Beef Soup sent by Lucille White, of Bangor, given to her by her neighbor, Wilma Lynch, wins on all points. Lucille says that soups and stews are a big part of her cool weather cooking, and wrote, "This soup not only tastes great but is

{ SERVES 8 TO 10 }

economical to make. I don't know of anyone I've passed this recipe on to who doesn't love it." I called her up and we talked about whether it should have onion in it or not, and did she think moose meat or venison burger would work, and what about more celery. Yes on onion, if you like it, and yes on deer burger.

Lucile says that Wilma usually uses more celery, and has tried boxed beef stock instead of bouillon cubes. And it can have more or fewer beans or more cabbage, too. In short, this is pretty flexible stuff.

1 POUND GROUND BEEF, MOOSE, OR VENISON

1 LARGE ONION CHOPPED (OPTIONAL)

2 CLOVES GARLIC, MINCED

2 TO 4 RIBS CELERY, CHOPPED

1 LARGE CAN, OR 1 QUART HOME CANNED TOMATOES,
CHOPPED WITH JUICE

1 MEDIUM CAN, OR 2 CUPS SOAKED AND COOKED KIDNEY BEANS

½ MEDIUM CABBAGE

1 BAY LEAF

3 TO 4 CUBES BEEF BOUILLON

SALT AND PEPPER, TO TASTE

In a large, heavy-bottomed soup kettle or Dutch oven, brown the ground meat, adding a little oil if the meat is very lean. When the meat begins to brown, add the onion, garlic, and celery and cook until the meat is done. Crumble the cooked meat, then add all the rest of the ingredients plus 3 ½ cups water. Bring just to a boil, reduce heat, and simmer for at least an hour. Taste and adjust the seasonings

It is ready to serve, but is better the next day.

Potato Parsley Soup

An all-purpose potato, like my favorite, Carola, that I grow annually, is best for this soup. My favorite parsley is the flat leaf Italian style. You will need a big bunch.

I used chicken broth as the recipe suggested but instead of yogurt, I used a cup of cottage cheese that I was afraid would go by, and a dollop of sour cream. Ricotta would work as well and so would evaporated milk, if that is what you have. You can actually leave out the milk products altogether and still have a fine soup.

If you like creamy soup, put the potato mix in a blender and puree it. Since I like things a little lumpy, I just used a masher on it, and only pureed a couple of cupsful.

4 MEDIUM POTATOES, DICED

1 MEDIUM ONION, DICED

¼ CUP (½ STICK) BUTTER

¼ CUP OLIVE OR VEGETABLE OIL

1 TEASPOON CURRY POWDER (OPTIONAL)

1 TABLESPOON WORCESTERSHIRE SAUCE

2 PACKED CUPS PARSLEY, PICKED OFF THE STEMS

3 CUPS CHICKEN BROTH

1 CUP YOGURT, MILK, CREAM, OR SOUR CREAM

SALT AND PEPPER, TO TASTE

Put the potatoes, onions, butter, olive oil, and curry powder into a heavy cook pot and cook until the onions are softened. Add 1 ¼ cups water and Worcestershire sauce, bring to a boil, reduce the heat, and cook until the potatoes are very tender. Mash it well or let cool and put it into a blender or food processor to puree into a creamy soup. Then put the parsley and broth into a blender and process until you have a green sauce. Add that to the potato mixture, add the yogurt, milk or cream, reheat and taste, then adjust seasonings.

{ SERVES 4 TO 6 }

{ ADVICE }

This recipe works just as it stands, but you can also consider it a soup base for lots of variations. Keep it vegetarian by using water or vegetable broth. Add broccoli or cauliflower, or add some cooked chard or spinach whirled up in the blender. Use meat broth or add meat to the soup. Smokey or spicy sausage would be terrific in it. Ham works as an addition; so does cheddar cheese. Add sautéed leeks in either the vegetarian or meat version. Feel free to cut loose with this. Scour your fridge for flavorful bits and pieces to add.

Peasant Soup

Mim Hart, in Hampden, shared this recipe. She said it started out as a plain lentil soup she found in *Gourmet*. "Then over the years," she wrote, "I added more veggies so it would be more nutritious, and tasty with more spices, and the vinegar for pep!"

I like this a lot, and felt terribly virtuous eating it because it has that good-for-you combination of legumes (lentils) and grain (brown rice), which creates a complementary protein. Then all the vegetables added their minerals and vitamins.

Mim's idea about the vinegar for pep is a good one. A dry sherry will work well, too. A long time ago, a friend of mine vastly improved a pot of pea soup I made with a generous splash of sherry, and I have used it since in all kinds of pea, bean, or lentil soups. Of course, most of us peasants are more likely to have vinegar.

{ ADVICE }

As it stands, this could be a vegetarian soup with the substitution of vegetable broth for the chicken broth. Conversely, you could add meat like a little bit of browned beef or slices of kielbasa. (If you are aiming for low-fat, you can use turkey sausage.) I thought about using chicken, but since lentils just can't keep themselves from turning into a kind of muddy sludge, I think red meat might hold up better in the appearance department.

1 CUP LENTILS

1½ QUARTS CHICKEN BROTH OR THE EQUIVALENT MADE WITH
  CHICKEN BOUILLON CUBES

1 CUP CHOPPED CARROTS

1 CUP CHOPPED CELERY

1 CUP CHOPPED ONION

1 CUP UNCOOKED BROWN RICE

2 MEDIUM CANS DICED TOMATOES

5 CLOVES GARLIC, MINCED

1 BAY LEAF

½ TEASPOON CURRY POWDER

1 TEASPOON DRIED BASIL

1 TEASPOON DRIED OREGANO

1 TEASPOON CUMIN

4 TABLESPOONS CIDER VINEGAR OR SHERRY

SALT AND PEPPER, TO TASTE

Pour all the ingredients plus 2 cups of water into a large stock pot. Simmer uncovered for 50 minutes. Add the vinegar or sherry at the last minute. If soup seems too thick, add more broth. Taste and add salt and pepper to taste.

Quick Breads

SOMETHING BAKED to go with supper or have as breakfast bread.

Pumpkin Bread

I waited years to find pumpkin bread I was enthusiastic about. My island neighbor Ruth Hartley gave me this recipe and for a change I didn't fiddle with it. The great error in most pumpkin breads is too much sugar, though some of you won't think so. Feel free to dump in more if you like very sweet quick breads. If you like raisins, add some of those. Since this makes two loaves, eat one and freeze one, or halve the recipe, easily done.

{ MAKES 2 LOAVES }

3¾ CUPS FLOUR

2 TEASPOONS BAKING SODA

1 TEASPOON CINNAMON

1 TEASPOON NUTMEG

1½ TEASPOON SALT

2 CUPS COOKED, WELL-DRAINED PUMPKIN OR CANNED PUMPKIN

4 EGGS

3 CUPS SUGAR

1 CUP COOKING OIL

⅔ CUP COLD WATER

Preheat the oven to 350 degrees. Grease and flour two bread pans. Sift together the flour, baking soda, cinnamon, nutmeg, and salt. Put the pumpkin, eggs, sugar, oil, and water into a large mixing bowl and beat. Add the dry ingredients and mix thoroughly. Divide into the two pans. Bake for 1 hour, or until the top rises and cracks, and a tester inserted comes out clean. Cool on a rack before turning out.

Pumpkin Waffles

{ SERVES 4 TO 6 }

{ ADVICE }

Sometimes if I suspect a stored pumpkin is tending towards spoiling, I cook it up and freeze it in one cup batches for recipes like this one. I put the pumpkin into freezer bags, flatten them so they stack neatly on the freezer shelf. I need only remove the specified number of cups for a recipe.

If you like waffles and if you like pumpkin bread, then you will like pumpkin waffles. Lest you find the ingredient list too long, remember four of the dry ingredients are spices. Separating eggs may also seem like one too many things to do, but it really makes for a tender waffle. If you find that one batch of batter makes more than you want to eat in one sitting, bake the rest and turn them into toaster waffles for another day.

2½ CUPS FLOUR

2 TABLESPOONS SUGAR

4 TEASPOONS BAKING POWDER

½ TEASPOON SALT

½ TEASPOON GROUND GINGER

¼ TEASPOON GROUND NUTMEG

⅛ TEASPOON GROUND CLOVES

1½ CUPS MILK

⅓ CUP VEGETABLE OIL

1 CUP COOKED AND DRAINED PUMPKIN

3 EGGS SEPARATED

PINCH OF CREAM OF TARTAR

Preheat your waffle iron. Sift the flour, sugar, baking powder, salt, and all spices together. Beat the egg yolks into the milk, add the oil and pumpkin, and beat the wet ingredients until they are smooth, then stir them into the dry ingredients. Beat the egg whites with the cream of tartar and fold them into the waffle batter. Bake the waffles according to the directions for your iron.

Oat Scones

As a bit of an Anglophile during my teens, I was entranced by the idea of making scones to accompany a cup of tea. Then when I was twenty years old, I worked one summer at a bill collection agency where one of my co-workers was a pleasant Englishwoman named Eleanor Nabbs, who gave me this recipe for oat scones. Among the plentiful scones in coffee shops and bakeries and the recipes that have appeared since my youth, I still haven't come across a recipe quite like these homey, chewy scones. Mrs. Nabbs cut the dough in wedges, which I have always done, but you can use a round cutter if you wish.

{ MAKES 6 TO 8 }

1 CUP FLOUR

1 CUP ROLLED OATS

½ TEASPOON SALT

2 TEASPOONS BAKING POWDER

1 TABLESPOON SUGAR

¼ CUP BUTTER

½ CUP MILK

Preheat the oven to 425 degrees. Mix all the flour, oats, salt, baking powder, and sugar together in a bowl, then cut in the butter with a pastry cutter or two knives. Dribble in the milk and toss the mixture until it all sticks together like biscuit dough. Flour a board and pat the dough out to a half-inch thick circle. Cut into wedges and lay on a greased baking sheet. Bake for 15 minutes, or until they are golden brown.

A Treat at the End

YOU'VE EATEN ALL YOUR DINNER, had your vegetables and main dishes, cleaned your plate, and now here is a wicked little sweet treat.

Caramel Corn

{ MAKES 4½ QUARTS }

{ ADVICE }

The recipe is written for microwave popcorn and the serving size on a package says it makes four and a half cups of popcorn. Two bags then would be nine cups. When I made my popcorn from scratch nine cups looked like a measly amount. So I went for twelve. The recipe makes a lot of caramel candy, and to tell the truth I think you could cover up to sixteen cups of popcorn decently. You decide. If you like it really slathered on, then stick to ten cups. If you want the candy covering to go further, add more popcorn.

Islesboro sets up its polling place in the public safety room and by custom the pre-school holds an Election Day Bake and Lunch Sale next door in the firehouse garage. All morning long we poll workers catch tantalizing whiffs of homemade soup, chowder, and chili and usually we run in on our breaks to see what else there is. One Election Day, Sarah Randlett made this caramel corn from her mom Susie's recipe, and I was so impressed with it, I asked Sarah for the recipe. It is simply delectable.

What I like about this recipe is that I don't need a candy thermometer as long as I stick to the instructions to boil five minutes. I set a timer for that because five minutes can whip by in a flash. (The older I get the faster it whips, too.) And, yes, you get one heck of a sticky roasting pan. Fortunately the baked on sugar mixture soaks right off.

10 TO 16 CUPS POPPED CORN OR 2 TO 4 BAGS OF PLAIN
   MICROWAVE POPCORN

1 CUP (2 STICKS) BUTTER

1 CUP LIGHT BROWN SUGAR

1 CUP DARK BROWN SUGAR

1 TEASPOON SALT

½ CUP LIGHT CORN SYRUP

½ TEASPOON BAKING SODA

1 TEASPOON VANILLA

Preheat the oven to 225 degrees. Put the popped corn in a deep roasting pan (greased if you wish). In a heavy saucepan, melt the butter and stir in the sugars, salt, and corn syrup. Stirring constantly, bring this mixture to a boil, which happens quickly. Then boil for 5 minutes without stirring, adjusting the heat slightly downward to keep it from boiling over. After 5 minutes, remove it from the heat, stir in the baking soda and vanilla. The soda causes it to foam. Stir and dribble the mixture over the popcorn, stirring the corn gently to coat it with the syrup.

Bake for 1 hour stirring it every 15 minutes then let it cool, break it up, and store in a lightly-covered container.

Modern Maine Cooking

MODERN MAINE COOKING

I am so old that I remember when the only lettuce we knew about was iceberg, foreign cooking was spaghetti and meatballs, and no one I knew cooked with wine or cilantro. I was thirteen before I ate pizza, and in my twenties before I had quiche, eggplant, or an artichoke. Words like latte, pesto, hummus, risotto, and sushi had not entered our vocabularies, all rice was white, seaweed stayed in the ocean, and red and yellow bell peppers were unusual.

So much has changed with food in just the past thirty years that unless you have been hiding under a rock in Washington County you can't have missed hearing about Thai or Tex-Mex, encountered salsa, and being treated to artisanal bread.

Even home cooks now keep olive oil on hand, use balsamic vinegar, and know what to do with feta cheese.

The recipes in this section reflect fairly recent trends in Maine home cooking, though some more sophisticated households may have served up some of these even in the mid-1900s. I have met up with these dishes at potlucks, dinners with friends, or ordered them at restaurants and wanted to try them at home, too, just as you do.

Some Dishes to Start a Meal

TO TELL THE TRUTH, I could make a whole meal out of a selection of appetizers. If you have company coming, though, you might like to have a few dips and nibbles, or hot and savory items to pass, either as your whole offering with drinks or as prelude to a full meal.

Tapenade

Tapenade is so delicious that I could just eat it with a spoon, but most people use it as an appetizer spread on crackers or bread, or they dip veggies in it. It hails from Provence, France, and is made of finely chopped black olives, sometimes green ones also, plus a few capers, olive oil, garlic, and usually some anchovies or anchovy paste. Thyme, basil, or parsley appears in some recipes. Most of us never heard of it until the last decade or two. Now you can get prepared jars of it, not only in specialty food shops, but almost any chain grocery store, too.

Keep your eyes open for large containers of capers. I get mine from a wholesale place in Rockland and never, ever buy the skinny jars that only hold a few ounces. Capers are so handy and add such an interesting flavor to all kinds of otherwise plain fish, chicken, and vegetable dishes, that I really hate to be without them.

{ ADVICE }

What got me going on tapenade was a recipe calling for it as an ingredient in a potato dish. Now, as you know, if I think I can make something cheaper myself, that is what I will do, and tapenade is one of those things. Not that I want to deprive a specialty food producer of a living, but the ingredients are so easy to find and assemble that I can make buckets of it for the price of a little containerful. My niece, Sarah Oliver, of Belfast, makes a wonderful tapenade, enhancing hers with an orange-flavored brandy and a tablespoon or two of red pepper or garlic jelly.

¾ CUP PITTED BLACK OLIVES

1 CLOVE GARLIC, MORE TO TASTE

2 TABLESPOONS WELL-DRAINED CAPERS

1 TABLESPOON LEMON JUICE, MORE TO TASTE

ZEST OF HALF A LEMON

½ TEASPOON DRY THYME

3 TO 4 LEAVES FRESH BASIL OR PARSLEY (OPTIONAL)

¼ CUP OLIVE OIL

SALT AND PEPPER, TO TASTE

Pulse everything except the oil in a food processor until it is finely chopped. Add the oil gradually until you have a spreadable paste. Taste and add pepper and salt as needed. Store in a covered container in the fridge.

HOW TO USE TAPENADE:

1. Spread it on French bread or crackers as an appetizer.

2. Use it mixed with mayo in a chicken sandwich.

3. Add to scrambled eggs.

4. Add to sautéed spinach or swiss chard.

5. Add to cooked pasta as speedy sauce.

6. Put on baked potatoes.

Smoked Salmon Spread

This spread is pretty much of a free-for-all.

{ MAKES 1¾ CUPS }

My island neighbor Joanne Pendleton says she just takes whipped cream cheese and beats the smoked salmon into it. That's it. Can't get any easier than that.

Deborah Rollins and Ruth Thurston offered slightly more complex recipes, with which anyone can play fast and loose.

Ruth's recipe included mayonnaise, dill weed, Tabasco, and chopped olives. Ruth didn't have any olives on hand when she tried the recipe, and didn't think she'd like them anyway. She did hers in a mixer and says the mixer had a hard job of it. She also wrote to say that she thought when it is time to serve it, something green on the mounded-up spread improves it.

Deborah's recipe recommended lemon and capers with the salmon and cheese mix with yogurt added to adjust the consistency. Her recipe calls for Neufchâtel or cream cheese and provides a lot of leeway in the salmon department: a quarter of a cup to one cup, "depending on how salmony you want it, or how much you bought." In winter, she eats hers on bagels and in summer on thin rye crackers. She says that it is good on baked potatoes, and she sometimes thins it out with milk, stock, or vodka! for pasta sauce. So, have a party, make more spread than you need, and have it the next night on pasta.

8 OUNCES CREAM CHEESE OR NEUFCHÂTEL CHEESE

8 OUNCES SMOKED SALMON

¼ CUP YOGURT OR MAYONNAISE

SALT AND PEPPER, TO TASTE

LEMON JUICE OR TABASCO, TO TASTE (OPTIONAL)

CHOPPED DILL, TO TASTE (OPTIONAL)

A FEW CHOPPED OLIVES OR CAPERS, TO TASTE (OPTIONAL)

Throw all the ingredients into a food processor or mixer and whirl until you have the texture you like, either very smooth or a bit lumpy. Taste and adjust seasonings. Mound it on a plate and serve with crackers or crusty bread.

Cowboy Caviar

I met this dish in Amherst, Maine, at a potluck lunch with the Upper Union River Historical Society. Marie Bassett, of Osborne, supplied the recipe for this wholesome dip with vivid, fresh flavor. Use scoopy little corn chips to eat it as a dip. It also works as a salad dressing on greens.

{ADVICE}

Marie used what is called shoe-peg corn — tiny kernels that add yellow color and a contrasting texture. Use parsley if you hate cilantro. How much heat from hot peppers you add is up to you. Marie used finely chopped jalapeño pepper, but you might prefer a milder sort, like an Anaheim, or you might like the smokiness of chipotle pepper. If you don't have peppers, you can use hot sauce.

2 CUPS BLACK-EYED PEAS

1 CUP OR SMALL CAN OF SHOE-PEG OR WHOLE KERNEL CORN

1 SWEET RED OR GREEN PEPPER, VERY FINELY CHOPPED

1 MEDIUM RED ONION, FINELY CHOPPED

JALAPEÑO PEPPER, FINELY CHOPPED, TO TASTE

2 TABLESPOONS CHOPPED CILANTRO

⅓ TO ½ CUP SUGAR

½ TO ⅔ CUP CIDER VINEGAR

¾ CUP OLIVE OR CANOLA OIL

Mix all the ingredients together in a bowl and let marinate for a few hours. Before serving, drain the marinade. Provide large corn chips or scoop-shaped chips.

Wild Mushroom Soup

{ SERVES 6 TO 8 }

For years I didn't know that I liked mushroom soup. My mom served canned soup, and that white pasty stuff with the gray blobs in it didn't look very appealing. Then when I was in my late twenties, a co-worker brought to work some homemade mushroom soup that his wife had made from fresh mushrooms and I took a taste. What a revelation. I've been a mushroom soup enthusiast ever since.

There are so many different fresh mushrooms available now in stores, some even fairly exotic, and with the addition of dried wild ones, the range of possibilities for soups and sauces is really generous. I used mixed dried wild ones, plus plain button and baby bellas, a mini-portabella. Don't be shy about mixing them up.

My island neighbor Jennifer Whyte offered the following just plain delicious recipe. Her recipe calls for pureeing the soup at the end. Generally I like things chunky, so I pureed only half of the potful. Suit your own taste on this.

1 OUNCE DRIED WILD MUSHROOMS, OR MORE TO TASTE

6 CUPS CHICKEN OR VEGETABLE STOCK

2 TABLESPOONS BUTTER

2 MEDIUM ONIONS, COARSELY CHOPPED

2 CLOVES GARLIC

2 POUNDS BUTTON OR OTHER FRESH MUSHROOMS, SLICED

SALT AND PEPPER, TO TASTE

1 TEASPOON DRIED THYME

½ TEASPOON GRATED NUTMEG

2 TO 3 TABLESPOONS FLOUR

½ CUP Madeira OR SHERRY

½ CUP SOUR CREAM

CHOPPED CHIVES OR PARSLEY FOR GARNISH

Rinse the dried mushrooms in cold water, tossing and shaking to remove sand or dirt. Put them into a small saucepan with 1 cup of stock and bring to a boil. Remove from heat and let soak for 40 minutes.

In a heavy soup pot, melt the butter over medium heat and cook the onions until they are softened and golden. Stir in the garlic and fresh mushrooms and cook until they soften, then add the salt, pepper, thyme, nutmeg, and flour. Cook, stirring, for 3 to 5 minutes.

Drain the soaked, dried mushrooms through a sieve and add them to the pot. Strain the soaking liquid through a piece of cloth or filter paper to remove any grit and add it and the rest of the stock and Madeira to the pot and cook for 30 minutes or so over medium until the mushrooms are very tender.

Puree the soup in a blender or food processor, put back in the pot, and add the sour cream and bring back up to temperature. Serve garnished or not.

Shrimp Pesto Roll

This hot hors d'oeuvre showed up at a holiday party I attended. It would also make an elegant accompaniment to a soup or salad for supper or lunch. Use Maine shrimp in it or shrimp from away. If you buy fresh shrimp, dunk it in salted boiling water for only a minute and drain it quickly. Dry it a bit on a paper towel before putting it into the roll.

I buy the puff pastry. My life is too short to make puff pastry from scratch, but if you want to, more power, and a gold star to you.

> 1 PACKAGE PUFF PASTRY, 2 SHEETS, THAWED ACCORDING TO
> PACKAGE DIRECTIONS
> 10 OUNCES SHRIMP, CLEANED AND BOILED
> 4 TO 6 TABLESPOONS PESTO
> ½ CUP GRATED CHEDDAR CHEESE

Preheat the oven to 425 degrees. Open out the puff pastry sheets and spread the pesto over the surface. Arrange the shrimp across the middle of the pastry slices and sprinkle the cheese over all. Fold over to cover the shrimp, dampen the very edges and pinch them shut. Bake for 15 to 20 minutes, reducing the oven to 400 degrees after the first 15 minutes. Slice to serve.

Pumpkin Soup with Thai Seasonings

I was looking in the cupboard one day for evaporated milk to add to pumpkin soup when I spotted a can of coconut milk. The only reason I have coconut milk is to make the occasional Thai dish with that wonderfully hot and spicy sauce that you season the milk with to make into a sauce for chicken or pork on rice noodles. Something clicked, and I thought, why not use the coconut milk instead of evap and use Thai chili sauce with other Thai seasonings in the soup? This is the result.

2 TABLESPOONS VEGETABLE OIL

1 MEDIUM ONION, FINELY CHOPPED

2 CLOVES GARLIC, CRUSHED

1 SMALL PUMPKIN, PEELED AND CUT INTO SMALL CHUNKS

2 CUPS WATER

1 MEDIUM CAN OF COCONUT MILK

1 TABLESPOON THAI CHILI SAUCE, OR TO TASTE

1 TABLESPOON GRATED LEMON RIND

1 TABLESPOON FISH SAUCE OR SOY SAUCE

SALT AND PEPPER, TO TASTE

FRESH CILANTRO

In a heavy pot, sauté the onion and garlic in the oil until the onion is just soft. Add pumpkin, water, coconut milk, chili, lemon rind, and fish, or soy sauce. Simmer for 30 minutes until the pumpkin is soft enough to mash. Mash it in the pot or let cool and puree in a blender until smooth. Add salt and pepper, taste, and adjust seasoning. Chop the cilantro and add to the soup at the last minute, or use it to garnish the bowls.

Maine's Other Seafoods

LOBSTER SO DOMINATES MAINE SEAFOOD that it is easy to overlook the fine crab, scallops, mussels, shrimp, and salmon we find here. Our rock-hard crabs are a pain to pick, but Maine crab is some of the best tasting that you will find anywhere. Our tiny winter shrimp are sweet and delicate. Mussels abound, growing wild on mooring lines and rocks, and are farmed as well. Maine salmon was famous in past times, and is another fish farmed in Maine water. Maine fishermen go scalloping in winter. There's lots more to Maine seafood than *Homarus americanus*.

Mussels in Wine

Shortly after asking readers for a recipe for steamed mussels, I was in the Island Market, in what passes for downtown Islesboro, where I live, and my neighbor Julia Pendleton asked if I'd found a mussel recipe yet. I said I had a few that were sent in, and asked her how she did hers, and she said, "I put a can of beer in and steam them on top of that." Neila Ambrose, in Millinocket, does that, too, and adds onions and garlic.

Then Linda Durkee said, "What about peppercorns; don't you grind up some pepper to put in?" And then she told me about the garlic and wine steamed mussels she has at a restaurant in Florida where she goes for the winter (Maine mussels and Mainers *both* to Florida). And Helen Barrett chimed in, "I use lots of onions and garlic and a good wine," usually Chardonnay, and "parsley, flat, Italian parsley, because the curly doesn't have any flavor." Helen reports that her mussel broth ends up tasting like a very fine onion soup when she is done. I asked her how much water she puts in, and she said none, and my neighbor Adrienne Durkee had recommended "very little."

So this grocery store conversation among my island neighbors pointed out to me that they, and probably you, too, if you cook mussels, don't exactly have a "recipe" of the quarter cup of that and half teaspoon of this ilk, but rather you have a "way" of doing it. Isn't that the case with so much cooking?

{ SERVES 2 TO 3 }

{ ADVICE }

Leftover mussels are also handy as an hors d'oeuvre. Save one shell from each leftover one, and lightly toss the cooked mussels in vinaigrette, and put one on each shell with a shred of pimiento.

Ruth Thurston, in Machias, wrote that she found a way of preparing them in the 1986 Maine's Fishermen's Wives Association seafood cookbook. She said, "I'd never cooked mussels before, but I decided to try when I read your request." She liked the results. Anne Feeley, in Belfast, also offered a recipe. Here is our collected wisdom.

2 TABLESPOONS OLIVE OIL

2 TABLESPOONS BUTTER

1 CELERY RIB, MINCED

2 CLOVES GARLIC, MINCED

3 TO 4 MEDIUM ONIONS, CHOPPED

1 CARROT SLICED (OPTIONAL)

1 BAY LEAF (OPTIONAL)

2 POUNDS MUSSELS

2 TO 3 CUPS DRY WHITE WINE

½ CUP OR MORE PARSLEY

Put the olive oil and butter in a large heavy pot, and heat them until the butter is melted and bubbly. Add the vegetables and cook them until the onions are soft and translucent. Clean the mussels, removing the beards and checking to see that the mussels are tightly closed. If not, discard. Add the wine, and when it simmers, put in the mussels. Add the parsley. Steam them until they are all wide open.

Serve in soup bowls with the vegetables, alone, or on pasta or rice or bread for dipping — if you wish.

Orzo, Feta, and Shellfish

{ SERVES 4 }

My friend Sharon Daley, who is the telemedicine nurse on the Seacoast Mission's boat *Sunbeam*, which visits Maine islands and coast, has been managing her cholesterol by careful eating. She told me about this new favorite quick, easy, and low-fat recipe. It is sumptuous with shellfish, satisfying with the pasta, and as flavorful as you want with the extra stuff you can add in.

Sharon says the original recipe she had calls for scallions, but she uses roasted red peppers. I've used leeks and also stirred in a tablespoon of roasted garlic puree that I had. Why not pesto?

Consider using little Maine shrimps, or a combination of shrimp and scallops, or scallops alone. If your scallops are the big ones, consider cutting them up.

1 CUP ORZO

1 POUND SHELLFISH

4 OUNCES FETA CHEESE

5 OR 6 SCALLIONS, OR ONE LARGE SHALLOT, CHOPPED

¼ CUP CHOPPED ROASTED RED PEPPER

SALT AND PEPPER, TO TASTE

Preheat the oven to 350 degrees. Cook the orzo according to the directions on the package. Mix together the cooked orzo, shellfish, feta, vegetables, and salt and pepper. Bake for 30 to 40 minutes, or until the feta is melted and bubbly.

Crab Strata

I picked up this luscious recipe in Stonington-Deer Isle from Caroline Rittenhouse who got it from the Stonington artist Michie Stovall O'Day. It is just the ticket for a special occasion brunch or breakfast, because you can assemble it ahead and bake it the next day when you want it. You can also use lobster and mix it with the crab, or go with either alone. When those lovely little Maine shrimp are available, consider using them in this dish.

{ SERVES 4 TO 6 }

{ ADVICE }

Caroline and Michie like to use leftover baguettes for the bread, and you can use that, too, or any firm bread, as long as it is not so assertively flavored that it diminishes the crab. Whether or not you take the crusts off, is up to you.

4 TO 6 SLICES OF BREAD, OR AS NEEDED

8 OUNCES SHREDDED CHEDDAR, MILD OR SHARP ACCORDING
   TO TASTE

16 OUNCES CRAB MEAT

4 TABLESPOONS OF BUTTER, MELTED

3 EGGS BEATEN

1 PINT HALF-AND-HALF, OR LIGHT CREAM

½ TEASPOON DRY MUSTARD

¼ TEASPOON CRUSHED RED PEPPER FLAKES, OR HOT SAUCE,
   TO TASTE

SALT AND PEPPER, TO TASTE

Grease a 9 by 13 glass or ceramic casserole dish. Lay the bread in bottom of the casserole. Sprinkle most of the cheese over it, then the crab, and drizzle with the butter. Beat together the eggs, half-and-half, and seasonings, and pour that over the layers in the casserole. Top with the remaining cheese. Cover and refrigerate overnight.

In the morning, pre-heat the oven to 350 degrees and bake the casserole for about 1 hour, uncovered, until it is puffy and golden.

Crab Quiche

{ SERVES 4 TO 6 }

When Connie MacDuffie, of Newburgh, wrote, saying, "I'm looking for a recipe for crab quiche and have had no luck in my cookbooks. Do you have such a recipe?" she was recalling one she had in a Belfast restaurant and enjoyed it so much that she wanted to make it for herself. My Islesboro neighbor Linda Gillies sent a recipe for a very rich and flavorful crab quiche that she found in a Charleston (South Carolina) cookbook, *Mrs. Whaley Entertains*. She said, "Delicious, though one must take a break from cholesterol watching. Good served with a green salad and tomatoes of some kind — salad or roasted." Linda uses store bought piecrust, but you can make your own favorite if you want. She says it takes about an hour of preparation time.

1 UNBAKED 9-INCH PIE CRUST

2 LARGE EGGS, WELL BEATEN

½ CUP MAYONNAISE

2 TABLESPOONS FLOUR

½ CUP MILK

⅛ TEASPOON MACE

2 CUPS GRATED SWISS CHEESE

2 TABLESPOONS BUTTER

4 CHOPPED SCALLIONS, WHITE AND GREEN PARTS

8 OUNCES CRABMEAT

PAPRIKA FOR SPRINKLING (OPTIONAL)

Preheat the oven to 400 degrees. Line the quiche pan with the pastry, prick it all over with a fork, and bake until light brown. If it puffs up, gently press down the puffed parts with the fork. Remove from the oven and cool.

Reduce the oven temperature to 350 degrees. Whisk the eggs and then add the mayonnaise, flour, milk, mace, and 1 cup of the swiss cheese, mixing thoroughly. Set aside. In a small skillet, melt the butter over medium-low heat. Add the scallion and sauté until soft, but do not brown. Remove from heat.

Fold the scallions and crabmeat gently into the mayonnaise mixture, being careful not to break up the crab lumps. Pour the filling into the pre-baked pie shell and sprinkle the remaining swiss cheese over the top. Sprinkle with paprika if desired. Bake for about 40 minutes, until the quiche is set and golden brown on top. Let it rest for about 10 minutes before serving.

The quiche can be cooked a day ahead, chilled, brought back to room temperature, and re-heated for 20 to 25 minutes at 350 degrees. Freezes well.

{ ADVICE }

The whole question of crab quiche recipes, however, made me think about how I make quiche, which is basically to line a quiche pan with pastry and dump anything I like or have into the pan, then top it off with eggs and cream beaten together and seasoned with a little nutmeg, salt and pepper. Bake it and voila! — quiche. I have put broccoli, crumbled bacon, cheese, red peppers, lobster, and chopped ham into quiche — not, mind you, all at one time. I figured that if I had to, I could just provide my standard old quiche recipe with crab added. So while I have ended up with a perfectly recognizable and tasty quiche using my method, I may not have ended up with really good quiche, which Linda's is.

Crab Cakes

{ ADVICE }

Just the tiniest bit
of seasoning is needed:
some finely minced
shallot, a sprinkle of
Old Bay Seasoning, or
parsley, tarragon, or
chives work. I usually
save all the powerful
flavors for the sauce:
ketchup with grated
horseradish stirred into
it for a cocktail sauce, or
a homemade pickle relish
stirred into mayonnaise
for tartar sauce. You can
put on the dog by adding
to the tartar sauce a
few chopped capers and
tarragon to taste. Or
doctor up prepared sauces
to suit yourself.

Lobstermen loathe bait-eating crabs that clutter up their traps, and
they are usually happy to take a few out of circulation for free. If you go
to a great deal of trouble to pick crab, or spend a fair amount to buy it,
then when you eat a crab cake you ought to taste crab and not have it all
thinned out with miscellaneous fillers.

Once I watched my neighbor Sarah Randlett make her delicious
crab cakes for dinners at a bed-and-breakfast inn we used to have on the
island. Her secret was using a mild fish to help bind the flavorful little
threads of crab together; the trick was grinding the fish up raw, which
made it downright sticky. The fish took up crab flavor and held the cakes
together. I know that some folks use a little mayonnaise as a kind of glue
for crab cakes, and if you think you want the security of extra stickiness,
then drop in a dollop.

To end up with a pleasantly crusty exterior, breadcrumbs and some
beaten egg are all that is required. Fry them in a blend of butter and
olive oil. Just please don't deep fry them.

Three crab cakes can be enough for an entrée with vegetables and
rice or pasta on the side. You can consider making them smaller, and
using them for hors d'oeuvres.

1 ½ CUPS, ABOUT 12 OUNCES, PICKED CRAB

½ CUPS OR ABOUT 4 TO 6 OUNCES FRESH WHITEFISH

   (COD, HADDOCK, CUSK, ETC.) GROUND IN A FOOD PROCESSOR

1 SHALLOT, OR 3 OR 4 SCALLIONS, FINELY MINCED

2 OR 3 SPRIGS PARSLEY, FINELY MINCED

SALT AND PEPPER, TO TASTE

MAYONNAISE (OPTIONAL)

1 BEATEN EGG

DRY BREADCRUMBS

BUTTER

OLIVE OIL

Toss the crab and ground fish together in a bowl, add the shallot, or
scallions, parsley, and a sprinkle of salt and pepper. Pick up a soup
spoonful and form it into a patty about 2 inches in diameter, and about
a ½ inch thick. If the patty will not hold together, add some mayonnaise

or beaten egg until it will. Dip each patty into beaten egg and then into breadcrumbs, both sides. Set on a baking sheet or pan and refrigerate for 1 hour or more until you are ready to fry them.

Melt 2 tablespoons of butter in a fry or sauté pan and add 2 tablespoons of olive oil, and allow it to get very hot (so that a drop of water jumps in the pan). Put the cakes into the pan, reduce the temperature somewhat, and cook them until crusty on both sides, about 5 minutes per side. Keep warm until you are ready to serve.

Salmon Quiche

This salmon quiche from Nina Scott, in Friendship, is so tasty! Canned salmon is handy stuff, and this recipe puts it to good use. If you have some leftover baked or poached salmon, use that in this dish. Serve it with a green vegetable and a tossed salad for a pretty supper or brunch.

I pedal back a little on the cheese and butter in this recipe, and that does no harm. Nina's recipe called for an unbaked pie shell, but, either out of habit or superstition, I pre-bake mine a little anyway.

{ SERVES 6 }

9-INCH PIE SHELL WITH A HIGH RIM

½ STICK (3 TABLESPOONS) BUTTER

1 SMALL ONION, FINELY CHOPPED

¼ CUP FLOUR

SALT AND PEPPER, TO TASTE

1 CAN EVAPORATED MILK

3 EGGS

2 TABLESPOONS LEMON JUICE

1 CAN OR 2 CUPS SALMON

1 TEASPOON DILL WEED

½ TO 1 CUP GRATED CHEDDAR CHEESE

¼ CUP PARMESAN CHEESE

{ ADVICE }

I admit to being lazy about piecrusts. A recipe calling for a crust stops me dead in my tracks. I don't use ready-made crusts, and I suppose I ought to just get over it. (My prejudice comes from my not being willing to ingest the unidentifiable items in the ingredients list.) My usual, favorite recipe, however, makes two crusts, and so I can help myself out a bit by making one recipe, rolling out a one-crust pie or quiche, then putting the other crust in the freezer for another time.

If you wish to prebake the piecrust, preheat the oven to 400 degrees and line the pie or quiche pan with the pie dough. Bake it for 10 minutes. Reduce the oven temperature to 375 degrees. Drain the salmon, reserving the liquid and removing bones and skins. Add water to the liquid to make 1 cup. Melt the butter in a sauté pan and cook the chopped onion until it is transparent. Add the flour, salt, and pepper, and stir to cook the flour until bubbly. Add the fish liquid and the evaporated milk and simmer, stirring steadily. Beat the eggs and add them gradually to the sauce until the sauce thickens slightly. Arrange the fish in the crust and dribble in the lemon juice, then sprinkle on the dill and cheddar and Parmesan cheese. Pour the sauce into the crust and shake the pan to settle the ingredients. Then bake for 30 to 40 minutes, depending on how deep your pan is. The quiche should be puffed and beginning to be brown. Let stand for 10 minutes before serving.

Deviled Scallops

{ SERVES 3 }

As with most shellfish, the main thing with scallops is not to overcook them. A recipe from that nice Ruth Thurston, in Machias, showed how to make a casserole of them, simply assembled with mushrooms and onions with slivered almonds sprinkled on top. She also sent along a scallop stew, in which the scallops are gently cooked in butter and simmered in scalded milk, with a splash of Worcestershire.

If you are in the mood for scallops without sauce, however, this recipe shared by my island neighbor Maggie Aston will work beautifully.

{ ADVICE }

Maggie adapted this deviled scallops recipe from her 1996 *Fanny Farmer Cookbook*. You can jack up the spiciness to your taste on this one. I go easy on the cayenne — too easy, probably. Maggie said she thought we could cut back on the butter and crumbs a bit, and so I do. I cut the scallops down so they are all a similar size. Add a little minced garlic.

She wrote that the recipe "is delicious, simple, and practically foolproof. These are baked and always come out perfect." And they do. Twenty minutes! Just enough time to throw together a salad, or steam a little asparagus or broccoli, and make a little batch of couscous, and it is a spiffy dinner in a half hour if you move quickly.

1 POUND SCALLOPS

3 TABLESPOONS SOFTENED BUTTER

½ TEASPOON DRY MUSTARD

DASH CAYENNE PEPPER

⅓ CUP FRESH BREADCRUMBS

Preheat oven to 375 degrees. Butter a small baking dish (I used a glass pie plate) or scallop shells. Rinse the scallops and pat them dry. Cream together the butter, mustard, and cayenne. Put the scallops in the dish, dot them with the butter and spice mixture, and then cover them with breadcrumbs. Bake for 20 minutes exactly, then take them from the oven. Serve.

Recipes from Away

MAINERS ARE VERY LIKELY to describe someone who is not from Maine for generations as "from away," which is, of course, anywhere not Maine. Maine, therefore, is surrounded on all sides by "away" and is increasingly populated by people from away, too, who have brought recipes with them. Plus, modern life being what it is, with television and the Internet, it is impossible to miss new wrinkles in cookery or downright foreign fare.

Mediterranean Chicken Salad

{ SERVES 3 TO 4 }

{ ADVICE }

Most stores these days
sell many kinds of olives:
black pitted and un-pitted,
big green, small, and
wrinkled black ones in oil,
green with garlic, etc. I
like getting olives from
this selection because
I am very suspicious
about canned black olives.
Someone told me once
that manufacturers
take green olives, bleach
them, then dye them
black. Yuck. I don't know
if that is true, but
with honest to goodness
ripe black olives, who
needs the canned ones?
Kalamatas were my first
experience with real black
olives, and I thought,
"Where have you been
all my life?" If you have
olives with pits in them,
here is what to do: put
the olive on a cutting
board, then smack it with
the flat side of a chef's
knife. That breaks the
olive and leaves the pit
easy to pick out.

This chicken salad just oozes flavor.

I think a chicken salad ought to have a little of dark and light meat, but that is up to you. If you start with uncooked meat, the trick is to poach it until it is cooked but not overdone, because it toughens up if it boils hard. The poaching water can be chicken broth if you have some. If not, start with water and add salt, a bay leaf, a few peppercorns or a few grinds of a pepper mill. If you feel ambitious, chuck in a quartered onion, a carrot, a stalk of celery, a garlic clove or two. When the chicken is cooked, you will have a useful broth to stash in the fridge or freezer to cook rice in, or to use in a cream-of-something-or-other soup.

The rest of the ingredients — capers, olives, tomatoes, green beans — I think are somewhat optional. Asparagus or snap peas are potential additions. This is a fine chance to use cherry tomatoes. Capers are a terrific addition to this salad, too, a little salty and exotic. Italian parsley, the flat kind, has the best flavor. Save the curly for garnish.

A WHOLE COOKED CHICKEN, BREASTS AND A THIGH

1 BIG FISTFUL GREEN BEANS

2 TABLESPOONS CAPERS

A DOZEN BLACK OLIVES, PITTED AND CHOPPED

HANDFUL OF CHERRY TOMATOES (OPTIONAL)

⅓ CUP OLIVE OIL

JUICE OF 1 LEMON

DRIED OREGANO

FINELY MINCED PARSLEY

SALT AND PEPPER, TO TASTE

WASHED AND TORN LETTUCE OR BABY GREENS

Pull the meat from the bones and cut into bite-size pieces. Put into a bowl. Snap the beans and blanch them in hot water, or cook until tender — your choice. Add them to the chicken. Sprinkle capers on to taste, add the olives, slice the tomatoes in half, if you wish, and add them. In a small jar, shake the olive oil and lemon juice together and dribble over the salad to taste. Sprinkle on some dry oregano, parsley, and add salt and pepper to taste. Let rest at room temperature. Serve the salad on the lettuce.

Squash Risotto

Risotto is that trendy Italian rice dish to which you can add vegetables, seafood, or chicken. Sometimes recipes for it make it sound very involved and fussy, but I remember one time visiting Nancy Jenkins in Camden and she threw together risotto for lunch. I was just standing around watching, and when it finally occurred to me what she was making, I thought, "Wow, that's easy."

Nancy says the wine gives it a bit of fruitiness, but if you wish you can omit it. She also says that after you have added the last bit of stock and it has cooked in, take the pan off the heat, and let it rest for 5 minutes.

I found I could add hot liquid, stir it in, then go tear up lettuce for the salad, come back, add more liquid, stir, set the table, and so on. Just be aware of it, and don't let it get all stuck on the pan.

{ SERVES 6 }

{ ADVICE }

There are only a few risotto must-dos, and they are no big whoop. You do have to use the short-grain Arborio rice. You do have to toast the rice in the oil before adding liquid. You do have to keep hot water or broth boiling to add gradually while cooking the rice. You can't put all the liquid in at one time and waltz off somewhere for 20 minutes, but neither do you have to hover over it every minute.

3 TABLESPOONS OLIVE OIL

1 SMALL ONION, CHOPPED

2 CLOVES GARLIC, MINCED

1 POUND SQUASH, CUT INTO ½ INCH DICE

1½ CUPS ARBORIO RICE

½ CUP WHITE WINE

6 TO 8 CUPS BOILING HOT VEGETABLE OR CHICKEN STOCK

¼ CUP GRATED PARMESAN CHEESE

PARSLEY, OPTIONAL

SALT AND PEPPER, TO TASTE

Put the oil, onion, and garlic into a heavy, wide-bottom saucepan. Sauté until the onion begins to look translucent, add the squash, and cook until it just begins to soften. Add more oil if needed. Add the rice and cook for a couple of minutes. Then add the wine and when it has cooked away begin to add the stock, stirring in a ladleful at a time and cooking until the rice has absorbed the liquid. Stir as needed to keep it from sticking. Add more liquid and repeat the stirring and cooking until the rice is just al dente. Add the Parmesan, or put it on the table for people to add to their own servings. Add parsley, salt, and pepper to taste. Take the risotto off the heat, put a lid on the pot, and let it rest for 5 minutes while you put the rest of the dinner on the table.

Winter Squash and
Black Bean Enchiladas

When I saw sweet potato and black bean enchiladas on the menu of a local restaurant, I thought right away of a new way to use my homegrown winter squash. Sweet potatoes and squash are both orange, have similar textures, and can be cooked up about the same way.

The enchiladas came out very tasty, richly flavored with the spiced squash and substantial with beans for a main dish. Of course, if you have sweet potatoes, or like them better than squash, then you can use those instead. It is a great way to use leftover cooked squash, too.

OLIVE OR VEGETABLE OIL

3 TO 4 CUPS OF DICED WINTER SQUASH OR 3 CUPS OF
  MASHED COOKED SQUASH

2 TO 3 TEASPOONS OF GROUND CUMIN, OR TO TASTE

2 CLOVES GARLIC, FINELY MINCED

1 CUP COOKED BLACK BEANS

1 TO 1 ½ CUPS ENCHILADA SAUCE

8 CORN TORTILLAS, OR WHEAT, IF PREFERRED

CHEDDAR OR JACK CHEESE

Lightly coat a heavy frying pan with the oil, and when hot, add the squash and cook at a high temperature, turning the squash over from time to time, until it is just tender, about 15 minutes. Sprinkle on the cumin, chili powder, and the garlic and stir until you can smell the seasonings, then add the black beans.

Preheat the oven to 350 degrees. Spread enough enchilada sauce in the bottom of a baking pan to cover it. Dip the tortillas one at a time in the sauce, and fill with the squash and bean mixture, roll up and lay in the pan. Spread a little more enchilada sauce over the top, and top with a little grated cheese if desired. Bake for 30 minutes. Serve with sour cream and salsa if desired.

Veal Scaloppini

Scaloppini just means thin slices of veal.

I have never seen the word "scaloppini" attached to any packages of veal at the store, but when I was looking for something flat and not very thick, it came in the form of slices of leg meat. They were already pretty thin, but I pounded the thicker ones until they all matched — a little less than a quarter of an inch thick. They were also very lean, and since veal all by itself is not very flavorful, all the saucing really makes the difference. I kept thinking, why veal? Wouldn't chicken pounded flat be just as good, or better? and certainly cheaper. Well, that is a question for you to decide.

Eleanor Maxim, of Unity, sagely pointed out that there is a workable recipe in *Fanny Farmer* to use. Jean Belanger, of Bangor, sent along two recipes, one from her adopted Canadian mother's recipe for the dish and another from a friend with whom she was stationed at Charleston Air Force Base back in the sixties. Jean writes, "Sometimes I put slices of cheese (mozzarella) and slices of prosciutto on top and put it in the oven at 375 degrees until the cheese is melted. Canadian bacon and swiss cheese may be used also," and she serves it over noodles. For the one with tomato sauce, she serves rice and a salad.

Following are instructions for veal scaloppini a couple of different ways, based loosely on the selection of recipes these good folks shared.

{ SERVES 4 TO 5 }

For the veal:

3 TABLESPOONS BUTTER

2 TABLESPOONS OLIVE OIL

8 SCALOPPINI OF VEAL

¼ CUP FLOUR WITH PAPRIKA, SALT, AND PEPPER STIRRED INTO IT

8 OUNCES MUSHROOMS, SLICED

1 GARLIC CLOVE, MINCED

1 SMALL ONION, CHOPPED

¼ CUP WHITE WINE

For the cream sauce:

½ CUP CREAM

¼ CUP GRATED SWISS OR GRUYERE CHEESE (OPTIONAL)

A FEW SLICES OF PROSCIUTTO, SLIVERED (OPTIONAL)

For the tomato sauce:

½ CUP TOMATO PASTE

½ CUP CREAM

¼ CUP CHOPPED, PITTED BLACK OLIVES (OPTIONAL)

SMALL JAR OF ARTICHOKE HEARTS, CHOPPED (OPTIONAL)

Melt the butter in a large, heavy sauté or fry pan, and add the olive oil. Dip both sides of the veal into the flour, shake off the excess, and fry each at a high temperature for about a minute per side. Remove and keep warm. Add the mushrooms, garlic, and onion to the far left in the pan and cook until they are tender. When they are done, remove, and set them aside. Reduce the heat to medium. Put the wine into the pan and cook and scrape up the browned bits until the pan is cleaned.

At this point decide whether you want a cream sauce or a tomato sauce.

If cream sauce, add the cream to the pan and simmer just until it is slightly thickened. Return the veal and mushrooms to the pan, and heat them until they are warm all the way through. Remove to a platter and sprinkle on the cheese and prosciutto slivers. You may put this into the oven briefly to warm, if you prefer.

If tomato sauce, add the tomato paste to the pan, dilute it a little with a bit more wine or with water, then the cream. Simmer as above; if too thick, add a little water or broth. Put the veal and mushrooms back into the pan and simmer it very gently until warmed through.

Serve on noodles or pasta.

Arroz Con Pollo

The first time I ever had *arroz con pollo* was at my Ecuadorian-born college roommate's house. Her grandmother, who lived with the family, made it for dinner that night. So as I tried this recipe out at home, it hit me: this is Spanish rice with chicken in it!

{ SERVES 4 TO 5 }

Zelma Merritt found her version of the recipe "in an old Mary Margaret McBride encyclopedia of cooking that I purchased from Graves Shop-and-Save when they were in Caribou." Josephine Ross, from Hampden, sent along a recipe from a club in Panama, where she and her husband used to enjoy it when he was stationed there. These two recipes could not have been more different.

The McBride one was pretty stripped down: chicken, rice, tomatoes, lightly seasoned, and done in the oven. The Panama recipe, on the other hand, was elegant and full of all kinds of interesting stuff from raisins to sherry and served with peas and pineapple and garnished with pimento. As Josephine said, "It is delicious and as pretty as a picture." Of course, it takes a bit more effort to produce, but it makes a major presentation on the table.

I averaged them out in order to come up with something similar to what I remembered at my roommate's house. I borrowed the browning instructions, the tomato quantity, and the chicken with bones in from Zelma's recipe, and I put in raisins, sherry, vinegar, Tabasco, and more liquid per Josephine's recipe. Both called for onions.

3 TO 4 POUND CHICKEN, CUT UP

2 TABLESPOONS OLIVE OIL

1 LARGE ONION, CHOPPED

3 CUPS STEWED OR DICED TOMATOES

1 TEASPOON SALT

½ TEASPOON PEPPER

1 BAY LEAF

1 TEASPOON OF TABASCO (OPTIONAL)

2 TO 4 CLOVES OF GARLIC, TO TASTE (OPTIONAL)

½ CUP RAISINS (OPTIONAL)

¼ CUP SHERRY (OPTIONAL)

1 TABLESPOON VINEGAR (OPTIONAL)

1½ CUPS RICE

Put the cut-up chicken in a heavy pot with the olive oil, and brown on all sides at a medium-high heat for about 15 minutes. Add the onion, tomatoes, salt, pepper, 2 cups of water, and any or all of the optional ingredients, reduce the temperature, and cook altogether for about 45 minutes to 1 hour. 30 minutes before you wish to serve it, add the rice, cover the pot, and simmer for another 30 minutes. Check halfway through to make sure there is enough liquid for the rice, and, if necessary, add a bit of hot water.

When you are ready to serve, take the chicken out and put it on a platter, surround it with the rice, and garnish to taste. I like the idea of green peas and/or green pepper rings.

Fish Tacos

{ SERVES 4 }

My neighbor Mike Boardman, whose family has inhabited Islesboro since the beginning of settlement here, learned to love fish tacos when he lived in San Diego for a while, where for a couple of bucks he could buy them from street vendors for lunch. Mike showed me how to make them.

He asked me to bake a filet of fish before he arrived for supper. I seasoned it merely with salt and pepper, but you could experiment with other seasonings, if you wish. (Baking the fish instead of using a breaded, fried fish is one way of keeping calories down, in case that concerns you.) Once here, Mike made the sauces, and we assembled the tacos.

He made a creamy sauce out of sour cream or yogurt, thinned-out with lime juice. Then he assembled fresh *pico de gallo* with raw tomato, onion, cilantro, and lime juice. Mike made the *pico de gallo* really quickly, and put quite a lot of cilantro in it, and chives for color and flavor. You may have a favorite salsa you might prefer to use, and you could even tinker with it, adding more or different seasonings. For Mike, a fish taco has to have the *pico de gallo*, and I agree, as long as you can get reasonably flavorful tomatoes.

Mike likes using shredded cabbage for greens, though shredded lettuce is acceptable. Warmed soft corn tortillas are best, because they wrap around the fish and greens, making them easier to handle.

For the Pico de Gallo:

2 TO 3 TOMATOES, DICED

1 SMALL RED ONION, DICED

JUICE OF 1 TO 2 LIMES

BUNCH OF CILANTRO, CHOPPED

BUNCH OF CHIVES, CHOPPED

For the fish:

1 POUND WHITEFISH

2 TABLESPOONS OIL

SALT AND PEPPER OR OTHER SEASONING (OPTIONAL)

For the sauce:

½ PINT SOUR CREAM OR YOGURT

1 TO 2 TABLESPOONS LIME JUICE

For the filling:

¼ HEAD OF CABBAGE, FINELY SHREDDED

8 TO 10 SOFT CORN TORTILLAS

1 LIME, QUARTERED

Assemble the *pico de gallo*. Put the tomatoes and onion in a bowl with the lime juice, cilantro, and chives. Set in the fridge to chill for 1 hour.

Heat the oven to 350 degrees and put the fish on a lightly oiled pan, then sprinkle it with salt and pepper to taste. Bake until the fish flakes apart, 20 minutes or less. Wrap the tortillas in a slightly damp towel and put into a warm 200 degree oven.

Assemble the sauce. Stir the sour cream or yogurt with the lime juice until it is liquid enough to dribble it.

Put the fish, cabbage, *pico de gallo*, and sauce on the table and let everyone assemble their own taco. First put the fish in the center of the tortilla, dribble sauce on it, add cabbage, then the *pico de gallo*. If you like hot sauce, serve that and the quartered lime on the table, so each can add it to their taco to taste.

Savory Eggs

{ SERVES 1 }

One annual, seasonal treat for breakfast is eggs with basil, garlic, and Parmesan. I met up with this combination years ago at a little breakfast place where the cook called it Italian eggs.

There are no tricks with this except to use fresh basil and fresh garlic as opposed to dried basil and powdered garlic.

{ ADVICE }

The operating principle here is the combination of a fragrant herb with something aromatic like onion, pepper, or celery, and an agreeable cheese to sprinkle on the top. So a little bit of cilantro, a piece of hot chili pepper finely chopped, and a grating of jack cheese might make it a Tex-Mex egg. Chervil or tarragon, plus minced shallots, and a bit of grated Gruyere cheese might make you think of France or Switzerland.

1 TABLESPOON BUTTER

1 TABLESPOON OLIVE OIL

BASIL OR OTHER FRESH HERB

A LITTLE MINCED GARLIC OR SHALLOTS, OR RED OR GREEN PEPPER

2 EGGS

PARMESAN CHEESE OR CHEESE OF YOUR CHOICE

Melt the butter in a frying pan with the olive oil over a low heat. Lay the basil leaves in the pan and add the minced garlic, heating them until you can smell them and the herbs are wilted. Break the eggs on top of the herbs, grate some Parmesan on top, and put a lid on the pan. Cook over a low heat until the whites are set. Alternatively, run the eggs under the broiler briefly to cook the eggs and melt the cheese.

Dishes from Our Granola Heritage

BACK-TO-THE-LANDERS flocked to Maine in the seventies and built their own houses, dug gardens, and many promoted whole grain, vegetarian fare. Nowadays lots of these folks are eating meat and keeping their gray hair fairly short, but vegetarian fare has gone mainstream, and lots of restaurants have vegetarian options on the menu. We owe artisanal breads, most of our goat cheese, and storefront coops to our ageing granolas' influence. Here is a batch of granola-style recipes starting with — granola!

Handel Whole Wheat Bread

Maine is so blessed with artisanal bread bakers that fewer of us are making our own whole-wheat bread these days. Still, Lucy Johnston, who works in Greenville, wrote "I would like to find a really good recipe for home-baked whole grain bread."

This recipe came from the Handels, an elderly couple I knew about thirty-five years ago in Rhode Island. I wrote their bread recipe into the "Notes" section of my copy of the *Tassajara Bread Book*, which you had to own to be a certified back-to-the-lander and which itself is a great source of bread recipes. The Handels had gone back to the land before some of us had been born, using the anthroposophist principles of Rudolf Steiner to raise gorgeous vegetables. Mrs. Handel always made their bread.

- 2 CUPS HOT WATER
- 2 CUPS HOT MILK
- 6 TABLESPOONS VEGETABLE OIL
- 6 TABLESPOONS HONEY OR MOLASSES
- 3 TEASPOONS SALT
- 3 TABLESPOONS DRY YEAST (3 PACKETS)
- 9 CUPS WHOLE-WHEAT FLOUR (OR 6 CUPS WHOLE-WHEAT
  PLUS 3 CUPS OF RYE OR OATS)

Put the water, milk, oil, honey, or molasses, salt, and yeast into a large bread bowl. Beat for 5 minutes while adding 5 cups of the flour. Beat until the dough is very sticky. Add more flour, very nearly the full 9 cups until it is stiff enough to knead. Knead dough in the bowl for a while, then turn it out on a very lightly floured board, oiling your hands to knead until the dough is elastic enough that when you poke it, it springs back. Allow to rise in an oiled bowl for about 2 hours in a warm place.

Punch it down, turn it out, and divide into thirds. Re-knead and shape into 3 loaves, which you put into greased bread pans. Preheat the oven to 375 degrees. Let rise for about 1 hour, or until it begins to rise slightly over the height of the sides of the pan. Bake for 15 minutes, then reduce the oven to 350 degrees and continue baking for 40 minutes or less. It will be done when you hear a hollow sound when you tap it and it slips from the pan.

{ MAKES 3 LOAVES }

{ ADVICE }

Whole-wheat bread is a bit tricky because the whole grain rapidly absorbs moisture, yielding a dry texture. That's why you need to handle the dough with as little extra flour as possible. One way would be to use your electric mixer with a dough hook on it. Another way, instead of flouring your hands to keep the dough from sticking to you, is to oil your hands before kneading, and re-oil lightly as it begins to stick so much that it is hard to knead.

Red Zinger and White Grape Juice

{ SERVES 6 }

A charming visit to Bayside to spend the day with old friends in the Witherill and Gates families reminded me how good it is to have something cold to drink that's reasonably wholesome, sometimes fizzy, and not loaded with high-fructose corn syrup.

My friend Beth Gates Code made a terrific refreshing and light Red Zinger tea drink sweetened with white grape juice. It held up well to ice, and its bright red color appealed to me a lot and it went well with white wicker porch furniture on a hot day, as welcome as the breeze we had off the water.

6 TO 8 BAGS OF RED ZINGER (OR OTHER ROBUST HERB TEA)

6 CUPS BOILING WATER

⅓ CUP THAWED WHITE GRAPE JUICE CONCENTRATE

Brew the tea and allow to cool. Add the concentrate, sample, and adjust to taste. Serve on ice. Refrigerate or refreeze the rest of the concentrate for the next batch.

Homemade Granola

{ MAKES 1 QUART }

As far as both price and wholesomeness are concerned, homemade granola is a great alternative to packaged cereal. When I read the ingredient list on the average box of flakes, puffs, or crunches, and calculate the number of servings per box, I wonder why anyone would want to buy it. You can, of course, buy ready-made granola at health food stores and specialty markets, but some of them are pretty lush and costly, too.

Measure the ingredients the first time you make this, but observe how the mixture looks. The next time don't bother measuring. Just toss together the oats and nuts and experiment with the sweetening until you find a proportion and mixture that you and your family enjoy.

3 CUPS ROLLED OATS

½ CUP WHEAT GERM AND, OPTIONALLY, GROUND FLAX SEEDS

1 ½ CUPS OF A MIX YOUR CHOICE OF NUTS, SUNFLOWER OR PUMPKIN

    SEEDS, SESAME SEEDS, FLAKED COCONUT

⅓ CUP SWEETENING LIKE MAPLE SYRUP, HONEY, OR BROWN SUGAR

    MIXED WITH A LITTLE WATER

¼ CUP VEGETABLE OIL

OPTIONAL DRIED FRUITS LIKE RAISINS, CRANBERRIES, BANANA

    CHIPS, APPLES, MANGO, PINEAPPLE

Preheat the oven to 300 degrees. Toss the oats, wheat germ, nuts, and seeds mixture together in a 9-by-13 roasting or baking pan. Heat the sweetening and oil in a small pan and add just a little water and dribble it over the dry ingredients, tossing to distribute the wet mixture until there are no obviously damp clumps. Bake for 20 minutes, stir it, then bake for another 20 minutes. Repeat until the granola is golden brown, about 1¼ hours or so. Let it cool in the pan, then add dried fruits if desired. Store in a container with a tight-fitting lid.

Whole-Wheat Potato Dinner Rolls

{ MAKES 3 DOZEN ROLLS }

I find bread pretty darn forgiving and flexible. It is possible, you know, to make bread using only flour, water, salt, and yeast. No sugar, no butter, no milk, no eggs. You can experiment with most bread recipes at a fairly low risk of failure.

It seems to me that the main trick is to add flour gradually and knead the dough well between additions and then to stop adding flour when the bread is smooth and elastic. Someone once told me that the dough should feel as smooth as a baby's bottom, and I always look for the dough springing back when I poke it. If your finger hole just sits there and you don't see much movement, then it hasn't had enough flour and/or hasn't been kneaded enough.

2 RUSSET POTATOES

2 ENVELOPES DRY YEAST

1 STICK PLUS **3** TABLESPOONS BUTTER, SOFTENED

½ CUP SUGAR

2 EGGS, BEATEN

3 TEASPOONS SALT

1 CUP MILK WARMED TO BODY TEMPERATURE

5 CUPS FLOUR

2 CUPS WHOLE-WHEAT FLOUR

Peel, boil, and mash the potatoes, reserving the liquid. Cool ½ cup of the reserved potato liquid until warm, add the yeast to it, and stir to dissolve. Let stand. Meanwhile, in a large bowl, cream together the butter and sugar, then add 1 cup of the mashed potato, eggs, and salt. Beat well. Add the milk and the potato/yeast mixture to it. In a separate bowl, blend together the white and whole-wheat flours.

Mix 4½ cups of flour into the potato/yeast mixture, beat well, and then add the rest of the flour, ½ cup at a time, switching from using a spoon to using your hands as soon as sticky dough forms. Knead the dough in the bowl for about 3 minutes, then cover with a damp cloth, and set to rise in a warm place until it doubles in volume, about 1 hour. Punch it down and knead again until the dough springs back when you poke it.

To make cloverleaf rolls, grease 3 muffin tins and pinch off pieces of dough and roll into balls, about 1 inch to 1½ inches in diameter. Put 3 balls in each muffin tin cup and let rise until doubled, about 1 hour.

Preheat the oven to 400 degrees and bake the rolls until golden, about 20 to 25 minutes. If you want brown and serve rolls later, take them out after 10 minutes, cool them, and put them in the freezer. To use them, preheat the oven to 400 degrees, put the rolls on a baking sheet, and reheat them for 5 to 10 minutes or until they are golden brown.

{ADVICE}

Judy Hakola, in Orono, wrote, saying, "I have come across a number of good yeast bread recipes in my cooking magazines lately, most of which are for use in bread machines. I don't have a bread machine, nor do I want one. I prefer kneading dough on my Finnish mother-in-law's homemade breadboard, which I brought from Montana after her death in 1969. Do you have or know of any guidelines for converting bread machine recipes to "regular" old-fashioned versions?" Barbara Stephens, in Holden, recommended *Whole Grain Breads by Machine or by Hand* by Beatrice Ojakangas. "It includes two hundred recipes all in one book and saves having to cut recipes from magazines and storing them somehow," Barbara said.

Wheat Berry Salad

One of the things Carol Pierson, of Islesboro, likes about this chewy and flavorful recipe is that since it keeps well and needs to be chilled for a while anyway, she can double it and make it ahead if company is coming. It would be fine for lunches or a side for dinner. It would be good for a picnic. Plus it is so doggone wholesome, I recently experimented with whole grains of rye, which I grew myself, to make this recipe, and it worked just as well.

There is a fair amount of chopping and fussing going on here, but you can do that while the wheat berries are cooking. Carol prefers smoked Gouda cheese over plain, and uses a lot of the green part of the scallions. Dried cranberries are wonderful, but if you are fresh out, use raisins.

{ SERVES 4 }

{ ADVICE }

Even though Maine granolas have been cooking with wheat berries for decades, they still require a bit of scouting to find in stores. In large grocery stores you want to look in the natural foods section for the words "whole-grain wheat." In various cooperative stores or natural food stores you might be able to buy them as a bulk item.

1 CUP UNCOOKED WHEAT BERRIES

½ CUP MINCED SHALLOTS (2 TO 3 LARGE ONES)

¼ CUP CRANBERRY OR ORANGE JUICE

3 TABLESPOONS VINEGAR, FLAVORED IF YOU HAVE IT

1 TABLESPOON BALSAMIC VINEGAR (OPTIONAL)

2 TABLESPOONS VEGETABLE OIL

2 TEASPOONS DIJON-STYLE MUSTARD

½ TEASPOON SALT

½ CUP COARSELY CHOPPED DRIED CRANBERRIES

½ CUP OR 2 OUNCES DICED GOUDA CHEESE

4 TO 5 SCALLIONS, SLICED

⅓ CUP TOASTED SLIVERED ALMONDS

¼ CUP DRIED CURRANTS

¼ TEASPOON PEPPER

Combine 3 cups of water and the wheat berries in a heavy saucepan and bring to a boil, reduce the heat, cover, and simmer until the water is absorbed and the berries are tender. While they are cooking, whisk together in a large bowl the shallots, juice, vinegars, oil, mustard, and salt. Let stand. As soon as the wheat berries are done, rinse them in cold water and add them to the bowl, then add in all the rest of the ingredients, toss together, cover, and let stand 4 hours or even overnight.

Barley Pilaf

This recipe sneaks another sort of whole grain into our diet besides oatmeal and brown rice. I found it in an old James Beard cookbook that someone gave me, lo, forty years ago when I started living on my own. The cover and title page are long gone, and half the index has fallen off. I still can locate the barley recipe, though.

You can jazz it up, of course. It calls for onion, and there are always mushrooms, celery, and parsley. It is brainlessly simple to make, and I extended the method to wheat berries, grains of whole wheat. At times I use some of each.

It comes out pretty beige, so consider serving it with something green on it, like snipped chives or parsley or scallions. Toasted almonds or some toasted seeds, like sunflower or pumpkin seeds, are a nice touch.

2 TO 4 TABLESPOONS BUTTER AND/OR OLIVE OIL

1 LARGE ONION, CHOPPED

1 CUP PEARL BARLEY

2 CUPS CHICKEN OR BEEF BROTH, OR WATER

SALT AND PEPPER, TO TASTE

Preheat the oven to 350 degrees. Melt the butter in a heavy pan and a sauté the onion in it until the onion is soft. Add the barley and brown it a little, then put the barley into a buttered baking dish and add 1 cup of the broth and the salt and pepper. Bake for about 25 minutes, and when the liquid has been absorbed, add the second cup of broth or water. Bake for another 20 minutes or until that liquid is absorbed, too. Garnish to taste.

Caper Sauce

This is fast food. Fifteen minutes if all you do is serve it on pasta.
Salad on the side and you are good to go. Jennifer Whyte, one of my
neighbors, who gave me this recipe, uses this sauce on all kinds of
things: chicken, fish, or plain pasta. It would be tasty on pork chops or
slices of pork tenderloin, turkey breast, cauliflower, tofu, almost anything
that can stand a little zing.

Anchovies are a little controversial, but anyone in Maine who likes
smelts ought not to have a problem with anchovies. In this recipe, the
anchovy is all mashed up. If you really dislike the texture of anchovies,
use a squirt of anchovy paste, but don't leave it out.

{ MAKES 1 CUP }

2 TABLESPOONS OLIVE OIL

½ STICK BUTTER

½ SMALL ONION, FINELY CHOPPED

1 ANCHOVY FILET, MASHED

1 TABLESPOON FLOUR

2 TABLESPOONS RINSED CAPERS

1 TABLESPOON FINELY CHOPPED PARSLEY

4 TABLESPOONS WHITE WINE VINEGAR

4 TABLESPOONS BALSAMIC VINEGAR

Heat the olive oil and half the butter in a small, heavy saucepan, and
slowly cook the onion in it. When it is soft, add the anchovy, mashing it
into the onion. Then sprinkle the flour in and stir to mix it well. Add the
capers and parsley. Stir in the wine vinegar and 4 tablespoons of water
and cook over a low heat to thicken the sauce. Just before serving, add
the rest of the butter and the balsamic vinegar.

Desserts of Maine

DESSERTS OF MAINE

Mainers have as many sweet teeth as anyone else, and the state is full of home cooks who make and bake from scratch. Traditional desserts from the 1800s made with blueberries, rhubarb, apples, and pumpkins were joined by chocolate and exotic fruits in the 1900s.

I fashion desserts around seasonal fruits, and hankerings for chocolate or ginger and spice. Lots of times when asked for a particular kind of cake or pie recipe, readers sent along widely varying recipes for it, as you will see with the spice cake and blueberry pie recipes below. I learned a lot from them about variations on a theme. And even though I always thought baking required more precision with measurement and care with proportions and procedures, I learned that many recipes were very flexible, indeed. Be sure to read about my Peach Kuchen near-debacle, and you will see what I mean.

Seasonal Fruits

FIRST UP IN THE SPRING comes rhubarb. I greet those tightly curled, dark green knobs that unfold on long red stalks with joy. Then we have strawberries, and soon blueberries, each marked by festivals. Peaches ripen on my yard in August, and by September there is a glorious plenty of apples enough for a winter supply. Pumpkins keep into winter, too, and lend themselves to sweet dishes.

Rhubarb Crisp

Over the years I have taken to baking this crisp in a 9-by-13 Pyrex baking dish, doubling the amount of rhubarb and making one and a half times the topping. You can do whatever you please about that. If you like a deep, juicy filling, then you will prefer a deeper baking dish. My island friend Anne was telling me that she uses cardamom as one of the spices. The recipe calls for cinnamon, but she always adds an equal amount of ground cardamom. That turns out to be a great idea if you like that spice as much as I do.

In May 1988, when I moved to Islesboro, the radio station WERU had just come on the air. The early morning hours featured a program co-hosted by Karen Frangoulis and Jim Campbell. One morning Karen offered this crisp recipe, and since rhubarb was the only domesticated edible growing on the property that May, I wrote the recipe down and made a panful as soon as my rhubarb plant was ripe and ready to pick. It has become a favorite. In fact, I found this topping is perfectly suited to blueberry and apple crisps as well, each in their own season.

For the filling:

4 CUPS CHOPPED RHUBARB, ABOUT 5 OR 6 STALKS

¾ CUP SUGAR

¼ CUP FLOUR

½ TEASPOON CINNAMON, OR MORE TO TASTE

½ TEASPOON CARDAMOM (OPTIONAL)

½ CUP WATER

For the topping:

1 CUP FLOUR

1 CUP ROLLED OATS

⅔ CUP BROWN SUGAR

½ CUP BUTTER, MELTED

Preheat the oven to 375 degrees. To make the filling, mix everything together and put into a greased baking dish. To make the topping, mix together the flour, oats, sugar, and butter until you have a lumpy looking topping. Distribute evenly over the filling. Bake for 30 minutes until the top is golden and you see bubbling on the bottom.

Rhubarb Custard Pie

Rhubarb custard pies! Yum. Sometimes it is called rhubarb crème pie, and unlike the Beebopareebop Rhubarb pies that Garrison Keillor of *A Prairie Home Companion* says will take the taste of shame and humiliation out of your mouth, this style of rhubarb pie is very smooth and sweet. I've tasted this kind of rhubarb pie, liked it very much, but never really caught onto how it was made. Fortunately, Lois Farr, up in Dover-Foxcroft, and Blanche Davis, on Deer Isle, sent along recipes that revealed all.

Blanche doesn't remember where she found her recipe, but surmised that she got it from "some of the girls where I worked," a great place to get recipes (and ideas for what to make for dinner, too).

PIE DOUGH FOR 2 CRUSTS

2 TO 3 EGGS

1¼ TO 2 CUPS SUGAR

2 TO 4 TABLESPOONS FLOUR

½ TEASPOON NUTMEG, OR MORE TO TASTE

A COUPLE TABLESPOONS MILK

3 TO 4 CUPS CHOPPED RHUBARB

2 TO 3 TABLESPOONS BUTTER

Preheat the oven to 400 degrees, and line a pie plate with dough. Beat the eggs slightly, and add the sugar, flour, nutmeg, and milk, if needed. Add the rhubarb and toss until the rhubarb is lightly coated in the egg mixture. Turn into the pie plate and dot with bits of butter. Top with a lattice crust or a solid one with vents cut into it. Bake at 400 degrees for 10 minutes and then reduce the oven temperature to 350 degrees and bake an additional 45 to 50 minutes.

{ MAKES A 9 TO 10-INCH PIE }

{ ADVICE }

Both Blanche and Lois recommended a 10-inch pan for this one, and one said a lattice crust. I don't have a 10-inch pie pan and crammed my recipe into a 9-incher, and it was fine. I did use a lattice top, which I often use for pies that I think will get runny.

Strawberries, Sour Cream, and Brown Sugar

The easiest strawberry dessert on the planet is this one that I learned from my friend Pam Gordinier, who lives in Stonington, Connecticut. It is best if you make bowls of sour cream and brown sugar available within arm's reach of each person fortunate enough to eat some.

If, like so many of us, you are watching your fat intake, you can use fat-free sour cream or extra-thick yogurt.

LARGE STRAWBERRIES, PREFERABLY WITH STEM STILL ON

A DISH OF SOUR CREAM OR VERY THICK YOGURT

A BOWL OF LIGHT BROWN SUGAR

Pick up a strawberry, dip it into the sour cream, then into the light brown sugar. Eat it. (Is that all? Yes!)

Peach Kuchen and the Comedy of Errors

{ SERVES 4 TO 6 }

I didn't think it had a chance, but the kuchen came out all right anyway.

My friend Kristina King, of Rockland, and I were making supper together, visiting in my Islesboro kitchen. I really wanted to do something with some of my own canned peaches, and I remembered a kuchen recipe a friend gave me a long time ago, but I couldn't find it anywhere. I looked up kuchen in the *Tassajara Cookbook* (not many under forty-five years old will remember that one), and found a recipe, but that wasn't quite as I remembered it, either. So I decided to wing it.

The first wrinkle was that Kristina has to be careful about wheat, but I wasn't worried, because I have spelt flour. The second wrinkle was that I thought I remembered using yogurt for the custard, but the *Tassajara* recipe didn't call for that.

I thought, oh, what the heck, and I went ahead with the *Tassajara* crust recipe using spelt flour (but you can use whole-wheat or all-purpose or a combination). When you use spelt, you have to pack it tightly into the measuring cup, which I did after Kristina reminded me.

Then instead of using a cup of sour or heavy cream, I substituted low-fat yogurt, though I bet you could use just about any yogurt. Vanilla would work. The recipe calls for two eggs, though I got lucky since one egg was a double yolker.

The instructions (which I know you are supposed to read through carefully before you begin to assemble the ingredients, but I don't always remember to do) said to press the crust firmly into a baking pan and bake it for 25 minutes at 400 degrees. But guess who forgot that step? So I decided to bake the whole thing for 10 minutes at 400 degrees, then dropped the temperature to 350 degrees. After consulting with Kristina who said, "I bet it will bake in 30 minutes," instead of the 40 specified, I set the timer for 30 minutes. You know, it was fine, and we really enjoyed it.

So here is my so-called recipe for kuchen. Clearly it takes a lot of abuse. No peaches? Try blueberries or apples sliced thinly.

2 CUPS FLOUR

¼ TEASPOON BAKING POWDER

½ CUP (1 STICK) BUTTER

1 MEDIUM CAN SLICED PEACHES (I USED A PINT OF HOME-CANNED)
   OR 2 CUPS SLICED FRESH PEACHES

1 CUP YOGURT

2 EGGS, BEATEN

1 CUP LIGHT BROWN SUGAR

1 TEASPOON CINNAMON

Preheat the oven to 400 degrees. Mix the flour and baking powder together and cut the butter into it (I use a food processor). Press into a 10-inch pie plate or a 10-inch square baking pan, making sure to bring the edge up an inch or so. Distribute the peaches over the crust. Beat together the yogurt, eggs, sugar, and cinnamon, and pour it over the peaches. Bake the kuchen for 10 minutes at 400 degrees, then reduce the temperature to 350 degrees and bake an additional 30 minutes. It is done when the custard has set.

Blueberry Pie

For this pie, I took a few ideas from the *Joy of Cooking* and my favorite blueberry crisp recipe. For a variation of your own, you could put a crisp topping on it instead of a pastry crust.

Obviously, the pie is best made with fresh blueberries and the recipe is meant for the little wild ones. When I use frozen berries or have larger domestic ones, then I think a little more thickening is in order, and my favorite is a tablespoon or two-size sprinkle of instant tapioca. If you lack tapioca, you can use more flour, but I think the tapioca gives the pie a better texture overall. I personally don't like the glueyness of cornstarch, though it might not bother you.

The lemon juice and nutmeg are must-haves. If you like your lemon a bit more noticeable, you can grate in a little lemon rind. Also, I prefer a lattice-top crust for blueberry (and other berry) pies.

PASTRY SUFFICIENT FOR TWO CRUSTS

1 QUART BLUEBERRIES

1½ TABLESPOONS LEMON JUICE (HALF A LEMON)

FRESHLY GRATED NUTMEG

¼ CUP LIGHT BROWN SUGAR

¼ CUP WHITE SUGAR

¼ CUP FLOUR

2 TABLESPOONS TAPIOCA, IF BERRIES ARE JUICY

Preheat the oven to 425 degrees. Put the berries into a large bowl with the lemon juice and toss. Add the other ingredients and toss until the berries are well coated with the flour and sugar mixture. Line the pie plate with the dough for the bottom crust. Put the berries into the pie plate and top with a solid or lattice-top crust. Bake for 35 to 45 minutes until it is bubbly and the crust is golden.

1

Combine the
berries, lemon
juice, flour, and
other ingredients
in a large bowl.

»

2

Roll out one chilled
disc of dough, line
the pan, put in
the berry filling.

⌄

How to make
Blueberry Pie

⌃

4

Brush on egg
glaze and put
into a 425
degree oven.

«

3

Roll out the
remaining dough,
and cut long
ribbons, assemble
the lattice crust
and crimp edges.

Open-Faced Blueberry Pie

{ MAKES A 9-INCH PIE }

As an alternative to the traditional two-crust baked blueberry pie before, here is an open-faced, fresh blueberry pie. You will need a pre-baked pie shell, and you will spend a little time at the stove preparing part of 2 quarts of blueberries that you will use. You will cook part of the berries with a thickener, sweeten and season them, mix in fresh berries, and then chill it. The uncooked berries pop in your mouth when you eat them, and you get a burst of fresh blueberry flavor.

Recipes varied so much that it seems to me you can use anywhere from one to two cups of berries cooked and the rest raw; you can make them as sweet as you like, use cinnamon or lemon zest, and add butter or not. Just make sure to cook the cornstarch and berries until the mixture is glossy and shows no cloudiness. Otherwise, feel free to fiddle and come up with what your family likes best.

1 PRE-BAKED 9-INCH PIE SHELL

4 CUPS BLUEBERRIES, DIVIDED INTO 1 CUP AND 3 CUPS

¼ TO 1 CUP SUGAR

2½ TO 3 TABLESPOONS CORNSTARCH

1 TABLESPOON BUTTER

½ TEASPOON CINNAMON OR MORE, TO TASTE

LEMON ZEST (OPTIONAL)

In a heavy saucepan, cook 1 or more cups of blueberries with the sugar, cornstarch, and up to 1 cup of water until the mixture is thickened and glossy, about 10 minutes. Stir in butter, cinnamon, and lemon zest. Put the rest of the berries in the pie shell and pour the cooked mixture over the top carefully enough to keep the raw berries evenly distributed. Chill and serve topped with whipped cream.

A NEW WRINKLE IN BLUEBERRY PIE MAKING

Fresh, unbaked blueberry pie has not been around that long. JoDelle Rolerson, of Belfast, got her recipe from her great-aunt Lytle Wood, who headed the Waldo County Extension program that published this recipe in 1974. She uses a tablespoon of tapioca as well as cornstarch and says the recipe never fails. Judy Herrick, in Sedgewick, said, "This pie was my late husband's favorite — he was a blueberry grower but didn't like the traditional one." Dorothy Simmons suggested that instead of water, you use blueberry juice if you have some. Sherry Ryan, of Bancroft, whirls one cup of berries with water in a blender and then cooks it with the sugar and cornstarch. Gene Stinson, of Lincolnville, uses two cups of blueberries in the cooked mixture and two cups of raw in the shell. In Machias, Ruth Thurston's favorite calls for six cups, two cooked and four raw, and nutmeg for spice.

Corinne Ness, in West Levant, said her recipe was one her mother found in *Good Housekeeping* magazine in the 1980s. This recipe was different from the others in that it called for only one-quarter cup of sugar and her procedure was to mash one cup of berries in a saucepan with the cornstarch and sugar with no added water and to cook it until it was thick.

Then there are the ones with cream cheese or sour cream mixtures added. Sharon Goguen, of Belfast, sweetens cream cheese with powdered sugar, then adds a touch of lemon juice and spreads it over the bottom of the crust, then tops it with the raw and cooked blueberries. Sherry Ryan's recipe calls for an egg, sour cream, and sugar custard poured over two cups of blueberries in a graham cracker crust. Yum.

Anne Black, in Harborside, Jean Anderson, of Islesboro, Rena Day, on Deer Isle, and Iris Brown, all shared variations on this recipe.

Apples

FEW DESSERTS ARE BETTER than a simple baked apple, especially if you are in a hurry, because all you have to do is core them, put a few raisins in the hole with a bit of brown sugar, a sprinkle of cinnamon, and a tiny dot of butter. Bake them at 350 degrees for 30 to 45 minutes or more until they split and foam a bit. Served hot with some cream or ice cream — they are suitable even for company.

If you bake a few more than you absolutely need for dinner, they make a terrific breakfast.

Chunky Applesauce

{ SERVES 2 TO 4 }

When Katelyn Keresey, of Alton, an Old Town Leonard Middle School student, was twelve years old, she won the 2007 University of Maine's Page Farm and Home Museum's Apple Fest apple recipe contest with a chunky applesauce made from apples she picked in her yard the same day she entered the still warm sauce in the contest.

Katelyn, a twenty-first-century child, took a more scientific approach to her applesauce than most of us oldsters usually do, having learned about the chemistry of sugar in her home economics class. Katelyn explained, "Sugar helps the apples hold together better." She added sugar to the sauce, she said, at the point when softening apples reached the "desired chunkyness." Here is her recipe.

5 MEDIUM APPLES, PEELED AND CORED

1 TABLESPOON SUGAR

1 TEASPOON CINNAMON

⅓ CUP BOILING WATER

Cut the apples up and put the pieces into the boiling water. When they have cooked into the desired "chunkyness," add the sugar and cinnamon. If you wish a smoother applesauce, mash them up completely, then add the sugar and cinnamon.

Apple Crisp

When Cathy Bean, of Searsmont, asked for a recipe for an "old-fashioned cafeteria apple crisp" she remembered from grade school, she was recalling the flour, sugar, and butter topping that bakes up all crisp and golden. Her recollection was it didn't seem to have so much brown sugar in it and that it tasted like "heaven." My mom used to make her crisp like that, with streusel topping, fifty years ago. One early name for apple crisp was apple paradise, so Cathy's memory of "heaven" is right on.

When I make apple crisp, really the only recipe I need is for the topping. I figure on one cored and sliced apple per person and one tablespoon of flour and one of sugar for each apple. I sprinkle cinnamon sparingly over the apples, about half a teaspoon for four apples. Whether you peel the apples or not is a matter of personal taste. I don't do a lick more of work than is absolutely necessary, and apple peeling doesn't qualify as necessary around my house. Serve warm with ice cream.

For the filling:

4 APPLES, CORED AND SLICED

4 TABLESPOONS FLOUR

4 TABLESPOONS SUGAR

½ TEASPOON CINNAMON

For the topping:

1 CUP FLOUR

⅓ CUP LIGHT BROWN SUGAR

⅔ CUP OF WHITE SUGAR

½ CUP (1 STICK) BUTTER

Preheat the oven to 350 degrees. Toss together the apples, flour, sugar, and cinnamon. Grease a 9-by-13-inch baking pan, spread the apples in it, and add ½ cup water. Blend together topping ingredients using a pastry cutter, two knives, food processor, or your fingertips, until it appears crumbly. Spread the streusel topping over the apples. Bake 45 to 50 minutes until the topping is golden and the apples are tender.

Sweet Apple Dumplings

Baked apple dumplings are literally as easy as pie and one step shorter. Start with the same cooking apples you like for pie: Cortlands, Baldwins, Granny Smiths, Empires, and Honeycrisps work well. Maybe you are lucky and have an old apple tree in your yard that you can harvest from. Otherwise, visit a local orchard and see what they recommend. Maine still has small orchards growing traditional apple varieties, and you'll enjoy the break from the old Delicious and McIntosh scene with an apple like a Wealthy or Wolf River.

> PASTRY ENOUGH FOR TWO 9-INCH PIE CRUSTS
>
> 6 TO 8 BAKING APPLES
>
> RAISINS
>
> 2 TEASPOONS LIGHT BROWN SUGAR PER APPLE, MORE OR
>   LESS TO TASTE
>
> A SHAKE OF CINNAMON PER APPLE
>
> DOT OF BUTTER PER APPLE (OPTIONAL)

Preheat the oven to 375 degrees. Divide the pie crust loosely into 6 to 8, 2-inch balls of pastry and chill it. Prepare the apples by coring them (I use a melon baller for coring) without breaking through the blossom end. Fill the core with raisins, brown sugar, cinnamon, and butter. Roll each ball of pastry into a 6- to 8-inch round and put the apple into the center. Draw the pastry up around the apple, pressing it gently together over the top. If you feel festive, decorate the top with a leaf shape cut from pastry and glaze with an egg-white wash. Set each into a baking pan, separated. Bake for 50 to 60 minutes or until the crust is golden — and a tester inserted on the apple's side shows the apple is tender. The baking time will vary depending on the apples you choose.

Savory Apple Dumplings

Inspired by the old saying, "Apple pie without the cheese is like a hug without the squeeze," I thought why not put cheese in the core hole of an apple for baking or a dumpling? Or a bit of crumbled bacon, or sausage or ham, even a bit of onion? That makes them more a savory than sweet dish, perfect for breakfast or brunch. In any case, you need a recipe less than a set of guidelines, which follow.

{ SERVES 6 TO 8 }

PASTRY ENOUGH FOR TWO 9-INCH PIE CRUSTS

6 TO 8 BAKING APPLES

1 TABLESPOON CRUMBLED COOKED BACON, SAUSAGE, OR
   SLIVERS OF HAM

SLIVERS OF CHEDDAR CHEESE

Follow the directions above for assembling and baking the apple dumplings.

Apple Pie

Gayle Crowley, of Bangor, won the University of Maine's Page Farm and Home Museum's 2008 Apple Fest's apple recipe contest in Orono. The combination of a bit of cream in the filling, sweetening it with both white and brown sugar, and baking it in an oil crust, made for an unbeatable combination. Gayle adapted her crust from Katherine Musgrave's recipe. You can use the oil crust recipe provided below or, if you prefer, use your own standard pastry. I chill oil by putting it into the freezer until it thickens up.

For the crust:

2/3 CUP VERY COLD CANOLA OIL

1/4 CUP VERY COLD WATER

2 CUPS FLOUR

For the filling:

APPLES ENOUGH TO FILL AN 8-INCH PIE PLATE, PEELED, CORED,
  AND SLICED

1/2 CUP SUGAR

1/4 CUP BROWN SUGAR

1/2 TEASPOON CINNAMON

1/4 TEASPOON FRESHLY GROUND NUTMEG

2 HEAPING TABLESPOONS FLOUR

1 TABLESPOON BUTTER, CUT INTO BITS

2 TO 3 TABLESPOONS CREAM

SUGAR FOR SPRINKLING ON TOP

Preheat oven to 400 degrees. Make the crust by whisking the oil and water together in a bowl until it is white and thick. Add to flour and mix with a fork. Divide in two pieces and roll out bottom and top crusts to fit an 8-inch pie plate.

To assemble the pie, toss the apple slices with the sugars, spices, and flour, and place in pie shell. Dot with bits of butter. Pour 2 to 3 tablespoons of cream into center. Add the top crust and sprinkle with sugar. Bake 40 to 60 minutes until lightly golden and you can observe the filling bubbling.

Apple Galette

The pastry for this rustic little apple dish is so delicious that it is worth every bit of from-scratch trouble you will go to. Carla Parsons, in Harrington, gave me the recipe. She and her mom, my neighbor Diane Ferris, used to run a bakery in the Finger Lakes region of New York State, so where pastry making slows me right down, Carla and Diane whip it right out. Assembling the galette once the pastry is chilled is easy. You can gild the lily by brushing the top of the pastry with cream or milk or beaten egg and adding a sprinkle of sugar.

{ SERVES 8 }

For the crust:

2 CUPS FLOUR

½ TEASPOON SALT

1 TEASPOON SUGAR

2 STICKS OF COLD BUTTER, MINUS ONE TABLESPOON

⅔ CUP ICE WATER

For the filling:

5 TO 6 APPLES, SLICED

¼ TO ⅓ CUP LIGHT BROWN SUGAR, ACCORDING TO THE
   APPLES' SWEETNESS

2 TABLESPOONS INSTANT TAPIOCA OR FLOUR

1 TEASPOON CINNAMON

GRATING OF NUTMEG (OPTIONAL)

To make the crust, whisk together the flour, salt, and sugar and cut in the butter until it is in small pieces. Toss the flour and butter mixture, with the cold water added gradually, until a dough forms, and then stop adding water, even if you have not used the full ⅔ of a cup. Pat it into a disc and chill it at least 1 hour.

Toss the apples, brown sugar, tapioca, cinnamon, and nutmeg together in a bowl.

To assemble the tart, preheat the oven to 400 degrees. Roll the dough out into a circle or oval until it is ⅜ of an inch thick. Place on a baking sheet. Pile the apples in the center and draw up the edges of the crust to hold the apples in place, but do not cover them entirely. If you wish, brush a beaten egg glaze on the pastry and sprinkle with sugar. Bake for 1 hour.

Pumpkin

PUMPKINS ARE AN ODD FRUIT. Like sweet potatoes, carrots, and some winter squashes, they can qualify as vegetables and as an ingredient for dessert as these recipes show.

Pumpkin Butterscotch Cookies

Whatever else can we do with cooked pumpkin? Nancy-Linn Ellis, from Stockton Springs, proprietor of Maine Temptations, sent along this recipe that she learned from a Pennsylvania friend. The texture — softly chewy with the contrasting sweet nuggets of the chips — is really appealing. To my horror, I personally ate four in a row.

{ MAKES 60 COOKIES }

{ ADVICE }

These cookies do not spread very much on the pan, so place them fairly close together.

2 CUPS FLOUR

1 TEASPOON CINNAMON

1 TEASPOON BAKING POWDER

1 TEASPOON BAKING SODA

¼ TEASPOON SALT

½ CUP BUTTER

1 CUP SUGAR

1½ CUPS COOKED PUMPKIN (APPROXIMATELY 1 CAN)

1 TEASPOON VANILLA

1 BAG BUTTERSCOTCH BITS (APPROXIMATELY 11 OUNCES)

½ CUP CHOPPED WALNUTS

Preheat the oven to 375 degrees. Grease baking sheets. Sift together the flour, cinnamon, baking powder, baking soda, and salt. Cream the butter and sugar together, beat in the pumpkin and vanilla. Add the dry ingredients. Mix well then fold in the butterscotch bits and the walnuts. The dough will be fairly stiff. Drop by teaspoonful onto cookie sheet. Bake approximately 15 minutes until they have risen and browned slightly.

Maple Pecan Pumpkin Pie

{ MAKES A
9 TO 10-INCH PIE }

I grow pumpkins and store them from October harvest time into the winter months. In February I watch them very closely for signs of little black spots, because, since they are living plants, I know that inside the pumpkins there are seeds seriously thinking about how to sprout and are hoping the orange flesh around them will rot away to let them out. My job is to make sure I cook it first.

This recipe from Alice Elliott, of Richmond, blends a Yankee dish — pumpkin pie — with a southern one — pecan pie. If you really like a pumpkiny mouthful, this pie won't do it, but, as Alice wrote, she likes this recipe because she thinks "pecan pie is too sweet and corn syrupy." Maple syrup takes corn syrup's place in the pecan topping. For a holiday meal, this pie is a wonderful variation on the traditional Thanksgiving dessert. You might want to make this one and an old-fashioned pumpkin pie, too.

Yes, it calls for a lot of eggs, and it is rich, and that is why it is perfect for a holiday meal.

{ADVICE}

One surprise with this pie is the relatively low oven temperature and the relatively long time it takes to bake it. You will bake this pie for 1 and ¾ hours, so, unlike me, who dawdled around the day I first tried it and had to rush to assemble it, make sure you plan ahead to give yourself plenty of time. Assembly is very easy, and even though the list of ingredients looks long, it goes together very quickly. Alice reserves pecan halves to lay around the perimeter of the pie, which looks very dressy.

SUFFICIENT PASTRY FOR A 9 TO 10-INCH PIE PLATE

For the filling:

2 CUPS COOKED PUMPKIN PURÉE

¼ CUP FIRMLY PACKED LIGHT BROWN SUGAR

2 TABLESPOONS SUGAR

1 LARGE EGG, BEATEN WELL

1 TABLESPOON HEAVY CREAM

1 TABLESPOON BUTTER, MELTED

1 TABLESPOON VANILLA EXTRACT

¼ TEASPOON SALT

¼ TEASPOON CINNAMON

PINCH OF ALLSPICE

PINCH OF FRESHLY GRATED NUTMEG

For the syrup:

½ CUP SUGAR

¾ CUP MAPLE SYRUP (DARKER IS BETTER HERE)

2 LARGE EGGS

1 ½ TABLESPOONS BUTTER, MELTED

2 TEASPOONS VANILLA

PINCH SALT

PINCH CINNAMON

¾ CUP PECAN PIECES

Combine all the ingredients for the filling in a medium-size bowl and set aside. In a separate bowl, combine all the ingredients for the syrup and set aside.

Preheat the oven to 325 degrees. Line a 9 or 10-inch pie plate with the pastry. Spoon the pumpkin filling into the plate, spreading it evenly to distribute. Gently pour the pecan syrup on top. Bake until a knife inserted in the center comes out clean, about 1 hour and 45 minutes. Cool and serve.

AS AMERICAN AS PUMPKIN PIE

Pumpkin pie is actually more American than apple pie. Apple pie was English, and came to America along with colonists and their apple trees. Pumpkins, on the other hand, were New World plants and Native Americans introduced settlers to them. At first, English settler housewives cut and cooked pumpkins in the same way they used apples, making sauce. The idea for pie came from custard-pudding like recipes incorporating fruit or vegetables often baked in pie shells, introduced to colonial America from England, particularly the one made from sweet potatoes. Lacking sweet potatoes, New Englanders substituted the mushy orange stuff from pumpkins instead, and there you have it: pumpkin pie, a truly native, invented-in-America pie. Tell your friends.

Pumpkin Cheesecake Pie

{ MAKES A 9-INCH PIE }

{ ADVICE }

The recipe only needs a
½ cup of cooked pumpkin,
and so you will want to
have another pumpkin
project in mind when you
open the can or cut up a
whole one. You could also
use any orange winter
squash that you like —
butternut, butter cup,
kubocha — take
out what you need for
this recipe and serve
the rest as a side
vegetable at dinner.

Ruth Thurston, from Machias, also sent along this recipe from the handout she prepared when she gave a talk on pumpkins to her extension group. She assembled recipes from various cookbooks in her collection. Don't be afraid to fiddle with the seasonings and even the sugar. Since I use a sweet graham cracker crust, I reduce the sugar somewhat.

ONE 9-INCH PIE CRUST (PASTRY OR GRAHAM CRACKER)

TWO (8-OUNCE) PACKAGES CREAM CHEESE

⅓ TO ½ CUP SUGAR

1 TEASPOON VANILLA

2 EGGS

½ TO ¾ CUP COOKED PUMPKIN

1 TEASPOON CINNAMON

¼ TEASPOON FRESHLY GRATED NUTMEG

DASH OF CLOVES

Preheat the oven to 350 degrees. Beat together the cream cheese, sugar, and vanilla until very smooth, then beat in the eggs. Set aside 1 cup of that mixture and beat the pumpkin and spices into the remaining batter. Pour the plain batter into the prepared crust and spread the pumpkin batter over the top of it. Bake for 40 minutes. The top should be slightly puffed and the center mostly set. Let it cool completely and firm up before cutting it. Top it, if you wish, with whipped cream.

Chocolate

WHEN IT WAS MANUFACTURED in convenient squares and cocoa powder by the early 1900s, chocolate nudged aside the robust flavors of brown sugar and molasses. Mainers still love their molasses and added chocolate to their repertoire, too.

Superb Brownies

The easiest, most delicious brownies I've ever tasted come from a recipe given me by my friend Jane Keener, of Stonington, Connecticut, who said she always heard that it was Katharine Hepburn's recipe. Whether the lady with the great cheekbones ever made these or not is a good question.

The brownies come out fudgy and richly flavored and you mess up only a saucepan, spoon, and a baking pan. I am not fond of nuts in brownies, so don't use any, but, of course, you can fold in some at the end. Substitute raisins for nuts if there is a nut allergy in your family.

½ CUP (1 STICK) BUTTER

TWO (1-OUNCE) SQUARES UNSWEETENED CHOCOLATE

1 CUP SUGAR

2 EGGS

½ TEASPOON VANILLA

¼ CUP FLOUR

Preheat the oven to 325 degrees. Grease and flour an 8-by 8-inch pan. In a heavy saucepan, over a low heat, melt the butter and chocolate together. Take off the stove and beat in the sugar, eggs, and vanilla. Stir in the flour. Pour the batter into the baking pan. Bake for 40 minutes or until a tester comes out clean and the brownies pull away from the sides of the pan somewhat.

{ MAKES A DOZEN }

{ ADVICE }

Some people like to frost brownies and the easiest way to do that is to sprinkle the top of still-hot-from-the-oven brownies with finely chopped chocolate pieces or chocolate chips that you spread when they soften.

Deep Dark Chocolate Zucchini Cake

In summer, with gardens virtually squirting zucchini, a great virtue of this cake recipe is that it uses *three* cups of grated zukes. Ethel Pochocki, of Brooks, and Iris Brown, of Baileyville, both shared this recipe with me. Even when I am not exactly tired of eating zucchini, I'm willing to sacrifice a vegetable to dessert as long as I have a cake as good as this one to dump it into. I make this in a tube pan, but you can use layer pans, a 9 by 13, or even loaf pans. It doesn't need icing, but I sprinkle confectioners' sugar on it because it is prettier that way.

{ MAKES 1 CAKE }

FOUR (1-OUNCE) SQUARES UNSWEETENED BAKING CHOCOLATE

½ CUP VEGETABLE OIL

2 CUPS FLOUR

⅓ CUP UNSWEETENED COCOA POWDER

2 TEASPOONS BAKING POWDER

2 TEASPOONS BAKING SODA

1 TEASPOON SALT

½ CUP (1 STICK) BUTTER

2 CUPS SUGAR

3 EGGS

2 TEASPOONS VANILLA

⅓ CUP SOUR MILK OR BUTTERMILK

3 CUPS GRATED ZUCCHINI

Preheat the oven to 350 degrees. Grease and flour a tube pan or other baking pan. Melt the baking chocolate with the vegetable oil. Sift together the flour, cocoa, baking soda, and powder, salt, and set aside.

Cream the butter and sugar together and beat in the eggs, then add the chocolate and oil mixture. Add the dry ingredients and sour milk and, when they are combined, fold in the zucchini. Put into the baking pan. If you make layer cakes, bake for 40 minutes or until a tester inserted comes out clean. If you bake in a tube pan, bake for 1¼ hours or until the tester comes out clean.

Steamed Chocolate Pudding

Steamed puddings are so old-fashioned and comforting, and, for many of us, chocolate is an essential food group. At their best, steamed puddings are like a moist cake, and this one is tender, chocolaty, and rose beautifully, a golden oldie for sure. For steaming I used a double boiler following a tip from my Islesboro neighbor, Sharon Hall. This idea is simpler than the old greased mold thing.

It takes two hours to steam, as it probably would if you used a coffee can or a pudding bowl. If you use a tube mold, it will steam more quickly — an hour and a half. Test as you would for any cake by inserting a knife or skewer: when it comes out clean, the pudding is done. Don't forget to dribble on cream for a sauce when you serve it, or make hard sauce, if you wish.

3 TABLESPOONS BUTTER

2/3 CUP WHITE SUGAR

1 EGG, BEATEN

2½ (1 OUNCE) SQUARES OF UNSWEETENED BAKING
   CHOCOLATE, MELTED

2¼ CUPS FLOUR

4½ TEASPOONS BAKING POWDER

¼ TEASPOON SALT

1 CUP MILK

Grease the top section of a 2-quart double boiler and set a kettle of water on to boil. Cream the butter, then beat in the sugar gradually. Beat in the egg and add the melted chocolate and mix well. Sift together flour, baking powder, and salt. Stir the dry ingredients into the chocolate mixture, alternating with milk. Mix until you have a smooth but fairly stiff batter, then spoon into the double boiler top. Put the hot water into the bottom of the double boiler and set in the top part with a lid on it. Keep it over a medium flame so it bubbles steadily, adding more hot water as it boils away. Check after 2 hours to test for doneness. If the very top is still a little sticky, you can let it boil another 15 minutes, or just relax and enjoy the gooiness. Turn out onto a plate for serving.

Spice Cakes

A QUERY ABOUT SPICE CAKES kicked up a cluster of recipes from lots of readers who offered advice and spice cake experience. Looking at all the recipes reveals that there are different species of spice cake. One is the old-fashioned spice cake, a flour-sugar-butter-egg-and-spices sort moistened with sour milk. Another is the gild the lily kind made with lots of eggs, sour cream, four kinds of spices, utterly grand and luscious. Then there is the spice cake with other stuff in it, including honey or applesauce or cocoa, whose first cousin seems to be that fascinating cluster of eggless, milkless, butterless cakes. What follows are examples of each.

Golden Glow Cake

This elegant variation on a spice cake with its orange frosting is easily one of the best cakes I have collected over the years. Mary Richard, of Bangor, sent it along, saying that it was just about the best tasting one she'd ever had. "The recipe," she wrote, "is from the late Lucille McDonough Gibbons, of Bangor. She taught a cooking class at our Catholic Youth Organization meetings around 1954. The recipe was one she provided us with for a cooking contest that was held at Frank's Bake Shop in Bangor in the 1950s."

Now that is what I call staying power. I can see why. It has a pleasantly spiced flavor, rises nicely, and can be frosted and garnished to make a lovely presentation. You can use a mixer if you want, though I do mine by hand. From measuring to mixing to baking, it takes only 1 hour, not counting frosting time. Add 20 minutes for that. I am such a klutz at frosting that I am sure you could do it faster than I do.

I use 8-inch pans and they bake in 30 minutes. Set your timer to check on them after 25 minutes of baking. You can make a simple white frosting with the recipe below by omitting the orange juice and zest.

2¼ CUPS SIFTED FLOUR

3 TEASPOONS BAKING POWDER

1 TEASPOON SALT

1 ¼ CUPS SUGAR

1 TEASPOON CINNAMON

½ TEASPOON NUTMEG

¼ TEASPOON CLOVES

½ CUP VEGETABLE OIL

¾ CUP MILK

2 EGGS

1 TEASPOON VANILLA

Preheat the oven to 350 degrees. Grease and lightly flour two, 8 or 9-inch pans. Sift together the flour, baking powder, salt, sugar, cinnamon, nutmeg, and cloves. Set aside. In a large bowl beat together the vegetable oil and milk. Add and beat the eggs and vanilla for 2 minutes. Add the dry ingredients and beat for 2 minutes. Fill the pans at least 1½ inches deep. Bake for 25 to 35 minutes or until a tester inserted comes out clean. Remove from oven and cool on racks slightly before taking cakes from the pans.

{ADVICE}

Mary said about the frosting: "I suppose orange juice could be substituted for the milk with a little orange zest. Coffee frosting also works well with this cake."

Orange Frosting:

4 TABLESPOONS BUTTER

2 CUPS CONFECTIONERS' SUGAR

3 TABLESPOONS MILK OR ORANGE JUICE

1 TEASPOON VANILLA

ZEST OF HALF AN ORANGE (OPTIONAL)

Cream the butter, sift the sugar, and add alternately with milk or juice. Beat until fluffy and thick enough to spread. Add the vanilla and orange zest.

Makes enough to cover top and sides of two, 9-inch layers.

Old-Fashioned Spice Cake

Here is a solid, classic version of a plain old-fashioned spice cake. I decided I wanted an orange icing on it, and the one that follows is from an old *Fanny Farmer* cookbook from the forties.

2¼ CUPS FLOUR

½ TEASPOON CINNAMON

½ TEASPOON CLOVES

¼ TEASPOON FRESHLY GRATED NUTMEG

¼ TEASPOON SALT

⅔ CUP BUTTER OR SHORTENING

1½ CUPS SUGAR

2 EGGS

¾ CUP SOUR MILK

1 TEASPOON BAKING SODA, DISSOLVED IN THE MILK

1 CUP FLOURED RAISINS (OPTIONAL)

Preheat the oven to 350 degrees and grease and flour a 9-by-13-inch pan. Sift together the flour, cinnamon, cloves, nutmeg, and salt, and set aside. Cream the butter and sugar. Beat in the eggs. Add the dry ingredients alternatively with the milk and beat until the batter is smooth. It is a stiff batter. Spread in the pan. Bake for 30 to 35 minutes, or until the center is firm and a tester inserted comes out clean. Let cool before icing.

Orange Icing:

¼ CUP BUTTER, MELTED

¼ CUP ORANGE JUICE

ZEST OF ONE ORANGE

2 CUPS OR MORE SIFTED CONFECTIONERS' SUGAR

Mix the butter and juice together in a bowl and beat in the confectioners' sugar until icing is a spreadable consistency. Beat in the zest.

{ ADVICE }

Barbara Piper, from Troy, and Mrs. Elaine Lowell, of Prospect Harbor, shared their recipes. All called for cinnamon, nutmeg, and cloves. When it came down to the taste test, though, it turned out that cloves lent a "spicier" flavor. I like nutmeg myself, grated it fresh. So I liked Mrs. Lowell's cake with a whole teaspoonful of nutmeg in it, plus a teaspoon of cinnamon and a quarter teaspoon of cloves. Mrs. Lowell, who was ninety-one and still cooking when she shared her recipe, wrote that her spice cake recipe came from her mother's collection. That makes it more than a hundred years old.

Eggless, Milkless, Butterless Cake

Houlton native Martha Dow, now residing in Midlothian, Maryland, asked for this cake recipe that, she recalled, "I had it for my birthday cake growing up. My mother had cut it out of the *Bangor Daily News* from Brownie Schrumpf's column. The recipe was called eggless, butterless, milkless cake. A friend has a young son with severe egg allergies and can't have dairy, either, and I thought of this recipe. Can you help me find it?" Anita Angotti, of Caribou, sent Brownie's recipe with a note saying, "The search for this recipe took me down Recipe Memory Lane — a wonderful journey."

This economical spice cake, born of seasonal scarcity and frugality, can be baked in a loaf, square, or round pan, as you wish. If you choose nuts, use walnuts or pecans. You can frost the cake or just dust it with confectioners' sugar.

1 CUP BROWN SUGAR, PACKED

1 CUP SEEDLESS RAISINS

⅓ CUP COOKING OIL

½ TEASPOON NUTMEG

1 TEASPOON CINNAMON

¼ TEASPOON CLOVES

2 CUPS FLOUR

½ TEASPOON BAKING POWDER

½ TEASPOON SODA

½ TEASPOON SALT

½ CUP NUTMEATS (OPTIONAL)

Preheat the oven to 350 degrees. Grease and flour a 9-by-9-inch baking pan. In a saucepan, combine the sugar, 1 cup of water, raisins, cooking oil, and spices, and bring to a boil for 1 minute. Cool. Sift together the flour, baking powder, baking soda, and salt, and stir into the cooled mixture. Add nutmeats if you use them. Bake for 45 minutes to an hour. When the cake is cool, frost it or dust it with confectioners' sugar as you wish.

BROWNIE SCHRUMPF

Mildred Greeley Brown Schrumpf wrote a cooking column for the *Bangor Daily News* for more than forty years, finally ending her writing when she was just a little over ninety years old. Nicknamed "Brownie," and trained in home economics, she worked for the University of Maine Extension Service as a 4-H leader and for the Maine Department of Agriculture, particularly during the annual Eastern States Exposition in Springfield, Massachusetts, where she promoted Maine products. Her column "Learn New Cooking Slants with Brownie Schrumpf" made her well known throughout the state. She compiled her recipes in several cookbooks.

Lemons & Limes

SOMETIMES A BRIGHT, citrus flavor is just the ticket after a rich meal.

Key Lime Pie

{ MAKES A 9-INCH PIE }

Before Nina Scott left Friendship for the winter one year, she very kindly called me up and told me about a really limey Key lime pie recipe she had just acquired from Sudi Blanchard, in York. "It is the best Key lime pie I have ever eaten," she said. This recipe knocked out all my other Key lime pie recipes. It cuts very smoothly, with none of that of sagging and dribbling business. It smoother, richer, doesn't have eggs, and, like a lot of these sorts of recipes, relies on condensed milk of which, you know, you can obtain a low fat version. Be sure to add the called-for bit of lime rind.

You can use sour cream or that very thick Greek-style yogurt widely available these days in the store dairy section. I always make my own graham-cracker crust, because I am too cheap to let someone else make it for me, but if you see company in your too-near future or you hate all that cracker crumbling, you might want to take the short cut and buy a pre-made one.

GRAHAM CRACKER CRUST FOR A 9-INCH PIE PLATE

2 CANS SWEETENED CONDENSED MILK

½ CUP SOUR CREAM OR GREEK YOGURT

¾ CUP LIME JUICE

ZEST OF 1 LIME

Preheat the oven to 350 degrees. Mix the condensed milk, sour cream, or yogurt, juice, and zest together in a bowl. Pour into the pie shall. Bake for 8 minutes. Then chill.

Lemon Cake

Where some people have a sweet tooth, others have a sour tooth: they like lemons, limes, and other pucker-provoking fare. That would be me. So when Marguerite Gallison, of Bangor, asked for lemon cake baked in a small tin, "yellow like cake, but more firm than cake," and when it is out of the oven, "drizzled with a tangy lemon glaze all over," a little spot at the back of my jaw tingled in anticipation.

Margaretta Thurlow, in Lincolnville, and Ruth Thurston, in Machias, both sent along recipes to try. I hybridized the two recipes, adding the grated lemon rind suggested in Ruth's recipe to the somewhat plainer cake in Magaretta's, and since the directions for the glaze from Ruth's seemed tangier I used that for the drizzle. It turned out very lemony. If it proves too tangy for you, leave out the peel, and add more sugar to the glaze.

{ADVICE}

Margaretta Thurlow got her recipe from a friend who, she reports, "dusts the greased surface of any cake pan with very fine bread crumbs instead of flour," a practice that Margaretta follows now. I baked it in two smaller pans, as Marguerite recalled, though you can make just one loaf out of it if you want.

For the cake:

1 SCANT CUP (OR 2 STICKS MINUS A TABLESPOON) BUTTER

1 CUP WHITE SUGAR

2 EGGS

1½ CUPS FLOUR

½ TEASPOON SALT

1 TEASPOON BAKING POWDER

½ CUP MILK

ZEST OF ONE LEMON

For the glaze:

4 TABLESPOONS LEMON JUICE

7 TABLESPOONS SUGAR

LEMON ZEST (OPTIONAL)

Preheat the oven to 350 degrees. Grease one 9-by-5-by-2 ½-inch loaf pan or two, 7½ -by-3 ½-by 2-inch pans. Cream the butter and sugar together, add the eggs, and beat well. Sift the dry ingredients together and add to the butter mixture, alternately with milk. Stir in the lemon zest. Bake for 45 minutes if you use the larger pan, for 35 minutes if you use the smaller pans, or until a tester inserted comes out clean. Make sure the loaf pan(s) are well greased and dusted with flour or very fine breadcrumbs.

To make the glaze, heat the lemon juice and sugar together to make sure the sugar is dissolved, and stir in additional grated peel, if desired. Take the cake out of the oven and let cool for about 3 minutes. Remove from the pans and put on a wire rack over a pan or a piece of aluminum foil to catch drips. Spoon the glaze all over the cake top and even tip them up on edge to dribble along the sides. Allow to finish cooling before serving.

Cookies, Cakes, & Bars

SOMETIMES A COOKIE or small piece of cake is just right at the end of the meal. It is a little like the period at the end of a sentence.

Almond Crescents

{ MAKES 60 }

I love going to Islesboro Island's Alice Pendleton Library on Sunday for recipes. I bet you are thinking, "She looks in the cookbook section." In our library, though, the best place for a new recipe is the refreshments table where one day I sampled a buttery, tender crescent shaped cookie. Diane Head had made them. When I called her, she said that she has made them all her life and the recipe was her mother's. "I used to make them for Christmas gifts," said Diane. I wish I had been on her list.

{ADVICE}

Diane gives two cautions with the crescents. First, chill them very well. She puts them in the freezer for a while. Second, watch them very closely as they bake, and take them out as soon as the bottoms look slightly brown. You can make small crescents that bake more quickly and produce a higher yield, or you can form a more generously sized cookie that may take as long as 20 minutes at the low oven temperature.

1 CUP (2 STICKS) BUTTER, SOFTENED, OR HALF BUTTER AND
   HALF SHORTENING

⅓ CUP SUGAR

⅔ CUP GROUND BLANCHED ALMONDS

1⅔ CUPS FLOUR

¼ TEASPOON SALT

½ CUP CONFECTIONERS' SUGAR

½ TEASPOON CINNAMON

Beat together the butter, sugar, and almonds. Sift together the flour and salt and mix into the butter, sugar, and nut mixture until a handful squeezed holds its shape. Chill the dough very well. Sift together the confectioners' sugar and cinnamon, and set aside to use later.

Preheat the oven to 325 degrees. Pinch off a piece of dough and roll it between your hands to make a "worm." Place it on an ungreased baking sheet and form it into a crescent shape. Bake 14 to 16 minutes if small, longer if larger. Bake only until they are set and brown on only the bottom. Take them from the oven and allow to cool slightly on the pan. Dip each cookie in the confectioners' sugar and cinnamon mixture. Cool thoroughly before storing.

Jam Pecan Bars

Another recipe from our island's library refreshment table is this one for cookie bars that Pat Hopkins made. I like the tart jam or jelly on a shortbread-like base and I especially like having a few ways to use the jam and jelly I make or receive as gifts. Actually, I probably like making jam more than eating it. This lovely recipe is adaptable enough that you can use almost any kind of jam you happen to have.

{ MAKES 1 PANFUL }

2 CUPS FLOUR (OR HALF WHOLE WHEAT AND HALF WHITE)

½ CUP SUGAR

¾ CUP (1½ STICKS) BUTTER

¼ TEASPOON SALT

½ TEASPOON VANILLA

1 CUP CHOPPED PECANS

1¼ CUPS JAM

Preheat the oven to 350 degrees. With a pastry blender or a mixer at a low speed, mix together the flour, sugar, butter, salt, and vanilla until mixture resembles small peas. Stir in a ½ cup of chopped pecans. Set aside ¾ cup of that mixture. Press the remaining crumb mixture into a 9-by-13-inch baking pan. Spread the jam over the top. Sprinkle with the reserved mixture and the other ½ cup of pecans. Bake for 35 minutes or until the jam bubbles and the topping is lightly browned. Cool. Cut into squares.

Carrot Cake

Maggy and another of my island neighbors, Charlotte Robinson, a prolific baker, were having a conversation, and Charlotte told her that she had a recipe for carrot cake that used pureed baby food carrots. Now when Maggy makes this cake she usually cooks up three or four regular carrots and purees them, and, if there is more puree than the recipe needs, she just eats it. Unless you have a prodigious sweet tooth, try to acquire unsweetened coconut for this recipe.

I store carrots from the garden in the cellar until it warms up enough in spring to encourage magnificent sprouting, at which point I put them in the fridge and plan ways to use them up. One way is carrot cake that I really like, especially with cream cheese frosting. Maggy Aston, who publishes the *Islesboro Island News*, shared her classic recipe. Maggy wrote, "This is my favorite carrot cake recipe. True, it does have as much sugar as flour and the dreaded coconut to boot, but I figure that's okay for the once or twice a year I make it." A girl after my own heart. Moderation, ladies and gentlemen. A full-flavored, rich, and moist carrot cake, *twice* a year. And after all, you aren't going to sit down and eat the whole thing all by yourself. (Are you?)

2 CUPS FLOUR

2 CUPS SUGAR

2 TEASPOONS BAKING SODA

2 TEASPOONS CINNAMON

1 TEASPOON CLOVES

1 CUP OIL

3 EGGS

2 TEASPOONS VANILLA

¾ CUP CRUSHED PINEAPPLE

1 ⅓ CUP PUREED COOKED CARROTS (3 TO 4 SLICED,
   APPROXIMATELY 2½ CUPS UNCOOKED)

1 CUP WALNUTS

1 CUP SHREDDED COCONUT

Preheat the oven to 350 degrees. Grease and flour a 9-by-13-inch baking pan or a tube pan. Sift together the flour, sugar, baking soda, cinnamon, and cloves into a large bowl. In another bowl, whisk together the oil and eggs, add the vanilla, pineapple, and carrots, and stir well to mix them. Add the wet ingredients to the dry and mix until you have stiff batter, then fold in the walnuts and coconut. Bake for 1 hour or until a tester inserted comes out clean.

Cream Cheese Icing:

4 OUNCES CREAM CHEESE

3 TABLESPOONS BUTTER

1 ½ CUPS CONFECTIONERS' SUGAR

½ TEASPOON VANILLA

1 TABLESPOON OF LEMON JUICE

{ MAKES 1 CUP }

Let the cream cheese and butter come to room temperature and then beat in the sugar, vanilla, and lemon juice until it is smooth and spreadable. Frost the cake after it has cooled.

Marble Cake

{ Makes 1 Cake }

When Susan Chase wrote asking: "I am trying to locate a recipe for a cake a friend made for birthdays when I was a little girl. The cake was called "Oogle" (rhymes with Google) Cake and was a combination of chocolate and white or yellow, as I remember. I have not been able to locate anything like this. Thanks for your help."

I Googled "oogle," by the way, and found no cake, but speculated that perhaps it was a marble cake, for which Adrienne Durkee, who lives just down the road from me on Islesboro, sent a recipe.

Some older versions of marble cake, ones dating to the early 1900s, called for molasses instead of chocolate to make the dark portion, but all the marble cakes I remember from my girlhood were chocolate and vanilla. Adrienne added a note that sometimes she bakes it in a Bundt pan. I baked it in a tube pan. I love chocolate and orange together, but, if you don't, you can use vanilla or rum extract instead for the light portion.

TWO (1-OUNCE) SQUARES UNSWEETENED CHOCOLATE

¼ CUP SUGAR

1 TEASPOON VANILLA

2 CUPS FLOUR

2 TEASPOONS BAKING POWDER

½ TEASPOON BAKING SODA

½ TEASPOON SALT

½ CUP BUTTER

1 CUP SUGAR

3 EGGS

¾ CUPS EVAPORATED MILK

1 TEASPOON ORANGE EXTRACT (OPTIONAL)

Preheat oven to 350 degrees. Grease and flour a tube or Bundt pan. In a small saucepan, melt the chocolate with the sugar and water over a low heat. Stir in the vanilla. Set it aside to cool. Sift together the flour, baking powder, baking soda, and salt. Cream the butter and sugar until the mixture is fluffy. Beat in the eggs, one at a time. Then beat in the flour mixture alternately with the evaporated milk. Add the orange extract. In another bowl, combine 1½ cups of batter with the chocolate mixture.

Drop the chocolate and yellow batters alternately in the pan and run a knife through the batter a few times to marbleize it. Bake 35 to 40 minutes or until a tester inserted comes out clean.

Prune Cake

{ MAKES 1 CAKE }

A few years ago, the prune producers of America tried to re-brand prunes as the more elegant sounding "dried plums" because they were weary of prunes' dowdy reputation, to wit, that they were, as my mother used to say, "good for what ails you." I don't think they succeeded, though, of course, there are lots of lovely things to do with prunes besides ingesting them as a daily necessity.

An island neighbor, Linda Gilles, brought this as a teacake for a church function. Rich, moist, and full of spices, the recipe hails from the South, the Beaumont Inn in Harrodsburg, Kentucky. It has buttermilk in it, both in the cake and the sauce. I was generous with spices. I started with dried pitted prunes, crammed a cup full of them, stewed them up, then took a potato masher to them. Serve it as a single layer cake with sauce on it.

For the cake:

2 CUPS FLOUR

1 ½ TEASPOONS BAKING SODA

1 TEASPOON CINNAMON

1 TEASPOON FRESHLY GRATED NUTMEG

1 TEASPOON ALLSPICE

1 CUP VEGETABLE OIL

3 EGGS, BEATEN

1 CUP BUTTERMILK

1 TEASPOON VANILLA

1 ½ CUPS SUGAR

1 CUP COOKED, CHOPPED PRUNES

1 CUP CHOPPED PECANS OR WALNUTS (OPTIONAL)

For the sauce:

1 CUP SUGAR

½ CUP BUTTERMILK

½ TEASPOON BAKING SODA DISSOLVED IN THE BUTTERMILK

1 TABLESPOON CORN SYRUP

6 TABLESPOONS (¾ STICK) BUTTER

½ TEASPOON VANILLA

Preheat the oven to 300 degrees. Oil your baking pan(s) and line them with waxed paper. Sift together the flour, baking soda, cinnamon, nutmeg, and allspice. Put the oil, eggs, buttermilk, vanilla, and sugar into a mixing bowl and beat well together, then add the dry ingredients. Fold in the prunes and nuts. Bake for 45 minutes or until the center springs back when you touch it. Make the sauce while the cake bakes. Mix sugar, buttermilk, corn syrup, butter, and vanilla together in a small saucepan and bring to a boil. Cook for 1 minute. Set aside. Invert the still-warm cake onto a serving platter. Spoon the sauce over and let it soak in, using all the sauce.

Remove from the oven and let it cool 10 minutes before adding sauce.

A Pair of Puddings

A LITTLE OLD FASHIONED, and both flavored with coffee, either of these two puddings make a charming dessert.

Coffee Carnival

{ SERVES 4 TO 6 }

During a visit to the Stonington and Deer Isle Historical Society a few years ago, I was treated to a lovely summery cold supper of salad, deviled eggs, ham, coleslaw, and smoked salmon from Stonington Sea Products. Lee Fay organized it, and her cousin, Rena Day, brought a dessert called coffee carnival, which I adored. The recipe came from Rena's and Lee's grandmother, Lillian Sylvester, who, with her husband, Fred, had a dairy farm on Deer Isle and occasionally took summer boarders. We all surmised that the recipe dated from the twenties or thirties, though why it is called "carnival," we can't quite tell. Festive sounding isn't it?

With its coffee-colored cream and little dark brown flecks of coffee-flavored tapioca all through it, it would be pretty spooned into parfait glasses, though Rena served it from clear glass bowls. Someone joked about calling Rena at two in the morning to tell her how good the dessert was, so if you have trouble sleeping after drinking caffeinated coffee, you might want to make this with decaffeinated coffee.

4 TABLESPOONS INSTANT TAPIOCA

¼ TEASPOON SALT

⅓ CUP RAISINS

2 CUPS STRONG BREWED COFFEE

½ CUP SUGAR

1 TEASPOON VANILLA

1 CUP WHIPPING CREAM

Put the tapioca, salt, raisins, and coffee in the top of a double boiler or in a very heavy saucepan and cook, stirring frequently, until the tapioca is clear, about 15 minutes. Add the sugar stirring until it is dissolved. Chill. Add the vanilla. Whip the cream and fold it into the coffee and tapioca mixture, then refrigerate it to let it chill thoroughly.

Spanish Coffee Cream

While this recipe is for coffee Spanish cream, remember that you can make a plain one by changing the coffee amount into all milk, and flavoring with vanilla or sherry. Even though the custard mixture looks thin and not very custardy when you fold in the egg whites, you can be sure that it will set up. Do you know the test for a custard? Dip the spoon into the custard and look to see if the custard coats the spoon, then run your finger through the custard coating, looking closely to see if the edges of the finger streak seeps. If it does not, it is done. (Lick your finger.) Use whole milk.

Barbara McLaughlin's Depression-era memory of a Spanish coffee cream unleashed a bunch of recollections and recipes. Another of those lovely old-fashioned desserts no one makes anymore, it asks only for good old eggs, sugar, gelatin, and a bit of time from the cook. The result is dressy, even elegant, and is delicious enough for company.

The fun thing about this dessert is that the fluffier egg white part rises to top off a solid jelly-like layer, but firms up to be quite mousse-like.

Many recipes say to put the cream into a mold to turn out for presentation, but unmolding creates more excitement than I need in my life, so I put mine into parfait glasses. If you don't have special glasses you can just use wine glasses or any other clear dessert dish. Garnish with whipped cream or a sprinkle of cocoa or those chocolate-covered coffee beans you can buy.

1 ½ CUPS WHOLE MILK

1 TABLESPOON (1 ENVELOPE) OF GELATIN

3 EGGS, YOLKS AND WHITES SEPARATED

½ CUP OF SUGAR

¼ TEASPOON SALT

1 ½ CUPS STRONG BREWED COFFEE

1 TEASPOON VANILLA

3 EGG WHITES

¼ CUP SUGAR

Put the milk into the top of a double boiler and sprinkle the gelatin over the milk and set aside for 5 minutes for the gelatin to soften. Heat the water in the bottom part of the double boiler and then put the milk on until it is hot. Beat the egg yolks with ½ of the sugar and salt and take a ladleful of the hot milk and add it to the egg yolks and mix well. Pour the egg yolk mixture back into the milk in the double boiler. Add the coffee and cook it all together until the custard coats the back of a spoon.

Take from the heat. Allow to cool and add the vanilla. Beat the egg whites with the remaining ½ cup of sugar until you have soft peaks. Fold into the custard and spoon into your glasses. Set in the fridge to chill.

SPANISH CREAM HISTORY AND MEMORIES

The earliest versions of this charming old dish date from the 1800s, but they are all descended from a family of desserts from even earlier, which included syllabubs and custards. In the later 1800s a convenient form of gelatin was finally manufactured and made it possible even for a middle-class family to have elegant desserts. Before that time, one had to boil calves feet to extract the gelatin, strain, and purify it and then make the dessert, a process not done casually. Then about mid-1800 we added the rotary egg beater to the list of conveniences and we were set for fancy desserts for all.

Barbara Elward, in Mattawamkeag, found the oldest Spanish cream recipe in an 1879 cookbook from Virginia. Anne Price, in Presque Isle, found her recipes in an Australian cookbook. Bev Boardman uncovered a first cousin to Spanish cream called coffee soufflé, which sounds very similar to the cream and which her mother called Spanish cream, but which doesn't make layers. Connie Seavey pointed out one in an old *Fanny Farmer*. Zelma Merritt found Spanish cream in a 1958 Mary Margaret McBride cookbook, which included a variation for a coffee-flavored one, and also for a macaroon Spanish cream with crushed macaroons folded into the beaten egg whites. I am going to bet that after the late fifties and early sixties this dessert would have just about disappeared from new cookbooks.

Then there was a half dozen of classic Spanish creams. Joan Belanger, of Bangor, found her offering in a well-worn 1923 Canadian cookbook that belonged to her grandmother, Mary Ann Belanger, who died in 1961 at eighty-nine years of age. My Islesboro neighbor, the late Midge Welldon, sent along Aunt Ada Perkins' recipe from the early 1900s.

Dorothea Mead, from Southwest Harbor, is eighty-three and said, "I hadn't thought of Spanish cream in *years*, but your mention of it rang a lot of bells." She still has her mother's 1923 *Fanny Farmer* and sent the recipe from it. Dorothea recalled her mother using sherry to flavor it instead of coffee. Another octogenarian, Arlene Krupsky, in Pittsfield, sent *her* mother's coffee Spanish cream recipe with the instructions to ladle it into sherbet glasses. Suzi Warholak, of Mount Desert, sent her grandmother's recipe found on a three-by-five card in her Aunt Elizabeth's handwriting. Her aunt, who died in 2000 at ninety-one years old, identified the recipe as her mother's, which set it in the early twentieth century.

Fresh and Seasonal

FRESH AND SEASONAL

One week, when I ran out of reader queries and wondered what to write about, my first *Taste Bud's* column editor, Lettita Baldwin, said, "Just tell them what happens in your kitchen."

What happens in my kitchen, besides rummaging around in the fridge to figure out what to do with leftovers, is what happens in my *garden*. Over the years, from the early spring spinach through the last stored winter squash and carrot, the vegetable population has determined daily menus. Most recipes that follow are the result of sometimes desperate measures to use gorgeously fresh vegetables, full of their own flavor and nutritious as all get out, while they are available in season.

Variations on themes like pasta salad, stir-frys, or vegetable soups pilot me through the year as vegetables come into and go out of season. As you will see, some of these recipes are less precise formulas than guidelines for delicious combinations, meant to be a springboard for your own creativity as you find vegetables in your garden, at farmers' markets, and stores.

The following recipes are organized according to the growing season, each vegetable arriving here in turn as it does in the garden, and accompanied by stored ones until they run out. I like celebrating each veggie as it comes into season, even if I can buy it at any time of the year. Trust me, asparagus from my garden in April is more delicious than asparagus from the store in January, and I'd rather wait, thank you.

Spring Arrivals

BY APRIL AND MAY, most of us are pretty hungry for something fresh and local. Even though we can find green stuff in the stores, the lettuce, green beans, and broccoli are travel weary, more raw than fresh. First out of the ground is parsnips, then soon after comes asparagus, spinach, chard, and welcome salad stuff.

Savory Parsnip Pie

{ MAKES A 9-INCH PIE }

This recipe was born when a recipe for a sweet parsnip pie along the lines of pumpkin or sweet potato pie just plain tasted funny, and I concluded that a savory version would be ever so much better.

Peel and cut up about three cups of raw parsnip to give yourself enough for this recipe. Use more, less, or no bacon, to your preference, and cook your onion in bacon fat or in oil, whichever you prefer.

3 CUPS PARSNIPS, PEELED AND CHOPPED

2 LARGE EGGS

1 CUP MILK

1 MEDIUM ONION, CHOPPED

5 SLICES OF BACON, COOKED AND CRUMBLED (OPTIONAL)

½ CUP GRATED CHEDDAR CHEESE

½ TEASPOON GROUND CELERY SEED

½ TEASPOON CHILI POWDER, OR MORE TO TASTE

SALT AND PEPPER, TO TASTE

PASTRY FOR 1 CRUST

Preheat the oven to 375 degrees. Steam the parsnips until very tender. Put them in a bowl and mash them very well, then beat in the eggs and milk. Cook the onion until it is soft and fold it and the bacon, cheese, and seasonings into the parsnip mixture. Taste and adjust seasonings.

Line a pie pan with the pastry and pour in the parsnip mixture. Bake for 35 to 40 minutes.

PARSNIPS

People who think they don't like parsnips never ate one dug in spring. Parsnips planted in summer and allowed to winter over in-ground lose their rooty earthiness by being frozen in the ground, turning sugary sweet by spring. Over-wintering means that parsnips are both the last vegetable to come out of the garden from the previous growing season and the first to harvest each year. In my farmhouse home, it is practically a ritual to eat parsnip stew here on the April day when I dig them.

Roast peeled and chunked parsnips in olive oil in a 375 degree oven for 30 minutes or until they are golden brown and as tender as you prefer.

Add parsnips to lamb or beef stew.

Make parsnip potato cakes by mashing cooked potato and parsnips together, forming into patties, and fry them in oil or drippings.

Parsnip Stew

This stew is only one of several things to make with them. Every time I make it I am reminded of chowder. In fact, to arrive at a decent parsnip stew, veteran chowder makers can easily substitute parsnips for whatever amount of fish they customarily use. Though I usually make parsnip stew with salt pork or a couple of strips of bacon, I have also made a vegetarian version with the substitution of butter, olive oil, or other vegetable oil.

A pretty deluxe version results if you use heavy cream, but I think milk is perfectly suitable. Half-and-half, light cream, and evaporated milk are also possibilities. Vary the proportion of parsnips to potatoes to taste. I like equal proportions.

3 SLICES OF BACON OR A 1-INCH SQUARE OF SALT PORK,
    DICED SMALL (OR 2 TABLESPOONS VEGETABLE OIL OR BUTTER)
1 MEDIUM ONION, CHOPPED
4 MEDIUM POTATOES, PEELED AND SLICED
5 TO 6 MEDIUM PARSNIPS, PEELED AND SLICED
SALT AND PEPPER, TO TASTE
WATER
MILK OR CREAM

Over a medium heat, fry the bacon or salt pork until the fat runs; remove any more than 2 tablespoons and add the chopped onion to the fat. You may choose to remove the bits of bacon or salt pork to use as garnish, or incorporate them in the stew. Sauté the onions until they are slightly softened, about 5 minutes. Add a layer of potatoes alternately with a layer of parsnips. Sprinkle a little salt and pepper on each layer. Pour in water, just enough to see it through the vegetables. Bring to a boil, then reduce the heat and let simmer until the vegetables are tender, about 20 minutes. Add the milk or cream and heat it through. Taste and add salt and pepper as needed.

Asparagus Pasta

For the recipe below, adapt whatever pasta size and shape you like or have on hand. Chop the asparagus small or leave it a bit larger. Use low-fat ricotta or whole milk. I like grating my own Parmesan, but this recipe calls for quite a bit, and you might not prefer to do that. I like adding a few chopped, pitted kalamata olives, but that can be optional.

With salad, this can be a meal by itself, or a side dish to accompany chicken or fish.

{ SERVES 4 }

16 OUNCES OF PASTA (FARFALLE, PENNE, ROTINI)

1 LARGE SHALLOT, MINCED

2 TABLESPOONS OF OLIVE OIL OR HALF BUTTER/ HALF OLIVE OIL

1 POUND OF ASPARAGUS

¼ CUP OF COARSELY CHOPPED, PITTED KALAMATA OLIVES

1½ CUPS OR 12 OUNCES OF RICOTTA, OR MORE TO TASTE

½ CUP GRATED PARMESAN AND MORE TO SERVE AT TABLE

SALT AND PEPPER, TO TASTE

Cook the pasta according to the directions on the package. Meanwhile, cut or break the asparagus into the desired lengths. In large heavy pan, sauté the shallots in the olive oil just until they are soft, then add the asparagus and sauté it until it is bright green. Drain the pasta when it is done and put into a large serving bowl, add the ricotta, and toss until the ricotta is evenly mixed with the pasta. Then add the asparagus, Parmesan, salt, and pepper, and fold in or, if you prefer, serve it with the asparagus on top. If the ricotta and pasta mixture needs to be moister, dribble in a little cream or milk.

Serve with additional Parmesan.

Spinach, Ricotta, and Pasta Casserole

{ SERVES 4 }

I was on the way to making green lasagna when I ended up with this dish. Since I grow spinach, I have to pick it over and wash it. I managed one night to get as far as the spinach ricotta mixture for the lasagna, then I foundered on the lack of time to cook the lasagna noodles and make layers. Instead I cooked up a batch of rotini, into which I stirred the cheese and spinach mixture, put half into a baking dish, added mozzarella, and then the rest of the spinach-ricotta mixture, with mozzarella on top of it all. In half an hour supper was ready, and it was delicious.

If you use frozen spinach, this whole process will be very easy for you. If you use bagged, washed spinach you will probably want to wash it again, then steam it and squeeze out the excess liquid. If you use spinach from your garden, as I do, well, get an earlier start than I did.

1 PACKAGE FROZEN CHOPPED SPINACH OR 1 POUND
   BAGGED FRESH SPINACH
1 TABLESPOON OF OLIVE OIL
1 MEDIUM ONION, CHOPPED

1 OR 2 CLOVES OF GARLIC MINCED (OPTIONAL)

1 PINT OF RICOTTA CHEESE

2 TO 3 TABLESPOONS OF PESTO (OPTIONAL)

8 OUNCES OF ROTINI OR BOW TIES

½ POUND OF MOZZARELLA, GRATED

If using fresh spinach, wash it, spin it to remove excess water, then blanch or steam it. Squeeze the water out of the cooked or frozen spinach and chop it up. Sauté the chopped onion and minced garlic in the olive oil until they are soft.

Preheat the oven to 350 degrees. Put the ricotta cheese in a medium bowl and stir into it the spinach, onions, and garlic. Add pesto, if you like, or your choice of herbs or spices. Boil and drain the pasta and mix it into the seasoned spinach and ricotta. Brush or spray a little oil in a 2-quart baking dish. Put in half of the mixture and sprinkle half the grated mozzarella over it, then add the other half, and top with the rest of the mozzarella. Bake for about 30 minutes until the cheese is melted on the top and it is heated through.

{ ADVICE }

If you want to make green lasagna, use the recipe above for the spinach ricotta filling. For a 9-by-13 baking dish, you'd probably want to double the quantities of filling and use a whole pound of mozzarella. If you like spicy food, you could add a little minced jalapeno to the filling. Oregano, parsley, or tarragon also work. And remember that you can bring down the calories by using low-fat ricotta and skim-milk mozzarella. Add more spinach if you want to. Or less. Lots of tinkering potential here (like using chard instead of spinach).

ASPARAGUS AND SPINACH

Spinach over-winters successfully, too, and I encourage you to try planting it in late September for the next spring. The spinach will come up but it won't grow to full maturity as the days shorten. As frost approaches, cover the bed deeply with mulch. As soon as the ground thaws in spring, uncover the spinach and you will find it beginning to sprout. You can enjoy luxuriant amounts cooked or raw in late April, all during May, and into June, until summer heat makes it bolt and your newly planted spinach is up and growing.

Asparagus usually comes up in April, as welcome a sight as any I can think of. The first few shoots that I harvest, I steam and drape artfully over some chicken or rice, and eat them very appreciatively, savoring each one. After I've devoured a big pile of stalks three or four times a week, I finally start chopping them up and using them in risotto, quiche, or pasta sauce.

Strawberry Spinach Salad

{ SERVES 3 TO 6 }

Combine fresh early summer spinach with new strawberries for a
virtuously wholesome salad.

4 TO 8 OUNCES OF SPINACH

½ LARGE RED ONION, OR TO TASTE

1 CUP OR LESS OF STRAWBERRIES

1 TEASPOON DIJON-STYLE MUSTARD

1 TABLESPOON RED WINE, MALT, OR BALSAMIC VINEGAR

3 TABLESPOONS OLIVE OIL OR YOUR FAVORITE VINAIGRETTE
   SALAD DRESSING

SALT AND PEPPER, TO TASTE

{ ADVICE }

By the end of June
in Maine, fresh ripe
strawberries are plentiful
and strawberry festivals
cluster around the
Fourth of July. A fresh,
local, sun-ripened berry,
red through and through,
and tender, is worth the
wait. I grew up thinking
strawberries were
only for dessert or at
breakfast, and now find
I can scatter them
around in salads, too.

Remove the big stems from larger spinach leaves and shred the spinach
into a bowl. Chop the onion finely and toss into the bowl with the
spinach. Slice the strawberries and add them to the spinach to suit your
taste. Whisk together the mustard, vinegar, and olive oil. Sample the
dressing by dipping a spinach leaf into it, and then add salt and pepper
to taste. Dress the salad lightly with the vinaigrette just before serving.

Spinach Salad

Piles of torn-up raw spinach with crumbled fried bacon, sprinkled in
along with a couple of finely chopped hard-boiled eggs, simply dressed
with vinaigrette makes a substantial dish.

FRESH WASHED SPINACH, 4 TO 5 OUNCES PER PERSON

2 SLICES OF BACON, PER PERSON, FRIED AND CRUMBLED

½ HARDBOILED EGG, PER PERSON, CHOPPED FINELY

OIL AND VINEGAR OR VINAIGRETTE (SEE PAGE 222) OR
   ITALIAN DRESSING

Tear the spinach into bite-size pieces and put into a shallow bowl.
Sprinkle the bacon and hardboiled egg onto the spinach, and, just before
serving, dribble the oil and vinegar or salad dressing all over the salad.
Toss lightly and serve.

Salad Dressings

Most of us living near the Down East coast enjoy cool-enough summers to allow lettuce to grow plentifully all season long. To ensure a continuous supply, I plant short rows of lettuce every two weeks or so — rows literally eighteen inches long, thinned down to four or five heads transplanted out to grow to size. I also plant short rows of mesclun and shave it off to allow it to sprout up again.

Salad needs dressing. There are lots of choices in stores, and sometimes I'm glad to put my hand on one in haste. Usually, I prefer to sprinkle oil and vinegar or make my own. Here are some favorites.

Basic Vinaigrette

{ MAKES 1 CUP }

I make this basic plain vinaigrette to keep on hand. Sometimes I vary it by using flavored vinegar, like raspberry or rice wine vinegar. It can also be the base for a blue cheese dressing — just add some blue cheese to it and give it a whirl in the blender.

1 TABLESPOON PREPARED MUSTARD (I LIKE MAINE-MADE RAYE'S)

4 TABLESPOONS OF RED WINE OR OTHER VINEGAR

1 TEASPOON OF GRANULATED SUGAR

SALT AND PEPPER, TO TASTE

PARSLEY, GARLIC, CHIVES (OPTIONAL)

½ CUP OLIVE OIL

In a bowl whisk together, or blend in a blender, the mustard, vinegar, sugar, salt, and herbs until they are thoroughly blended. Then add the oil very slowly whisking or blending constantly until all the oil is added and you have a thick mixture, ready to use.

Tarragon Vinaigrette

1 TABLESPOON RICE OR CIDER VINEGAR

JUICE OF HALF A LEMON

2 TABLESPOONS OF FRESH TARRAGON, FINELY MINCED

¾ CUP OF OLIVE OR OTHER VEGETABLE OIL

SALT AND PEPPER, TO TASTE

SUGAR

{ MAKES A SCANT CUP }

Using a food processor, blender, or bowl and whisk, combine the vinegar, juice, and tarragon, and slowly add the oil in a steady stream with the blade running or whisking continuously by hand. Add salt and pepper, taste, adjust seasonings, and if too tart, add a little sugar. The tarragon flavor will develop if you let the dressing rest for a couple of hours before you use it.

Shallot Salad Dressing

1 EGG

¼ CUP OR LESS GRAINY MUSTARD

⅓ CUP RED WINE VINEGAR

⅓ CUP OF RICE WINE VINEGAR

SALT AND PEPPER, TO TASTE

4 TO 5 SHALLOT CLOVES

2 CUPS OLIVE OIL

{ MAKES 3 CUPS }

{ ADVICE }

Turn this dressing into a garlic one by substituting four to five cloves of garlic for the shallots.

Drop the egg and mustard into a blender or food processor and combine. Add the vinegar and salt and pepper and blend. Then with the motor running, add the shallots, then add the oil slowly and steadily until all of the oil is incorporated.

Swiss Chard and Sausage Pie

{ SERVES 6 }

{ ADVICE }

Feel free to play with
the seasonings. I used
spicy Spanish chorizo,
but you could use Italian
sausage and herbs like
oregano, garlic, and
fennel seed, or you could
use a plain old breakfast
sausage and really load
up on onions and coarsely
ground pepper. Or you can
make a vegetarian one
with lots of dill, parsley,
thyme, or savory in it.
If you think this sounds
like something worth
trying, but you don't
have swiss chard, use
spinach instead.

The object of the game is "use as much swiss chard in one recipe as possible." Ruth Thurston, of Machias, and Marian Fowler, of Millinocket, rose to the challenge with some help from their favorite vegetable cookbooks. Ruth uses Marian Morash's *Victory Garden Cookbook*, published in 1982, as a companion to the PBS television show, and Marian is fond of *Too Many Tomatoes, Squash, Beans, and Other Good Things* by Lois M. Landau and Laura G. Myers.

Among the recipes Ruth and Marian spotted was this main dish one that uses a pound and a half of the stuff — or two giant handfuls. If you leave out the sausage you'll have a vegetarian dish.

PASTRY FOR A TWO CRUST PIE

1½ POUNDS OF CHARD, OR 3 TIGHTLY PACKED CUPS OF

   COOKED CHARD

½ POUND OF CHORIZO SAUSAGE (OPTIONAL)

1 TABLESPOON OLIVE OIL

½ CUP CHOPPED ONION

3 CLOVES MINCED GARLIC

¾ CUP RICOTTA

2 EGGS, BEATEN

½ CUP PARMESAN CHEESE

¼ TEASPOON RED PEPPER FLAKES

2 TEASPOONS WHOLE CUMIN SEED, SLIGHTLY TOASTED

SALT AND PEPPER, TO TASTE

Preheat the oven to 375 degrees. Trim your chard leaves by slicing out the ribs and setting aside to chop into ½ inch pieces while you steam the leafy portion. When the leaves are cooked, steam the rib pieces, and then recombine and squeeze firmly to remove excess moisture. Remove the sausage from its casing and break it up into a large sauté or frying pan; brown the sausage and drain it. Put the olive oil in the pan, add the onion, and cook it over a medium heat until it is soft. Add the chard and garlic and heat the chard through, stirring to allow moisture to evaporate. Combine by stirring the chard mixture with the cooked sausage, ricotta, eggs, Parmesan, and seasonings. Mix well.

Line a 9-inch pie plate with a crust and put in the filling and then the top crust. Crimp to seal. Bake for 35 minutes.

SWISS CHARD

Chard is an early summer garden arrival. You can find it in the grocery store year-round, but I always feel sorry for it because it has had to travel quite a way to arrive in Maine, and then it is rained on in the produce section under those greens sprinklers they have, which promote mushy leaves. It is never as satisfactory as garden-fresh stuff or chard from farmers' markets. In my garden, I grow the multicolored one called "Bright Lights," with pink, yellow, white, orange, and magenta stalks.

To prepare chard for cooking, I trim the leaves away from the stalk by sliding a sharp knife up through the leaf on either side of the stalk. Then I chop the stalk. I roll the leaves up in a bundle, then cut through it with a knife or scissors to shred them. Long ribbony shreds look pretty.

You will readily see that there is a kind of general principle involved here of sautéing green leafy stuff like chard, spinach, or beet greens in oil, then adding a little zest with vinegar, a little interesting flavor with garlic and capers, and then good old salt and pepper. You could as easily use a different kind of oil, and substitute lemon juice or vary the vinegar, use olives or pickled onions instead of capers to come up with your own variations.

You can even merely steam it and serve it with your favorite salad dressing.

Some cooks simply steam or sauté chard as they might spinach. Sooner or later the stuff grows so much that keeping ahead of it requires effort.

Summer Abundance

IN JULY, THE GARDEN continues to produce greens, and adds solid veggies like peas, broccoli, green beans, cauliflower, summer squashes, early cabbage, and young roots like carrots and beets, which I pull to thin the rows and allow for growth. Scallions and garlic scapes — the curly buds of garlic flowers that must be cut to promote bulb development — are useful for flavoring. I usually have basil, parsley, thyme, tarragon, chives, and cilantro growing as well.

Green Vegetable Salad

This supply-side salad resulted from a mixed bunch of vegetables I picked one day from my garden. It could also result from whatever vegetables you might have in your fridge.

I picked off two or three handfuls of green beans, a handful of snap peas, a few broccoli side shoots, maybe eight or so, and three tidy little green patty pan squashes slightly smaller than my palm. There weren't enough of any one of these to make a decent showing themselves. However, taken together, there was enough for a company supper. With a pile of green vegetables like this, I can make a competent hot or cold side dish, amplify it with chicken, ham, or shrimp, or send it off in a pasta salad direction.

Here is some general advice for creating a salad out of odds and ends.

{ADVICE}

I am a firm believer in blanching veggies if you are eating them raw or in a salad. They turn an appetizing bright green, and the flavor develops just enough, especially in green beans, squash, broccoli, and cauliflower.

■ **To prepare the vegetables:**

Take stem ends off the green beans and slice oversized ones lengthwise.

Take the strings off the snap peas and break in half.

Trim leaves off the broccoli, and, if necessary, cut into bite-size pieces.

Cut patty pan or other summer squash into bite-size pieces.

Dunk them all in boiling water for about a minute, then drain.

■ **To make a warm vegetable dish:**

Put a little butter, olive oil, and chopped onion or shallots in a sauté pan, heat them to soften them. Dump the blanched veggies into the pan, flip them around until they are hot, then serve them.

Or put salad dressing on warm blanched vegetables just before serving them (vinaigrette type dressings are my favorites for that).

If I expect company, I blanch the vegetables earlier in the day; at the last minute do the sauté to reheat them.

■ To make a cold vegetable dish:
Drain them after blanching and let them cool before dressing them.
Add diced cucumber, grated carrot, pickles if you wish. Consider using leftover cooked vegetables for salad.

■ To make a main dish with meat:
Add cooked chicken, ham, or shrimp.

■ To make a pasta salad:
Cook and add bows, penne, radiatore, rotini, or any prettily shaped pasta. You can use any leftover cooked pasta, even spaghetti or fettucine, cut up and tossed in with the vegetables.

■ To dress any of these dishes:
Use your favorite salad dressing, whatever it is. Plain vinaigrette is fine and so is mayonnaise with lots of herbs in it. Then there are all those bottled dressings.

Sesame, Noodle, and Napa Cabbage Salad

{ SERVES 16 }

I love going to potlucks, and this recipe came from a potluck in Winthrop when our community chorus sang with a choral group there who gave us supper after a joint concert. Among the many delicious dishes served was this interesting salad made with Chinese cabbage and a dressing with sesame seeds and little bits of ramen noodles. With some help from her fellow choristers, I tracked down the maker, Deb Petell, of Wayne, and asked how she did it.

The recipe follows, and you will see that it is mostly the dressing that makes it so flavorful. This recipe yields a large salad, a suitable alternative to slaw, enough for a big crowd. For a smaller batch, just halve it.

For the salad:

1 HEAD CHINESE (NAPA) CABBAGE

2 BUNCHES SCALLIONS

Slice the cabbage thinly and chop the scallions, mostly the white part, and some of the tenderest green parts. Put into a large bowl and set aside.

For the dressing:

¼ CUP RICE VINEGAR

½ CUP SOY SAUCE

½ CUP SUGAR

1 TABLESPOON SESAME OIL

½ CUP VEGETABLE OIL

For the topping:

2 PACKAGES RAMEN NOODLES

VEGETABLE OIL

1 CUP SLICED ALMONDS

½ CUP SESAME SEEDS

Mix and boil the dressing ingredients together briefly. Take from heat and set aside until you are ready to assemble the salad.

Open the ramen noodles. Discard the seasonings packet and crush the noodles inside the package. Put a little oil on a heavy frying pan and toast the noodles just until they begin to turn brown, then add the almonds and sesame seeds and toast until you can smell the nutty aroma. Remove from the heat and hold until you are ready to serve.

Toss together the cabbage and dressing and then sprinkle in the noodles, nuts, and seeds. Toss again and serve.

BOK CHOY

If you don't cook Asian dishes, maybe it wouldn't occur to you to use bok choy, which is perfectly acceptable as a kind of substitute for cabbage. Why not a slaw made of shredded bok choy and carrots with your favorite dressing on it? Or how about putting some oil with garlic, onions, or shallots in a pan and cooking shredded bok choy in that until it is just wilted. If you have something like toasted sesame seed oil, or just sesame seeds, add that to wilted bok choy. Treat chard and kale the same way.

Roasted Kohlrabi

{ SERVES 4 }

Kohlrabi is a funny-looking vegetable for sure, a turnipy little spaceship-like thing growing above ground, in green or purple, with leaves sprouting out of a smooth baseball-size round stalk. It is a cabbage family member and the leaves and the enlarged stalk are both good to eat. You can cook the greens as you would collards or kale and treat the bulb like turnips or broccoli stalks. I can just hear some of you saying, "I hate turnips and throw out broccoli stalks."

I don't blame you. Plainly boiling or steaming either is going to be a major snore. Think experimentally and less in terms of actual recipes than in ways of incorporating kohlrabi into other vegetable dishes. I always say, "When in doubt, roast it."

Why bother eating kohlrabi at all? Most of us need to eat more vegetables anyway, and this novel veggie has protein and fiber and is obligingly low in carbohydrates. Mainly, it's tasty, and it is fun to have something different more than occasionally.

1 TO 2 POUNDS FRESH KOHLRABI, ENDS TRIMMED, DICED

1 TO 2 TABLESPOONS OLIVE OIL

1 TO 2 CLOVES GARLIC CHOPPED (OPTIONAL)

SALT AND PEPPER, TO TASTE

RICE WINE OR MALT VINEGAR (OPTIONAL)

Preheat oven to 450°degrees. Toss the diced kohlrabi with olive oil, garlic, and salt in a bowl and then spread on a roasting pan so there is a single layer of vegetable. Or just toss the dice with oil and seasonings right on the roasting pan. After about 20 minutes, stir and then stir again after another 5 to 10 minutes. Roast for 30 to 35 minutes until the vegetable is golden brown. Sprinkle lightly with the vinegar and serve immediately.

Significant Salad

Deciding what to have for supper is the hardest part of cooking. An assortment of leftovers is a treasure because it can help you decide what to do, and frugally besides. The directions that follow came from a salad I put together based on miscellaneous contents of the fridge. Substitute at will for your own salad.

A word or two on cheese. I figure if I have some kind of interesting and flavorful cheese on hand — a blue cheese, like gorgonzola, or salty, crumbly feta — or a comforting cheddar or cottage cheese, then I can make some kind of meal, even without meat.

If a big salad like the one below doesn't cut it as a whole meal at your house, consider using it as the sole vegetable side dish with meat or fish, like salmon, or a bit of shellfish. You'll still use up all those pesky vegetable bits.

COLD BOILED POTATO

COLD ROASTED CHICKEN

BLANCHED GREEN BEANS OR BROCCOLI

CHERRY TOMATOES OR VERY RIPE TOMATOES, CUT IN WEDGES

SLICED CUCUMBERS OR CUCUMBER PICKLES

CARROTS CUT IN JULIENNE OR VERY THIN SLICES

LARGE BOWLFUL OF WASHED AND TORN LETTUCE OR MIXED GREENS

Cut the potato in small pieces, and, if you wish, add to it a bit of celery, scallion, or pickle, and dress with mayonnaise or vinaigrette. Set aside. Spread the lettuce on individual plates or on a large platter. Arrange the chicken, the potato salad, and the vegetables over the lettuce and garnish with the optional add-ons. Serve with vinaigrette or your favorite salad dressing.

Skillet Braised Fennel

Garlic-flavored orange juice is better than you'd think. You need it in this recipe that June Smith, in Perry, shared that calls for fennel, that bulbous, anise-flavored vegetable with feathery leaves. The thickened sauce works well for warming boring old boneless, skinless chicken breasts and it is a beautiful color.

{ SERVES 4 }

2 MEDIUM FENNEL BULBS, TOPS AND OUTER LEAVES REMOVED

1 TABLESPOON OF BUTTER

1 TEASPOON SUGAR, RAW OR LIGHT BROWN

1 CLOVE OF GARLIC, PEELED AND THINLY SLICED

¾ CUP OF ORANGE JUICE

SALT AND PEPPER, TO TASTE

Slice the fennel bulb lengthwise into ½-inch slabs. Melt the butter and sugar together in a large skillet, add the garlic, and cook it for a few moments. Lay the fennel in the skillet and brown over a medium high heat for about 4 minutes to a side. Add the orange juice, salt, and pepper — it will bubble violently at first. When it settles down, reduce the temperature to simmer, and let it cook, covered, for about 40 minutes, till the fennel is fork tender. Turn at least once. Take off the lid and let the sauce reduce, occasionally basting the fennel with it till the sauce is slightly thickened another 10 to 15 minutes.

{ ADVICE }

Lila Fortin, in Searsport, grows her own fennel, finding it hardy enough to survive Maine winters. She reminds us that fennel seeds, leaves, and bulbs are all delicious. Another fennel strategy is Lila's fennel parmigiana, in which you slice fennel bulbs thinly, boil till just tender, and then layer the slices in a baking dish with a dribble of butter (or olive oil), salt and pepper, and grated Parmesan. Bake that for 10 minutes at 425 degrees.

Corn Pudding

{ SERVES 6 TO 8 }

A few years ago I attended a potluck where a fair number of us old granola types were in attendance, along with some non-granolas old enough to be our mothers. There was a predictable array of whole-wheat pasta salads, dishes made with eggplants and squashes, spinachy things, millet and brown rice, all beloved of back-to-the-landers.

There was also a corn pudding that everyone absolutely adored and gushed over. Various ones of us asked for the recipe from the older lady who brought it. She said, as she wrote it down on an envelope, "Oh, it is very easy. This is all you need." What followed was a list of canned and packaged ingredients that most of us had given up buying twenty years ago.

The moral of the story is, it doesn't pay to be too snooty about your grub. I like cooking from scratch and using food I grow in my own garden and usually that doesn't include canned creamed corn or Jiffy Mix. I don't like to eat ingredients I can't pronounce, the ones listed on packages that are there to ensure a shelf life that will exceed my own. This pudding is an exception to my from-scratch habit.

1 SMALL ONION, CHOPPED

½ GREEN PEPPER, CHOPPED (OPTIONAL)

¼ CUP BUTTER

1 CAN CREAMED CORN

1 CAN WHOLE KERNEL CORN

ONE (8-OUNCE) BOX CORN MUFFIN OR BREAD MIX

3 EGGS

½ TO 1 CUP SOUR CREAM

½ TO 1 CUP GRATED CHEDDAR CHEESE

Preheat the oven to 350 degrees. Grease a 2-quart casserole. Sauté the onion and pepper in the butter until just soft. Mix the 2 cans of corn together with the muffin mix and the 3 eggs. Add the sautéed onions to the mix and spread it all in the casserole dish. Mix the sour cream and cheddar together and spoon it over the top of the mixture. Bake for 45 minutes or until golden and firm to the touch in the center.

{ADVICE}

Obviously, you can use your own frozen corn, an equivalent amount to what you get in a can, about 1¾ cup full and you can replace the creamed corn with another 1½ cups of corn in a homemade cream sauce, too. This recipe is a bit fatty, but, because most of the fattiest stuff — sour cream and cheese — goes on top, you can make a thinner layer of it. Or promise me you'll only eat this after you have been cross-country skiing or running a marathon all day.

CORN

It usually takes a couple of weeks to eat my fill of fresh corn straight from the garden. Once that happens, then I use corn as an ingredient in several favorite dishes. Corn oysters is usually the first, an almost ritual, annual treat. I also freeze corn simply by cutting it off the cob into a bowl and spooning it into quart-size freezer bags, which I flatten to freeze to save space. No processing required.

Genuine Creamed Corn

The gluey stuff crammed in a can and foisted off on us as creamed corn bears scant resemblance to the genuine article. At least once a season, when corn is fresh from the garden or farmstand, you owe it to yourself to make this recipe.

2 COBS CORN PER SERVING

1 TABLESPOON BUTTER PER SERVING

ALL-PURPOSE CREAM

SALT AND PEPPER, TO TASTE

Shave off the kernel tops with one pass of the knife, then repeat, cutting closer to the cob, then scrape the last bits and the milk off the cob with the back of the knife. Put the butter in a heavy pan and melt it, then add the corn and cook it until it changes to a deeper yellow color, stirring to keep it from sticking. Then add cream until the pan is flooded but the corn is not submerged entirely. Reduce the heat to a simmer and cook until the corn and cream becomes quite thick. Add salt and pepper to taste.

Corn Oysters

{ SERVES 4 }

This recipe won't work with frozen or canned cut corn. The corn has to be cut off the cob so that the milkiness joins the corn pieces. My old original recipe said to grate the corn from the cob, and you can do that if you wish, but I have found that if I cut the corn by slicing off the kernel tops in one pass, then cut close to the cob in a second pass, and scrape the cob with the back of the knife on a third pass, I accomplish much the same end.

2 CUPS CORN PULP, ABOUT 2 TO 3 EARS

2 EGGS, SEPARATED

2 TABLESPOONS FLOUR

2 TABLESPOONS MELTED BUTTER

SALT AND PEPPER, TO TASTE

Grate or cut the corn from the cobs and put into a bowl. Beat in the egg yolks, flour, butter, salt, and pepper. Beat the whites in a separate bowl until they form soft peaks, then fold into the corn mixture. Drop by spoonfuls onto a hot, oiled frying pan or griddle and cook until golden, then turn to brown the other side. Place in oven to keep them warm while you finish frying the whole batch.

Cauliflower Chowder

I wasn't looking for a vegetarian chowder among the choices offered at a box luncheon one time, but ended up with it by accident. It was a surprise, and I was impressed at how the cauliflower was very tender and its texture reminded me of cooked fish.

{ SERVES 6 }

If you are not avoiding meat, you can use bacon in this recipe to give it a little extra flavor, with butter or vegetable oil as an alternative. Otherwise, put it together just as you would any chowder, with onions, potatoes, and water or milk. See my chowder directions on pages 37-38. Cut the cauliflower fairly small. Feel free to fiddle with the proportions to suit yourself. You could even add in a bit of ham. This freezes well, so make some extra for when you need a supper or lunch in a hurry. As with most chowder it is better the next day.

Serve it with crackers or grated cheddar cheese.

3 OR 4 SLICES BACON, OR A SMALL PIECE OF SALT PORK,
    FINELY CHOPPED OR 2 TABLESPOONS VEGETABLE OIL
1 MEDIUM ONION, SLICED
3 MEDIUM POTATOES (ABOUT 1 POUND), PEELED AND SLICED
1 SMALL HEAD CAULIFLOWER (ABOUT 1 POUND), CUT SMALL
MILK
SALT AND PEPPER, TO TASTE

Fry the bacon or salt pork in the bottom of a heavy pot, and when it is done, layer in onions, potatoes, and cauliflower. Add enough water until you can just see it through the ingredients. Bring to a boil, reduce the temperature, and cook until the potato and cauliflower are tender, about 10 to 12 minutes. Add the milk, salt, and pepper to taste, and bring back up to a simmer. Do not let it boil, or it will curdle.

Cauliflower Macaroni and Cheese

{ SERVES 4 TO 6 }

{ ADVICE }

There are a couple of schools of thought on mac and cheese, including the cheesy sauce version and the cheese chunk-studded approach. People interested in deep flavor like sharp cheddars and lots of it, and those interested in lowering the fat content opt for ricotta or cottage cheese. Supply-side cook that I am, I usually opt for what is on hand, and even blend kinds of cheese, so if there are three tablespoons of cottage cheese in the fridge plus a small chunk of swiss and a sprinkle of mozzarella — well, it all goes in. One time, I made a cheesy sauce with a bit of butter, flour, milk, and cottage cheese and grated cheddar, which I poured over the top of the cooked macaroni and cauliflower mixture, then topped it with grated jack cheese.

Extending the idea that cauliflower is firm and white and so is pasta, I developed this version of macaroni and cheese. I aimed for an equal proportion of mac to cauliflower. You could even stir cooked cauliflower into the packaged mac and cheese beloved by children and teenagers (and some grown-ups) if you think they will stand for it. Otherwise, boil up as much pasta as you like.

1 HEAD CAULIFLOWER

1 TO 2 CUPS UNCOOKED MACARONI OR SHAPED PASTA

3 TABLESPOONS BUTTER

3 TABLESPOONS FLOUR

MILK

CHEESES OF YOUR CHOICE

SALT AND PEPPER, TO TASTE

DILL, PARSLEY, SCALLIONS, OR NUTMEG, (OPTIONAL)

Preheat the oven to 350 degrees. Cut the cauliflower into bite-size pieces and steam or simmer until just barely tender. Cook the pasta according to the directions on the package and drain. Mix the pasta and cauliflower in a lightly greased baking dish. Put the butter into a heavy pan over medium heat, melt it, add flour, and cook together until bubbly, then add milk. Whisk and cook until slightly thickened. Add the cheese. If the sauce is very thick, add a bit more milk. Whisk until smooth. Add seasonings. Pour the sauce over the pasta and cauliflower, stirring it a little to distribute it evenly. Top with a bit more cheese and bake until bubbly, about 30 minutes.

Stuffed Zucchini

{ SERVES 4 TO 6 }

When a zucchini shoots past the tender size suitable for steaming or sautéing, then I stuff and bake it, varying the filling quite a lot depending on what delicious things I have on hand. You know, if you are a two-person household, you can grow just one zucchini plant that keeps the zukes down to a dull roar.

ONE (8- TO 12-INCH) ZUCCHINI

1 SMALL ONION, CHOPPED

2 TABLESPOONS VEGETABLE OIL OR BUTTER

2 GARLIC CLOVES, MINCED

½ CUP FILLING (TOMATO, COOKED MEAT OR SAUSAGE,

SEAFOOD, RICE, ORZO, COUSCOUS, CHEESE, OR BREAD CRUMBS)

SALT AND PEPPER, TO TASTE

PARMESAN OR CHEDDAR CHEESE (OPTIONAL)

{ ADVICE }

Stuffed zucchini seasoning suggestions: pesto, or Italian-style seasonings, like basil, oregano, and garlic. Or use a southwestern-style combination with oregano, cilantro, chili powder, cumin, and red pepper. I have also tried curry powder or my own combination of turmeric, cumin, coriander, mustard, ginger, and cardamon. A simple combination of parsley, onion, salt, and pepper is fine, especially if you have just picked your zucchini. Possible savory additions include cooked burger, chicken or turkey, ham or bacon, or a favorite sausage. Crab and lobster are very elegant. Blue cheese and zucchini make a fine alternative. Sometimes I use rice or orzo or couscous.

Preheat the oven to 350 degrees. To hollow out the zucchini, cut it lengthwise. Remove the seeds and if they are coarse, discard. Scrape the pulp from the inside, reserving it; leaving a ½-inch thick edge and bottom. A melon baller works very well, but a spoon will work, too. Steam or parboil the hollowed-out zucchini for about 8 minutes, or bake inverted on an oiled baking sheet for 15 to 20 minutes. Remove, handling the halves carefully.

Meanwhile, put the chopped onion in a sauté pan with the oil or butter and cook until it is just soft, then add the minced garlic and zucchini pulp. Cook these together at a medium-high heat until the zucchini is tender, tossing occasionally, about 5 minutes. Take off the heat and add the fillings and seasonings of choice. Mix well. Spoon the filling into the zucchini shells loosely and top with cheese. Bake for 30 minutes.

OTHER WAYS WITH ZUCCHINI

Cut the squashes up coarsely and toss them with olive oil and a few garlic cloves and roast them at 425 degrees for about 10 minutes, then reduce the temperature to 350 degrees for another 20 minutes or so for a savory roasted zuke side dish.

Add some fresh tomatoes to the zucchini, prepared as above in the oven, for a fresh pasta sauce. They can be frozen in that condition, by the way, for use later.

Whirl roasted zucchini in a food processor with chicken or vegetable broth for hot soup or make a cold soup by adding cream or sour cream and chilling it.

Tomato Cheese Pie

{ SERVES 4 }

Too many tomatoes is not usually a problem I have, living as I do on an island surrounded by cold water. Our nights are cool and the poor tomatoes shiver and hope they might get lucky and end their days on a sunny kitchen windowsill. This recipe came from my friend Ann Chandonnet, who is descended from Mainers and lives in Vale, North Carolina, where I visited her one September. *She* had a ton of tomatoes, of course, and made this tasty open-faced pie. Her original recipe called for Fontina *and* cheddar cheeses, but Ann says she often uses all cheddar. She also said, "The best tomatoes to use are the least juicy — such as Roma," that is, plum tomatoes. "Don't forget to pat them dry," Ann says.

Ann also says that she found a pound of tomatoes is sufficient, and the mustard is a variable to-your-taste sort of thing. I found a tablespoon and a half or so was enough.

I am including Ann's piecrust recipe below, because it is an especially rich version that works well in this recipe. You may prefer to use your favorite pastry recipe instead.

For the crust:

1½ CUPS FLOUR

½ CUP GRATED PARMESAN CHEESE

1 STICK BUTTER

1 LARGE EGG

1 TABLESPOON ICE WATER

For the filling:

1½ TABLESPOONS DIJON-STYLE MUSTARD

1 CUP FONTINA OR SWISS CHEESE, GRATED

1 CUP COARSELY GRATED EXTRA SHARP CHEDDAR

1 POUND PLUM TOMATOES, SLICED AND PATTED DRY

2 TEASPOONS FRESH THYME OR OREGANO MINCED, OR A
   SPRINKLE OF EACH DRIED

SALT AND PEPPER, TO TASTE

Toss the flour and the grated Parmesan together in a bowl, and using your food processor or pastry blender, cut the butter into the cheese and flour mixture. Beat the egg into the cold water and add to the flour and butter mixture and toss until the dough comes together, adding more ice water, if necessary, a very little at a time. Pat the dough out into a flat disk and chill.

Preheat oven to 400 degrees. Roll out the dough on lightly floured board and lay in a 10-inch pie plate. Crimp the edges. Spread mustard over the pastry. Toss the cheeses in a bowl to mix and spread them over the mustard. Arrange tomatoes, slightly overlapping, in circles on top of the cheese. Sprinkle the thyme or oregano and salt and pepper over the tomatoes.

Bake the pie for about 30 minutes, then reduce the temperature to 350 degrees and bake until crust is brown and the tomatoes are cooked, about 10 minutes more. Allow to cool slightly, then serve.

Fall Vegetables

WHEN THE DAYS SHORTEN, especially after the autumnal equinox, and the weather grows cooler, the garden shifts down to a lower gear, with lots of greens again — spinach, chard, lettuce, and kale. By the now the leeks' stalks are thickened up and Brussels sprouts are tall and studded with fat little heads, each like baby cabbages. For years I have campaigned on behalf of Brussels sprouts, which many people think they dislike. The secret is to allow the sprouts to sit out in a hard freeze whereupon they become sweet and buttery, and even convinced sprout-haters have been converted. Available in fall, now even on the stalk, they often appear on holiday menus. I always store a few stalks in the cellar for use into early winter.

Warm Brussels Sprout Salad

{ SERVES 4 }

Since sprouts and broccoli (and cauliflower and cabbage) are all in the brassica family, I thought why not fix Brussels sprouts with that wonderful bacon, onion, raisin, and sweet and sour dressing that we sometimes use on broccoli or combinations of broccoli and cauliflower?

All I do is trim the outer leaves off up the sprouts and slice the larger ones in half. Brussels sprouts really are much better steamed until tender, but they do turn a kind of drab green. Too bad; close your eyes; it'll taste fine anyway. I put the crumbled bacon, chopped onion, raisins, and dressing on the hot sprouts and bring it to the table still a bit warm.

1 QUART CLEANED BRUSSELS SPROUTS

½ CUP MAYONNAISE

¼ CUP HONEY

1 TABLESPOON CIDER OR RICE VINEGAR

¼ CUP CHOPPED RED ONION (ABOUT ½ A SMALL ONE)

⅓ CUP RAISINS

5 SLICES COOKED, CRUMBLED BACON

Steam the Brussels sprouts until they are fork tender (time will vary depending on the size of your sprouts). Whisk together the mayonnaise, honey, and vinegar, and set aside. Crumble the bacon and chop the onion. As soon as the sprouts are done, put them into a bowl, add the dressing, onion, raisins, and bacon, and toss.

Brussels Sprouts in Cream Sauce

{ SERVES 5 TO 6 }

- 1 POUND BRUSSELS SPROUTS
- 1 TABLESPOON BUTTER OR OLIVE OIL
- 1 SHALLOT, CHOPPED
- 1 CUP CREAM
- ¼ CUP MARSALA OR COOKING SHERRY
- 1 TABLESPOON HORSERADISH, OR MORE TO TASTE
- GRATING OF NUTMEG
- SALT AND PEPPER, TO TASTE

Trim the sprouts, taking off the tough outer leaves. Steam or boil them until they are just fork tender, about 15 minutes or so. Heat the butter or oil in a sauté pan and cook the shallot in it for about 3 minutes. Add the cream and sherry and simmer until the cream is reduced slightly. Stir in the horseradish, nutmeg, salt, and pepper. Heat through, and taste, adjusting seasonings as needed. Put the Brussels sprouts in the sauté pan and toss them so they are coated with the sauce.

{ ADVICE }

You can steam or simmer Brussels sprouts in chicken stock or just plain, lightly salted water. One theme repeated in various recipes was sprouts with something added: mushrooms, pine nuts, almonds, bacon, butter or cream, horseradish, lemon, garlic, or mustard, or some other very sturdy herb that holds up to the sprouts' cabbaggy-ness. Chestnuts are a classic go-with, and I did that one year and thought, this is nothing to write home about. No doubt, with this recipe there is room to tinker.

Crispy Kale Chips

You probably won't convince a teenager or die-hard couch-potato chip-snacker that these are as satisfying as classic out-of-the-bag junk food, but I have fallen pretty hard for kale chips. They satisfy my longing for crunchy, oily, and salty, and look, Ma, no carbohydrates!

My Islesboro neighbor, Peigi Cole-Joliffe, first told me how she made kale chips, and since then I have encountered them elsewhere, most recently at Nebo Lodge on North Haven where I ordered them as an appetizer. Then the next day I visited Turner Farm, also on North Haven, where the lodge's kale was grown and Jen Porter, the farm manager, described how she makes them.

The directions below combine all the advice from these folks as well as my personal observations. Start with dry kale leaves. If you wash them, make sure you spin them in a salad spinner then pat them dry between dishtowels. Tear them in fairly large pieces because they do shrink.

Serve as an appetizer or garnish on salad or a plate of food. I just eat them straight off the baking sheet.

BUNCH OF KALE

OLIVE OIL

SALT, TO TASTE

Preheat the oven to 350 degrees. Prepare the kale leaves by removing the stems and heavy ribs. Tear into large pieces and put into a large bowl. Dribble only a little olive oil, less than a tablespoon, over the leaves and toss them, then massage the leaves by hand or use a pastry brush to spread the oil all over them. Sprinkle with salt. Spread the leaves in a single layer on a baking sheet and put into the oven for 8 to 10 minutes, taking them out once halfway through and turning them over gently. Remove to a serving bowl and repeat until all the kale has been toasted until crisp.

{ADVICE}

I grow Russian kale with a purple stem and also a long leaved one nicknamed "dinosaur kale," which looks like the kinds of plants you'd expect a T. Rex to prowl among, which has the proper name of Nero di Tuscana Lacinato kale (must've been an Italian dinosaur). Then I also have a standard curly leaved kale variety named Winterbor. I make crispy kale out of all the kinds of kale I grow, but I agree with Jen that the standard curly edged kale makes the best version. Just as well because that's the easiest sort for you to acquire if you don't grow it.

Leeks with Bacon and Hazelnuts

{ SERVES 1 }

This side dish caught my eye because I've been trying to think of interesting things to do with leeks besides put them in stew or soup. The recipe was written for four servings, but I realized that this recipe is one of those simple, easily multiplied ones. So the quantities below are fine for one serving (that is, one *hungry* person) so just multiply by the number of people you are serving.

This would be a lovely side dish for dinner. It also would be delicious on top of a baked potato or served over slices of ham, chicken, or turkey.

Don't forget to rinse the leeks to remove the dirt that collects between the layers.

1 LEEK, TRIMMED DOWN TO THE LIGHT GREEN PART

1 TABLESPOON COARSELY CHOPPED HAZELNUTS

1 OR 2 STRIPS BACON, CHOPPED INTO PIECES

SPLASH OF WHITE WINE OR RICE WINE VINEGAR

¼ CUP CREAM

SALT AND PEPPER, TO TASTE

Bring to a boil enough water to cover the leeks, and when it is boiling, put the leeks into it. Cook them for 10 to 15 minutes or until they are tender when you test them with a knife.

While the leeks are cooking, lightly toast the hazelnuts in a heavy pan (no oil), and set aside. Then fry the bacon until it is crisp. Let the bacon bits drain on paper and remove most of the bacon fat from the pan. Add the vinegar to the pan and cook off the little stuck on bits, then add the cream and cook until it is all bubbly and reduced somewhat. Add salt and pepper to taste.

Slice the leeks diagonally into 2-inch long chunks and add them to the cream, tossing a bit to coat and re-warm the leeks. Serve with the nuts and bacon sprinkled on top.

Winter Keepers

OUT OF THE CELLAR and into the kitchen nearly all winter long: carrots, beets, cabbage, potatoes, rutabagas, onions, and apples gathered from my own and neighbors' trees. Keeping one eye on them to watch for soft spots and sprouting becomes a regular wintertime chore. The reward? Homegrown fresh vegetables.

Since carrots and beets store so well in my cellar over the winter, I eat relatively few of them through the summer except very young ones that I pull out when thinning to allow plants to develop. I do plant early carrots, beets, and red and green cabbage for summer eating, but the emphasis is on the storage vegetables.

Curried Squash Apple Soup

Inspired by a recipe I read in Karyl Bannister's friendly and informative newsletter *Cook 'n Tell*, this soup is definitely adjustable to taste.

{ MAKES 2 TO 3 QUARTS }

It can be made for vegetarians, even vegans, or can be made with meat broth. You can add milk or cream for a cream of squash and apple soup, or not. I love it with curry powder in it though cumin and coriander would work. You can follow more advice from Karyl and use blue cheese. Actually, sharp cheddar and/or sprinkles of bacon or little bits of ham would make it more savory.

The recipe says to use your choice of optional ingredients. Start with a little and add more as you like. Taste as you go, adjusting it to suit yourself.

1 BUTTERNUT SQUASH

1 BIG APPLE

1 QUART BROTH OR WATER

1 TABLESPOON BUTTER

1 TABLESPOON OLIVE OIL

1 ONION, CHOPPED

1 STALK CELERY, CHOPPED

SALT AND PEPPER, TO TASTE

Your choice of optional ingredients:

RED PEPPER, CHOPPED

CURRY POWDER

CORIANDER

CUMIN

PARSLEY

CREAM OR MILK

SOUR CREAM

Peel, seed, and chop up the butternut squash. Core the apple and peel if you wish; chop it up. Put into a soup pot and add broth or water to cover them up, to a quart. Simmer these together until the squash is very tender, about 15 minutes. If you plan to puree it, take it off the heat to let it cool before putting it in the food processor. In a separate pan, melt the butter and oil together and add the onion and celery (and red pepper, if you choose) and cook until they are just softened. Add them to the squash mixture and puree or mash them together.

Put everything on a low heat and add whatever optional ingredients you choose. Adjust the seasonings and the liquid to obtain the texture and flavor you prefer.

Savory Squash Casserole

{ SERVES 6 TO 10 }

The idea for this dish came from my good old *Moosewood Cookbook* where it is called Chilean squash. The original recipe calls for a bit more in the egg and cheese department than I now desire and can actually metabolize. Sigh. Also it calls for green pepper, which I find I like less than ripe red ones. The seasonings include garlic, cumin, coriander, and chili, not all of which are in everyone's spice line-up, but you can use just the chili powder alone. I heartily recommend adding cumin to your supply if you don't have it because it works in many dishes. I have cumin both ground and as seeds, and when I toast the seeds, they are perfect for sprinkling on salads.

2 ONIONS, CHOPPED

2 TO 3 CLOVES GARLIC, MINCED

1 RED PEPPER, CHOPPED

VEGETABLE OIL

1 BUTTERCUP SQUASH (ABOUT 4 CUPS), COOKED AND MASHED

2 EGGS

2 CUPS COOKED CORN

1 TABLESPOON GROUND CUMIN

2 TEASPOONS GROUND CORIANDER

2 TEASPOONS CHILI POWDER

SALT AND PEPPER, TO TASTE

GRATED CHEDDAR OR JACK CHEESE

{ ADVICE }

Feel free to make twice
as much of this dish as
you need, because the
leftovers are terrific for
soup. Just add chicken
or vegetable broth to
whatever you have left
until it is as thick or thin
as you like, add a dollop of
sour cream, or not, stir
it up, taste, and adjust
the seasonings. Voila:
Savory squash soup.

Preheat the oven to 350 degrees. Put the chopped onions, garlic, and pepper in a sauté or fry pan with just enough vegetable oil to cook them until they are a bit soft. Put the squash into a mixing bowl and mash it together with the softened onions, peppers, and garlic. Stir in the 2 eggs, add the spices, salt, and pepper, taste, and adjust seasonings. Spoon into a greased casserole dish, sprinkle the cheese on top, and bake until it is hot all through and the cheese is browned, about 40 minutes.

WINTER SQUASHES

Butternut, buttercup, delicata, hubbard, acorn, kuri, kabocha, and pumpkins appear out from under their big leaves after frost withers them. Long before that I am on my hands and knees nosing around to see how many of what I can expect to harvest in fall. I keep them in a cool dry upstairs bedroom after cutting them off the vine and allowing their skins to toughen somewhat in the sun. From November through March, I have squash on hand for my favorite dishes. I use the large ones fairly interchangeably, preferring to slice delicata lengthwise and bake it.

Beet Relish

People seem to love or hate beets. Among my beet loving friends is Shirley Cherkasky, who lives in Alexandria, Virginia. Shirley has lived a very long time in the D.C. area and pulled this very easy and delicious recipe out of her collection of political party fund-raising cookbooks. I can't remember whether it was a Democratic or Republican one, but though there are beet partisans, I doubt there is anything partisan about beets.

The recipe calls for two cups of beets, but since beets don't come in convenient one or two-cup sizes, you may round it off to the nearest beet. If you dice the beets very small, say a quarter inch or so, you will end up with a relish. You can consider cutting them a tad larger so that the whole mixture looks more like a beet salad. The combination of flavors is good either way. Make this in advance, because the flavor needs a little time to develop.

2 CUPS DICED COOKED BEETS

1 SMALL ONION, FINELY MINCED

2 TO 3 TABLESPOONS HORSERADISH

¼ CUP CIDER VINEGAR

1 TABLESPOON SUGAR

SALT, TO TASTE

Combine and refrigerate. After a few hours, taste again, and adjust seasonings.

Winter Vegetable Soup

{ SERVES 8 TO 10 }

{ ADVICE }

As it stands, this a vegetarian dish, but if you prefer, you could use chicken or even beef stock or broth instead of water. I often make a big batch, even doubling the recipe, and freeze some of it for a quick supper or lunch on another day. If there are other stray vegetables in your fridge's veggie bin, well, in they go.

One of the first things I ever cooked on a fireplace hearth early in my food historian career, winter vegetable soup, dates to the early 1800s. It is so simple and so tasty.

The old recipe calls for equal quantities of basic root vegetables, cooked first in an alarming amount of butter, with water added to make a broth, and herbs to season it. I never use as much butter as the old recipe calls for, but instead mix butter and olive oil. I am also inclined to add celery and a wad of garlic, not originally called for. The historic recipe called for "sweet herbs," which I have interpreted to mean marjoram, sweet savory, thyme, and parsley. But here is where you choose your favorites, or even a favorite herb blend. In fact, instead of fresh celery or garlic, you could use dried powders.

1 POUND POTATOES

1 POUND RUTABAGA OR TURNIP, OR HALF OF EACH

1 POUND CARROTS

1 POUND ONIONS

1 POUND PARSNIPS, OPTIONAL

3 TO 4 STALKS CELERY

1 STICK BUTTER

¼ CUP OLIVE OIL

BROTH OR WATER

AT LEAST ½ TEASPOON EACH OF MARJORAM, THYME, PARSLEY,
    SWEET SAVORY

SALT AND PEPPER, TO TASTE

2 OR 3 CLOVES GARLIC, MINCED (OPTIONAL)

Cut all the vegetables into bite-size pieces. Heat the butter and olive oil in a large, heavy soup pot. Add all the vegetables and stir them around to cover with the oil and butter. Put the lid on and let them cook for 10 to 15 minutes. Add water or broth to cover the vegetables and cook for 2 hours or so. Add water or broth as needed to keep them covered. Add the herbs, salt, and pepper, or any other seasonings you like, and let cook a while longer, taste, and adjust the seasonings. If you wish, remove a couple of cups of the mixture, let cool slightly, puree it, and add it back to the pot.

Sweet Potato Soup

When I weary of squash, I acquire sweet potatoes. This soup is full of
bright color, and you will feel like you have a bowlful of sunshine and
vitamins to eat. And so little fat. It is terrible to feel so virtuous about
a meal. My friend, Leslie Fuller, in Cushing, sent me this recipe that
she found on the Internet. It became Leslie and her husband Ben's new
favorite soup. Perfect for the family vegetarian or even vegan, if you want a
bit of meat, you can add chicken, shellfish, like shrimp or scallops, or even
a little sausage. The soup itself is so flavorful that it doesn't need meat. Like
most soups, this one tastes better after a day or so, even after only six hours.

1 TABLESPOON VEGETABLE OIL

1 LARGE ONION, CHOPPED

2 LARGE STALKS CELERY, CHOPPED

1 TEASPOON DRIED OREGANO

1 TEASPOON DRIED BASIL

½ TEASPOON DRIED THYME

2 SWEET POTATOES, PEELED AND DICED

2 LARGE CARROTS, SLICED THINLY

ONE (28-OUNCE) CAN DICED TOMATOES OR 2 HOME CANNED PINTS

5 CUPS VEGETABLE BROTH OR WATER

1 CUP CUT GREEN BEANS

5 CLOVES MINCED GARLIC

CRUSHED RED PEPPER FLAKES (OPTIONAL)

SALT AND PEPPER, TO TASTE

Heat the oil in your soup pot at a medium heat. Sauté onion, celery,
and herbs until the vegetables are tender, then add the sweet potatoes,
carrots, tomatoes, juice, and all, and broth. Bring to a boil then reduce
the temperature and simmer until the vegetables are tender, about 30
minutes. Then add green beans, garlic, and red pepper, if desired, and
simmer briefly. Taste and adjust flavor with salt and pepper.

{ SERVES 8 TO 10 }

{ ADVICE }

I would not hesitate
to substitute some
richly flavored winter
squash, like a buttercup
or kubocha, or even a
pumpkin, for the sweet
potato. Also, I use
celeriac, which I grow
sometimes instead of
celery, which does not
fare so well in our soil.
We grow practically
everything in the soup
in our garden and
you might, too.

Waldorf Salad

{ SERVES 10 }

When Sharon Ray, in Brewer, wrote to ask if I had a recipe for Waldorf salad sufficient for fifty, I thought maybe someone would come up with one for ten that we could multiply. No one did, even though I know there are a lot of you out there who cook suppers for churches, granges, and lodges.

Maybe the reason no one sent a recipe is because no one uses a recipe to make a salad like this, which is one for the seat-of-the-pants kind of cooking that lots of us do all the time. Where cake ingredients really have to be mixed in certain proportions, a Waldorf, or any other kind of salad, has a lot of flexibility. The main trick really is not to make too much.

The following salad ought to be plenty for ten. Feel free to multiply or divide it.

6 TO 7 LARGE APPLES, CORED, PEELED, AND CUT INTO SMALL PIECES

2 TO 3 STALKS OF CELERY

1 SMALL RED ONION

WALNUTS, CHOPPED (OPTIONAL)

1 LARGE SPOONFUL OF MAYONNAISE

VINAIGRETTE DRESSING

SALT AND PEPPER, TO TASTE

Cut the celery into dice. Chop the onion finely and add the walnuts, if you wish. Toss these in a bowl, add the mayonnaise, sprinkle the vinaigrette, and stir thoroughly. Add more mayonnaise to taste. Add salt and pepper, taste, and adjust seasonings.

Sweet and Sour Cabbage and Apples

It took me the longest time to figure out that one reason I really like a bunch of dishes that I make was that they all have an element of sweet and sour. Vinegar and sugar in the same dish: Harvard beets, marinated cucumbers and onions, marinated cabbage, bread and butter pickles, and a little Thai sauce that is only sugar, vinegar, and fish sauce. Then my friend Alice Girvin was telling me about the braised cabbage and pears that the chef at Tall Pines in Belfast makes. He gave her the recipe and there it was again: sugar and vinegar, by gosh. I had a real "Oh, duh!" moment. Change the apples to pears if you want, use green cabbage if that is what you have, and it is fine to use white sugar instead of brown.

{ SERVES 4 }

1 MEDIUM ONION, CHOPPED

VEGETABLE OIL

1 SMALL HEAD RED CABBAGE, SLICED

2 MEDIUM APPLES, CORED, PEELED, AND SLICED

¼ CUP CIDER VINEGAR

⅓ CUP LIGHT BROWN SUGAR

SALT AND PEPPER, TO TASTE

Sauté the onion in a little oil until the onion is softened. Add the cabbage and apples and cook until the cabbage and apples begin to soften. Whisk together the vinegar, sugar, and ½ cup of water, add it to the vegetables, and simmer together for about 15 minutes. Some liquid will cook away a bit. Taste and adjust seasonings with salt and pepper, or even another sprinkle of sugar or vinegar if you think it needs it.

Carrot Apple Salad

{ SERVES 1 }

{ ADVICE }

If you have carrot apple salad leftovers take them for lunch the next day. I love having leftovers of a salad like this because I can toss them into a leafy green salad. The dressing marinates the carrots and apples a bit and makes a great starter for tossed salad.

Someone described this salad as "kid-friendly." It is for sure — it's sweet with carrots, apples, and raisins. If your kids tolerate onion flavors, add some chopped red onion, mild whites, or shallots. I use shallots because I grow them, and I like that amount of mild onion flavor in a raw salad.

What kind of dressing you choose to use is really up to you. Using mayonnaise or your favorite white creamy dressing is perfectly fine, and preserves the sweetness. If you want a little zing, then use a vinaigrette, or oil and vinegar.

This is such an easy salad that it's not accurate to call the following a "recipe." You don't need a lot of specifics for this one. I figure on one-half carrot per person, and half an apple per person. Everything else is to taste.

½ CARROT

½ APPLE

RAISINS, TO TASTE

SHALLOT OR ONION, TO TASTE (OPTIONAL)

MAYONNAISE OR SALAD DRESSING, TO TASTE

SALT AND PEPPER, TO TASTE

Pare and grate the carrots. Chop apples into small pieces. Add raisins. Chop shallot or onion very finely and add if desired. Toss with your dressing of choice and add salt and pepper to taste.

Well Preserved

WELL PRESERVED AND IN A PICKLE

Seasonal over-abundance is a good excuse to dig out the canner, lids, jars, jar lifter, ladle, funnel, and a few good recipes for homemade pickles, jams, jellies, and chutney.

It used to be in the past that putting food by was absolutely essential for survival and made a huge difference in a household's economy. Without the preserving process some foods were simply not available out of season, so, for instance, a pickled cucumber was the only way to eat a cucumber in January or April.

Now home cooks pickle to have variety on the table, and some put up preserves just for fun, and even buy the ingredients. As a gardener, my main goal has always been to put away whatever I can't use right away, though I own up to planting more cucumbers and green beans than I know I will eat so that I can make pickles out of them.

Pickled Vegetables

BEFORE YOU BEGIN PICKLING, go check your cupboard and fridge to see what you already eat. Dill spears or chips? Relish for hot dogs and hamburgers? Dilled green beans from the gourmet food store? Or do you have a pickle you fondly recall from your past? A bread and butter pickle? Mixed pickles that grandma used to make? Those are the pickles you might consider making for yourself. Recipes follow for a range of old and new fashioned ways to use garden and farm market produce.

Sweet and Sour Pickles

This is just about my favorite pickle recipe. Kristina King, in Rockland, told me about this recipe, which I like because it requires no processing in a canner. It uses lots of cucumbers, makes a home for undersized onions and stray extra green beans, and preserves garlic, tiny onions, and shallots for off-season use, too. Also, you can make batches in any size from one jar to several. In short, it is a very paragon of a pickle.

Besides, even though I am not a huge tarragon fan, I love the tarragon flavor in this recipe. I use pickling cucumbers 4 to 6 inches long, but use whatever you prefer or grow in your garden. Feel free to cut them in spears, slices, or chunks. Use little pearl onions or just small onions from your garden, 1 to 2 inches in diameter, peeled, and cut into halves or quarters to fit in the jar.

Important note: Though the recipe does not require canning with a boiling water bath, it recommends that you keep them in a cool place, possibly a refrigerator. I found they kept perfectly in the cellar stairway where the temperature varies from the high forties to low fifties. I trust in the brine and the fact that the jars lids create a seal as the brine cools in the jars to preserve them. If you are a worrier, refrigerate them.

1 GRAPE LEAF PER JAR (OPTIONAL)

1 STALK OF TARRAGON PER JAR

1 STALK OF PARSLEY PER JAR

CUCUMBERS, WASHED AND CUT INTO SPEARS OR SLICES

GREEN BEANS, OR OTHER GREEN VEGETABLES (OPTIONAL)

2 TO 3 CLOVES WHOLE PEELED GARLIC, OR SHALLOTS

SMALL PEELED ONIONS, WHOLE OR QUARTERED, DEPENDING
  ON THEIR SIZE

1½ TABLESPOONS SUGAR PER JAR

1½ TABLESPOONS KOSHER OR PICKLING SALT PER JAR

2 CUPS CIDER VINEGAR

2 CUPS WATER

Wash and sterilize the quart jars. Put the grape leaf, tarragon, and parsley in the bottom of the jar. Pack the cucumbers and green beans into the jar and top off with the garlic, shallots, and onions. Add the salt and sugar to each jar. Combine the vinegar and water and bring to a boil. (Make more brine as needed.) Pour it into the jar and put the lid on immediately. After the lid snaps, and is concave, you can put the jar away. Allow a week at least for flavor to develop.

{ADVICE}

It was Kristina's idea to put a grape leaf in each jar. You don't have to do that, but it helps keep the pickles crisp. I use wild grape leaves, picking medium-size ones from a vine growing in a friend's yard. You will get good pickles even if you don't use grape leaves. Grape leaves actually are a traditional way to keep pickles crisp, and I always use them for dill pickles, too.

Pickled Fiddlehead Ferns

Let me caution you about the lids on jars sold in the new-style, shrink-wrapped box. Be careful about using those lids for sealing your jars full of food. The lids are actually put on tightly enough to turn them into used lids, and they may not hold a seal for your preserves. It may irritate the dickens out of you to do so, and make you feel wasteful, but it is wiser to discard them rather than risk your jars not taking a seal. Why waste your canning effort with bad lids? Throw them out and use new ones!

Fiddlehead hunting is something that requires the taciturnity that comes naturally to some Mainers in order to keep plentiful patches a secret. Since I am not privy to one of those wonderful places where the ferns poke up their delicate, dark-green, curled little selves, I obtain mine at a local produce store. Having admired the specimens of pickled fiddleheads that I spotted at a specialty food shop, I decided to try making some for myself and asked for recipes.

Lois Baxter, of Orrington, came through with the recipe she adapted from dill pickles. Lois reported that she sent some off to her brother on a ship he served on, "and he got raves from sailors who had no idea what fiddleheads were!" Lois said she came up with the recipe one year when she had so many fiddleheads, she couldn't eat them all.

3 POUNDS FIDDLEHEADS, WASHED AND FREE OF BROWN SCALES

1 TEASPOON DILL SEED PER JAR

1 BAY LEAF PER JAR

1 CLOVE GARLIC PER JAR

1 PIECE DRIED HOT PEPPER PER JAR (OPTIONAL TO TASTE)

½ TEASPOON MUSTARD SEED PER JAR

¾ CUP SUGAR

½ CUP CANNING SALT

1 QUART WHITE VINEGAR

3 TABLESPOONS PICKLING SPICE TIED IN A CHEESECLOTH BAG

Pack 6 to 7 sterilized pint jars with the fiddleheads. Add dill, bay leaf, garlic, hot pepper, and mustard seed to each jar. In a non-reactive pot, mix together sugar, salt, vinegar, 1 quart of water, and the bag of spices. Bring to a boil and simmer together for 15 minutes. Ladle over the fiddleheads in the jars, leaving a quarter of an inch head room. Tap to remove air bubbles. Adjust caps and process 15 minutes in a boiling water bath.

Dilly Green Beans

I have had terrific luck with this dilly bean recipe, based on the one in *Putting Food By*. I always grow garlic and allow dill to sow itself all through the garden, so I always have quite a bit for any purpose. I often pick an additional dill flowerhead to put in the jar, too, to boost the dill flavor.

I usually snap off the stem ends and leave the pointy end. I put the dill heads in first, then garlic, and tip the jar sideways and lay in the beans. When it seems they are packed in as tightly as they can be, I stick my finger, or a chopstick, in somewhere and wiggle it around to see if I can't get one more bean in. Then I figure it is ready for the brine.

I have noticed that after processing, these beans often are wrinkled and, for some reason unknown to me, they lose that after a little while and return to normal in the jar. So don't be alarmed if that happens to you.

Some people — not me — like red pepper added to dilly beans.

6 PINTS GREEN BEANS

6 HEADS FRESH DILL SEED OR 12 TABLESPOONS DRIED SEEDS

6 CLOVES GARLIC

3½ CUPS WATER

2½ CUPS VINEGAR

6 TABLESPOONS PICKLING SALT

Snap off the stem end of the beans and size them for the jars. Set up your canner and begin heating the water for a boiling water bath. Sterilize the jars, then put the dill heads or 2 tablespoons of seeds, garlic, and beans into them. Bring 3½ cups of water, the vinegar, and salt to a boil and ladle it into each jar, leaving half-an-inch headroom. Adjust the lids and rings. Process in a boiling water bath for 10 minutes, or according to instructions for your canner. Remove and allow to cool.

{ MAKES 6 PINTS }

{ ADVICE }

Not all green beans are long and straight. When I have a freshly picked basketful, there are short ones, long ones, and curled ones. The short and straight go into pint jars and the longer ones go into quart jars. These I think of as pickles for the pickle dish. The curled ones I snap into two-inch or so lengths and pickle for use in salads.

Cornichons

Cornichons is French for small, gherkin-size pickles done up with tarragon and white wine vinegar. Classic sharp and bitey cornichons accompany particularly well an unctuous slab of country paté.

Both Ruth Thurston, in Machias, and Diane O'Brien, in Lincolnville, sent recipes. Diane free-wheeled her way through a recipe she found on-line, substituting as needed, and Ruth turned to the ever-useful *Better Than Store-Bought,* written by Helen Witty and Elizabeth Schneider Colchie in 1979. The recipe here incorporates some of Diane's substitutions. Don't use cheap distilled white vinegar instead of the more costly white wine vinegar, because it is very harsh and will defeat the tarragon and shallot flavors. Diane had only 1 cup of white wine vinegar, so she added a cup of *cider* vinegar.

You are supposed to give cornichons about a month to pickle. Diane had impetuously devoured half of hers three days after making them.

"They're delicious," she said.

"You mean, they *were* delicious," I said.

{ADVICE}

Cornichon-size cukes are not generally available in stores. Grow cukes or make friends with someone who does. Pick when they are an inch or an inch-and-a-half long.

1 ¼ POUNDS PICKLING CUCUMBERS, 1 TO 1 ½ INCHES LONG

3 TABLESPOONS PICKLING SALT

4 SHALLOTS

1 BAY LEAF

2 SPRIGS FRESH TARRAGON (OR 1 TEASPOON DRIED)

10 BLACK (OR RAINBOW) PEPPERCORNS

2 SMALL DRIED CHILI PEPPERS, OR HALF A TEASPOON OF
   RED PEPPER FLAKES

2 CUPS WHITE WINE VINEGAR

Wash the little cucumbers very gently to remove the spines. Mix them with the salt in a bowl and let stand 24 hours. Drain them and rinse in cold water. Spread the cucumbers between two towels and gently pat them dry. Put the shallots, bay leaf, tarragon, peppercorns, red pepper, and the cucumbers into a sterile 1-quart jar. Top the jar off with the white wine vinegar, cover tightly, and store in a refrigerator or cool, dark cellar for 3 weeks to a month.

Bread and Butter Pickles

Tomato soup, grilled cheese sandwiches, and bread-and-butter pickles
are the most perfect comfort food lunch I can envision for cold winter
days. I have been making these bread-and-butters for decades, since
1975 when a Mystic Seaport co-worker, Jan Virginski, gave me the
recipe. Long ago I decided I didn't like the green peppers in the recipe,
so have omitted them when I make the pickles, and in the recipe below
they are optional. The only thing I don't like about the recipe is slicing
all those darn onions, which I now do in a food processor, keeping the
lid on them until I dump them into the sliced cucumbers with my eyes
tightly shut. Still, I always cry. The product is worth it.

{ MAKES 8 PINTS }

1 GALLON SLICED CUCUMBERS

8 LARGE ONIONS, SLICED

2 GREEN PEPPERS AND 1 RED, SLICED (OPTIONAL)

½ CUP PICKLING SALT

5 CUPS SUGAR

5 CUPS VINEGAR

2 TABLESPOONS MUSTARD SEEDS

½ TEASPOON WHOLE CLOVES

1 TABLESPOON CELERY SEED

Layer the cucumbers, onions, and peppers, if using, and salt in a large bowl and let stand for 3 hours. Drain. Put the sugar, vinegar, and spices in a large non-reactive pot, bring to a boil, add the cucumbers and onions, then bring it all to a boil again and boil for 2 minutes. Put into sterilized pint jars, allowing for half-an-inch headroom. Adjust the lids and rings. Process in a boiling water bath for 10 minutes, or according to instructions for your canner.

Dill Pickles

This is the best plain dill spear recipe I have come across so far. I recommend a grape leaf in the bottom of the jar to keep them crisp, though you can make the pickles without the leaf. Use the freshest dill you can find for the sturdiest dill flavor. I grow pickling cukes, preferring the short blocky sort because they have smaller seeds and fit neatly into canning jars. The recipe is written so that you can put up any amount of pickles, a handy thing, because most gardens produce varying amounts of cukes. This recipe makes enough brine for about 10 quart jars of pickles.

For the pickles:

1 GRAPE LEAF PER JAR (OPTIONAL)

CUCUMBERS CUT INTO SPEARS, OR WHOLE SMALL PICKLING CUKES

1 CLOVE GARLIC PER JAR

2 HEADS FRESH DILL SEED OR 2 TABLESPOONS DILL SEED PER JAR

For the brine:

3 QUARTS OF WATER

1 QUART OF CIDER VINEGAR

1 CUP PICKLING SALT

Sterilize the jars and put a grape leaf in the bottom, the garlic, and then the dill heads, stems up, and pack the cucumbers into the jar as snugly as you can. Bring the water, vinegar, and salt to a boil. Pour the brine over the cucumbers in the jars allowing for half-an-inch headroom. Adjust the lids and rings. Process in a boiling water bath for 10 minutes, or according to instructions for your canner.

Pickled Beets

Beets keep perfectly well in a cold cellar, so while pickling them is not essential for preservation, I pickle them because I like to have them ready to use, and, besides, I welcome the sweet and sour flavor. It is also a grand way to use up the tiny beets among the larger ones that I pull out of the garden at the end of growing season, when it is evident that they are simply not going to get bigger.

Plan on using a pound to a pound and a half of raw beets per pint jar. Double that for quarts. Cook them just before you make the pickles so that they are hot for packing.

ONE PART VINEGAR (1 CUP)

ONE PART SUGAR (FOR EXAMPLE, 1 CUP)

HALF PART WATER (½ CUP)

WHOLE CLOVES OR WHOLE ALLSPICE (OPTIONAL)

HOT COOKED, PEELED BEETS, SLICED OR CHUNKED

Bring the vinegar, sugar, and water mixture to a boil. Pack the hot beets in sterilized jars, add the spices and vinegar mixture, allowing for half-an-inch headroom. Adjust the lids and rings. Process in a boiling water bath for 15 minutes, or according to instructions for your canner.

Relish and Salsa

WHEN I WAS GROWING UP in the fifties, for condiments we had ketchup and relish and mustard. That was it. No one in my Yankee family knew anything about salsa. Now we are eating bucket-loads of the stuff, and it seems you can make it out of almost anything as long as you include hot peppers.

Zucchini Relish

{ MAKES 6 TO 7 PINTS }

Basically, making relish seems to be about taking some firm bland vegetable that you have a lot of, chopping all up, adding spices, sugar, and vinegar, and putting it away to brighten up the flavor of dinner later on.

My island neighbor, Annmarie Mouw, started me on the zucchini relish search by wondering aloud what other people did to make it.

Mark Nadeau sent a recipe that he has been using for years. This year he had a yellow zucchini, but he added in a small green one to give it color. He usually cuts out the punky, seedy middles of large zukes. He doesn't bother paring the squash, so neither should we.

Phyllis Borns makes her relish to sell at her church fair, using "humongous, overgrown zucchini mysteriously left on my front porch." She probably ought to look around at her fellow churchgoers to see who is growing big zucchinis, since they can count on her to make it into relish for the fair. Paula Gillen, in Milbridge, found her relish in Patti Forbes' "The Camp Cook" section of the *Downeast Coastal Press*. Dorothy Lewis, in Camden, sent her recipe and noted that she weighed the zucchini once and found that about five pounds of squash gives her twelve cups ground.

Therese Lussier, from Ludlow, sent Grand-Maman's Zucchini Relish, writing that the recipe comes from her eighty-seven-year-old mom who lives south of Montreal, in Saint-Alexandre, and whose grandchildren are scattered from Quebec to North Carolina and Colorado and all look forward to receiving jars of her relish. The instructions say to cut the zucchini and peppers in "tiny cubes." Therese said, "She is very meticulous and cuts the ingredients in tiny, even sizes." Whew. God bless her.

You could invent your own relish as my young Islesboro friend Marie Fisk did by substituting over-grown yellow summer squash for zucchini in her grandmother's recipe. It turned out a gorgeous golden yellow color with little flecks of sweet red pepper in it, and it tasted just like any good relish will.

I use my old-fashioned hand-cranked grinder with a medium blade to grind the vegetables. Carefully pulsing them in a food processor also works, as long as you don't allow them to become mushy.

12 CUPS GROUND ZUCCHINI

4 CUPS GROUND ONIONS

1 RED PEPPER, GROUND

1 GREEN PEPPER, GROUND

½ CUP PICKLING SALT

2½ CUPS CIDER VINEGAR

4½ CUPS SUGAR

1 TABLESPOON DRY MUSTARD

¾ TEASPOON TURMERIC

1½ TEASPOON CELERY SALT OR SEED

½ TEASPOON PEPPER

⅛ TEASPOON CAYENNE (OPTIONAL)

¾ TEASPOON NUTMEG (OPTIONAL)

¾ TEASPOON CORNSTARCH

Put the zucchini, onions, and peppers in a large bowl and sprinkle in the salt; let stand at least 3 hours to overnight. Then rinse well in cold water and drain.

Combine the vinegar, sugar, spices, and cornstarch in a large pan and mix in the ground vegetables. Bring the mixture to a boil, reduce the heat, and simmer for 1 hour, stirring often enough to prevent sticking.

Spoon the relish into sterilized jars, allowing for a half-inch headroom. Adjust the lids and rings and process in a boiling water bath for 10 minutes.

Green and Red Tomato Salsa

{ MAKES 3 CUPS }

Homemade salsa experiments abounded for a while at my house when I realized I was *buying* salsa fairly frequently. So I poked through several of my favorite recipe books for condiments and preserves. Not surprisingly, the recipe that caught my eye was Helen Witty's green and red tomato salsa with red-hot peppers in her *Good Stuff Cookbook*. In her recipe the ripe tomatoes are outnumbered two to one by the green, perfect for Maine where, even in stellar garden years, we are very apt to have green tomatoes around at frost time. I altered the recipe to use lime juice instead of vinegar because I like the flavor of lime in salsa. I also rounded the amounts where I could to the nearest whole vegetable. The amount of hot peppers really is a matter of taste; sample as you cook and please yourself.

Helen intended for this recipe to be canned, and I did put up a couple of pints, but my happy discovery was that this is really as good as a fresh, *uncooked* salsa. Friends and I ate ourselves silly on the cupful I left out, scooping it up on tortilla chips.

2 CUPS COARSELY CHOPPED GREEN TOMATOES, ABOUT
   4 TO 5 MEDIUM
1 CUP COARSELY CHOPPED RED TOMATOES, 1 LARGE OR 2 MEDIUM
1 MEDIUM ONION, DICED
¼ CUP LIME JUICE
¼ A LARGE RED BELL PEPPER, DICED
2 TO 3 CLOVES GARLIC, MINCED
1 SEEDED, DE-RIBBED, AND FINELY MINCED HOT PEPPER, TO TASTE
1 TEASPOON SALT
1 TEASPOON GROUND CUMIN
ADDITIONAL CRUSHED RED PEPPER FLAKES OR HOT SAUCE, TO TASTE
CHOPPED FRESH CILANTRO, TO TASTE

For fresh salsa, merely combine all the above and allow to stand for a couple of hours for the flavors to blend.

To make the cooked version to can or to keep in the fridge to use later: Mix together everything except the cumin and cilantro and bring to a boil, then reduce heat, and simmer for about 30 minutes, or until only a little liquid runs from a spoonful set on a saucer. When it is thick enough, add the cumin, taste, and adjust seasonings, remembering that the heat from the hot peppers will continue to develop. Can in clean jars and seal according to your usual method for relish. Or put into jars and store in the fridge where it will keep for weeks. Add cilantro when you are ready to serve it.

Chutney

THE OPERATING PRINCIPLE behind chutney is to take a large mass of some kind of fruit (apple, rhubarb, green tomatoes, mangoes, peaches) to which you add raisins, onions, brown sugar, vinegar, and a bunch of spices and cook it until it is a fragrant sticky mess, more or less spicy according to your taste. That's it. Really.

Rhubarb Chutney

{ MAKES 8 CUPS }

I keep my rhubarb in good condition by ruthlessly cutting off the blossom stalks as they sprout up; otherwise the plants will think they had fulfilled their destiny, as far as procreation is concerned, and die back. I don't let them do that very quickly — greedy little rhubarb eater that I am.

This chutney recipe is based on one by Helen Witty, whose daughter, Anne, lives in Georgetown. Helen's *Fancy Pantry* and *Good Stuff Cookbook* are my two favorites because the recipes are so reliable and they taste very good, too. They have guided me through preserving over the years, and I recommend them highly. The recipe calls for fresh ginger, but I have substituted candied ginger when I had it on hand, and I have fortified the ginger flavor by adding a little ground ginger to the mixture, too. I also increased the onion and golden raisin content.

6 TO 7 CUPS DICED RHUBARB STALKS

2 CUPS COARSELY CHOPPED ONIONS

2 CUPS GOLDEN RAISINS

1½ CUPS WHITE SUGAR

¼ CUP LIGHT BROWN SUGAR

2 TABLESPOONS MINCED FRESH GINGER ROOT

1 TABLESPOON PICKLING SALT

2 TEASPOONS MUSTARD SEED

1 TEASPOON ALLSPICE

1 TEASPOON GROUND CORIANDER

½ TEASPOON CRUSHED RED PEPPER FLAKES, OR TO TASTE

¼ TEASPOON GROUND CINNAMON

¼ TEASPOON GROUND CLOVES

2 CUPS CIDER VINEGAR

Combine everything except the vinegar in a heavy bottomed pot and bring to a boil. Reduce the heat and simmer for about 30 minutes. Add the vinegar and cook, stirring very steadily to prevent sticking, until the chutney thickens up, and a spoonful dropped on a saucer does not weep thin liquid. Ladle into hot, sterilized jars, leaving a quarter-inch headroom, allowing half-an-inch headroom. Adjust the lids and rings. Process in a boiling water bath for 10 minutes, or according to instructions for your canner. Allow chutney to develop flavor for three weeks before using it.

Spicy Apple and Green Tomato Chutney

If you have more apples than green tomatoes, or vice versa, you can assemble this chutney to absorb more of your predominant ingredient. If you use more apples, you will have a sweeter result than if you use green tomatoes as the majority ingredient. Taste to adjust the seasonings. I often let the green tomatoes get the upper hand in chutney because at the end of the season there often are so many of them, and even though they will turn red on the windowsill as the season winds down, they never quite develop that same desirable, rich tomato flavor as those ripening on the vine.

{ MAKES 3 TO 4 PINTS }

3 OR 5 CUPS CHOPPED GREEN TOMATOES

5 OR 3 CUPS CHOPPED APPLES

1 LARGE SWEET RED PEPPER, CHOPPED

1 LARGE ONION, CHOPPED

½ CUP RAISINS

2 TABLESPOONS MINCED FRESH GINGER ROOT

2 TO 3 CLOVES GARLIC, MINCED

1 CUP LIGHT BROWN SUGAR

1 CUP CIDER VINEGAR

1 TEASPOON WHOLE MUSTARD SEED

1 TEASPOON GROUND CUMIN

1 TEASPOON GROUND CORIANDER

½ TEASPOON GRATED NUTMEG

¼ TO ½ TEASPOON CAYENNE, TO TASTE

2 TEASPOONS SALT

Mix all the ingredients in a large non-reactive pot and cook until the mixture will not seep liquid when a spoonful is placed on a plate. Spoon into hot, sterilized canning jars, adjust lids and rings, and seal in a boiling water bath for 10 minutes.

Sue Hess' Grandmother's Cranberry Chutney

{ MAKES 5 CUPS }

My island neighbor, Ruth Hartley, passed along this recipe that our mutual friend, Susan Hess, who lives now in Georgetown, gave Ruth. Sue had taken it to bridge club and regaled the group with stories from her grandmother, who made the chutney in the first place. Ruth observed about the smell of the chutney cooking, "So now, when the smell is wafting through the house on those anticipatory days when we have memories of past Thanksgivings and hopes for the future, it is a lot more than the cranberry!"

Isn't that the truth? Smell prompts some of our most powerful memories, and the combination of turkey, warming pies, and now cranberry chutney aromas ought to let loose a whole floodgate of recollections.

1 POUND FRESH CRANBERRIES

1 CUP WHITE SUGAR

½ CUP PACKED BROWN SUGAR

¾ CUP GOLDEN RAISINS

¾ TEASPOON CINNAMON

1 TEASPOON GROUND GINGER

¼ TEASPOON CLOVES

¼ TEASPOON ALLSPICE

1 CUP WATER

2 LARGE COOKING APPLES, PEELED, CORED, AND CHOPPED

1 MEDIUM ONION, CHOPPED

1 STALK CELERY, CHOPPED

Combine the cranberries, sugars, raisins, spices, and water in an uncovered saucepan. Bring to a boil over medium heat. Cook until the cranberries pop. Reduce the heat, and stir in apples, onion, and celery. Simmer uncovered 20 to 30 minutes, stirring occasionally, adding just a little water if needed to prevent sticking. Put into canning jars and process in boiling water bath for 10 minutes. Or chill and keep in the fridge up to 2 weeks.

Acknowledgments

One more time, let me acknowledge the contributions of many friends, neighbors, and readers of my newspaper column for their willingness to share recipes. Particular gratitude is due Letitia Baldwin, formerly at *Bangor Daily News*, who gave me the opportunity for the column that generated all these recipes.

Blessings on Kathleen Fleury, my editor at *Down East*, for engaging my interest in Down East's cookbook projects and for her steady support for this book, even as little Ella Fleur arrived on the scene. Dawna Hilton at *Down East* made intelligent and tasteful decisions in food styling as I cooked. Jennifer Smith-Mayo is the most energetic and fun photographer I have ever worked with. Jennifer Anderson brought it all to life with her magical design.

Toby Martin, a good home cook in his own right, and affectionately known to his colleagues at Madison, Connecticut's the Country School as "Captain Comma," painstakingly went over every word of this manuscript four times to ferret out erroneous punctuation and grammar, and help me avoid the many pitfalls of the English language. He also advised insightfully on organization.

Anna North Coit, in North Stonington, Connecticut, and Priscilla and Dudley Fort, in Islesboro, Maine, all gave me a place to live and work during a rough patch in my life at the beginning of work on this book, and many thanks to them.

Many thanks to Jamie MacMillan for all those beautiful vegetables he grew that inspired my cookery all those years.

Many thanks to Margie, Kay, Nancy, Nancy W., Allie, Pille, Hanna, Mary R., Mary Z., Val, and friends who weeded so I could write. Special thanks to Valerie Lester who unlocked the secret of how to get a book written.

Taste Buds Contributor List

Allen, Hannah

Alley, Martha

Ambrose, Neila

Anderson, Emily

Anderson, Jean

Andrews, Jo

Angotti, Anita

Aston, Maggy

Bannister, Karyl

Barrett, Helen

Baxter, Lois

Belanger, Joan

Black, Anne

Boardman, Bev

Boardman, Mike

Bodman, Gloria

Boothby, Judy

Borns, Phyllis

Braley, Helen

Brown, Iris

Campbell, Eleanor

Chandonnet, Ann

Cherkasky, Shirley

Clough, Diane

Code, Beth Gates

Cole-Joliffe, Peigi

Congdon, Marcy

Conn, Linda Jean

Crowly, Gayle

Day, Rena

Delicata, Genevieve

Dodge, Jan

Doyle, Gina

Durkee, Adrienne

Durkee, Linda

Elliott, Alice

Ellis, Nancy-Linn

Elward, Barbara

Estabrook, Patricia

Farr, Lois

Feeley, Anne

Ferris, Diane

Fortin, Lila

Fowler, Marian

Frangoulis, Karen

Frost, Sharon

Fuller, Leslie

Gannon, Peggy

Gay, Jeanine

Gillen, Paula

Gilles, Linda

Girvin, Alice

Goguen, Sharon

Gray, Georgia

Greene, Evelyn

Hart, Miriam

Hartley, Ruth

Harrigan, Janice

Head, Diane

Herrick, Judy

Hess, Susan

Hopkins, Patricia

Hughes, Bonnie

Hutchison, Mitch

Jandraeu, June

Jones, Jennie

Jordan, Nancy

Keener, Jane

Keresey, Katelyn

King, Kristina

King, Libby

Knight, Alice

Krupsky, Arlene

Landis, Mary

Landry, Vicki

Lewis, Dorothy

Littlefield, Louanne

Long, Linda

Lorizio, Marie	Pierson, Carol	Spencer, Cheryl
Lowell, Elaine	Piper, Barbara	Southard, Pat
Lussier, Therese	Pochocki, Ethel	Stephens, Barbara
Lynch, Wilma	Porter, Jen	Stinson, Evelyn
Maxim, Eleanor	Price, Anne	Stinson, Gene
Maybury, Betty Jean	Quimby, Dorothy	Stuart, Vivian
McCormick, Minnie	Randall, Charlene	Tibbetts, Sandra
McLain, Brenda	Randlett, Sarah	Thomas, Jacqueline
Mead, Dorothea	Ray, Sharon	Thompson, Carol
Merchant, Steve	Reynolds, Patricia	Thurlow, Margaretta
Merritt, Zelma	Richard, Mary	Thurston, Ruth
Mills, Betty	Rittenhouse, Caroline	Tracy, Nancy
Nabbs, Eleanor	Robinson, Charlotte	Varisco, Helen
Nadeau, Mark	Rolerson, JoDelle	Vaster, Sally
Ness, Corinne	Rollins, Alice	Warholak, Suzi
O'Brien, Diane	Rollins, Deb	Watson, Ruth
O'Day, Michie Stovall	Ross, Josephine	Welldon, Midge
O'Donnell, Gail	Ruckert, Baily	Whiles, Millie
Olson, Craig	Ryan, Sherry	White, Lucille
Olson, Melissa	Savage, Sonya	White, Susan
Olson, Olivia	Scott, Nina	Whittier, Phyllis
Oliver, Sarah	Seavey, Connie	Whyte, Jennifer
Parsons, Carla	Senter, Linda	Wilbur, Susie
Pendleton, Joanne	Seymour, Donna	
Pendleton, Julia	Simmons, Dorothy	
Petell, Deb	Smith, June	

* These are the *Taste Buds* contributors who sent recipes found in this book.

Ingredient Index

Recipe Index

CHEESE AND EGGS

PICKLES AND PRESERVES

CAKES AND COOKIES

Recipe Notes